Key Contemporary Concepts

Key Contemporary Concepts

From Abjection to Zeno's Paradox

John Lechte

SAGE Publications
London • Thousand Oaks • New Delhi

First published 2003

SAGE Publications Ltd
6 Bonhill Street
London EC2A 4PU

SAGE Publications Inc
2455 Teller Road
Thousand Oaks, California 91320

SAGE Publications India Pvt Ltd
32, M-Block Market
Greater Kailash - I
New Delhi 110 048

British Library Cataloguing in Publication data

A catalogue record for this book is available from the British Library

ISBN 0 7619 6534 3
    0 7619 6535 1

Library of Congress Control Number 2002108290

Typeset by C&M Digitals (P) Ltd., Chennai, India
Printed and bound in Great Britain by Athenaeum Press, Gateshead

For Gill
and my father,
John S. Lechte
(1921–2002)

Contents

Subject Index

Acknowledgements

I would like to give very special thanks to Gill Bottomley for the help and understanding she has given me during the writing of this book, at a very difficult time of her life due to illness.

I would also like to thank my friend and colleague, Mary Zournazi, who read most of the manuscript and made so many useful suggestions. Responsibility for the final product is, of course, mine.

Thanks also to my students and colleagues at Macquarie for responding – without always knowing it – to a number of entries in this collection.

A Note on the Text

Entries contain etymological and historical information about the concept, where this is relevant. The current meanings of the concept are given, along with an exposition and discussion of the term, with particular attention being paid to the use of the concept in the work of classical or contemporary thinkers or theorists. While I have endeavoured to be rigorous in referencing where this would be of help to the reader, mentions of very well known ideas in the work of classic authors (e.g., Plato, Kant) have not always been referenced. The overall aim is to give the reader a sense of the meaning and significance (especially current) of each concept, not to give a reading of the work(s) of specific authors.

Concepts which appear in entries other than their own are marked with an asterisk to facilitate cross-referencing. Asterisks are only to be found when the full concept appears. One term of a dual entry such as sacred (see sacred-profane), or difference (difference- individuality) is not asterisked, but the complete title appears in the list at the end of the entry.

KEY CONTEMPORARY CONCEPTS

Key Contemporary Concepts offers a map of where we are now as a society and culture at the beginning of the twenty-first century. From cybernetics to quantum theory, from ideology to power, from aesthetics to mimesis, from the sacred to work, this book is a guide to the present and the future, as it plumbs the depths of terms across the disciplines: social theory, art theory, politics, biology, cultural studies, religion and philosophy. This is the book for anyone who wants to gain an insight into the current scientific and intellectual state of society – a book that is ideal for the student and for academics who need to brush up on the latest in areas other than their own.

Each entry provides a history and current meaning of the concept in question. It then outlines its place in the work of a key author, while also offering an interpretation of the term's significance, both current and classical. Concepts are organised clearly in alphabetical order, and essential references are given for further research.

Not since Raymond Williams's *Keywords* has such an ambitious pedagogical and intellectual project been achieved with the same rigour, insight and breadth of knowledge. Specialist dictionaries are useful in their way; but how do concepts relate to each other across disciplinary boundaries? How do they work from an interdisciplinary perspective? *Key Concepts* shows us how.

John Lechte is Associate Professor of Sociology at Macquarie University in Sydney. He is well known for his writing on the work of Julia Kristeva and his book, *Fifty Key Contemporary Thinkers*. His latest writing is on cinema and the time image, and technologies of the word. He is one of the most accomplished interdisciplinary thinkers writing in the world today.

Introduction

THE COLLECTION'S RATIONALE AND STATUS

It is a truism to say that, during the twentieth century, knowledge and ideas, in both the humanities and social sciences, have expanded exponentially. Consequently, any selection of concepts deriving from this expansion will surely be skewed. My task is to provide the rationale governing the entries to be found in this collection. Before I embark on this, I would like to clarify the status of a collection of concepts such as this.

The book follows in the footsteps of my *Fifty Key Contemporary Thinkers: From Structuralism to Postmodernity* (1994) in which I aimed to engage with the work of thinkers within the framework of movements in modern thought. Rather than simply presenting an exegesis of an *oeuvre*, I endeavoured also to engage with that *oeuvre*: I pointed to difficulties and offered an interpretation, which it was then up to readers to accept or reject in light of their own research and interests. I had a clear framework to provide a sense of direction for my reading: in the first instance, French structuralism and its critics.

In a similar vein, I present here concepts that are becoming increasingly visible in light of developments in information science and philosophy. The concept of 'cyberspace' is particularly significant. In effect, many of the concepts have a link to (my version of) what drives contemporary reality: that is why 'image', 'icon', 'simulacrum', 'difference' and 'individuality' are included. This is the age of media (if not of the 'spectacle') and of the crisis of identity that accompanies it.

If it is true that humans only become fully conscious of their reality when they have concepts through which this reality is articulated, then certain concepts will assume a fundamental importance in enabling an understanding of the so-called present moment in history. Looked at in this way, 'contemporary concepts' are the vocabulary through which the experience of an epoch might be spoken and expressed.

While, no doubt, we should not proceed by linking concepts to context in a dogmatic or simplistic manner – thus opening the door to fashion for determining what concepts are relevant and illuminating – we should recall that concepts do not arise in a social and philosophical vacuum. Of importance here is the fact that, in a work of limited scope such as this – a work that makes no claim to be an exhaustive dictionary – choices must be made: the concepts included presuppose many that are excluded. Thus, 'code' is included while 'instinct' is excluded; for, in light of the structuralist revolution, together with the understanding of information technology as being based on the digital code, there is a call for a deeper understanding of the former concept, while, 'instinct' has come to have a far less visible role in explaining human experience, if not for explaining animal behaviour.

Does this mean that concepts arise and decline in light of historical developments, and that what was seen to be significant at one historical moment will become irrelevant at the next? The answer is decidely in the negative – first, because no researcher is in a position to choose concepts simply according to circumstances and relevance. The judgement of history is always retrospective. Secondly, and more importantly, it is not just the concept that is at issue, but also its interpretation. Concepts such as 'truth', the 'sacred' and 'justice' are not new; what is new is the range of possibilities of interpretation to which they have given rise. To grasp recent interpretations of these and other similarly enduring terms, however, often entails recourse to previous interpretations. 'Ideology' is a concept which illustrates this: beginning in the eighteenth century as the study of ideas, it became a synonym for doctrine (whether in a religious or political sense) and worldview and was finally understood in the 1960s and 1970s as a form of practice.

The concepts presented here are social, less because they are part of a (putative) social theory canon, and more because they are vehicles for illuminating our social present.

PREVIOUS WORK

To propose a book of concepts, those most relevant to the present moment, evokes Raymond Williams's project of the middle 1970s. Partly in the manner of the lexicologist, Williams, in his *Key Words* (1976), successfully distilled the sense of the fundamental terms of the decades after the Second World War. His list included words with important social and cultural overtones, words in common parlance which needed investigation and clarification ('family', 'image', 'native', 'nature'), including those of a more technical orientation with a strong Marxist flavour (bourgeois, capitalism, communism, class, dialectic, materialism, revolution), as well as those related to social life (civilisation, society, status), and a few directly related to Williams's own background and training in literary criticism (fiction, literature). The success of Williams's book is testimony to the fact that he tapped into a real desire for understanding. For a generation his text has been a crucial reference point for the humanities: for social scientists, literary critics and lay people who want help to find their way round modern social and cultural reality, and, latterly, around the theoretical terrain of Cultural Studies, a terrain that also offers itself as a key to knowing society.

Despite all this, *Key Words*, in retrospect, is of another era, and not simply because of the kinds of terms it included. Some of these (for example 'image', 'alienation') also appear in this volume. Nor is it of another era because Cultural Studies has now matured as an area of study (whatever has been said about its philosophical underpinnings). Rather, *Key Words* speaks to a different audience to that of today – first, because the ideological agenda which gave the work its impetus (humanist Marxism) is no longer so relevant: the communist wall has come down; 'man' has been decentred. Second, the scope of Williams's terms is severely limited as we head into the twenty-first century: key terms on the information society are truly multidisciplinary, deriving as much from mathematics, biology and philosophy as from sociology or cultural studies. To limit ourselves to the latter two fields is to fail to meet the needs of the moment.

Some concepts here will reiterate those of Williams, but they will be treated in a vastly different way. Instead of the etymological approach of the lexicologist, I focus on the historical and current *significance* (not exactly the same as their meaning) of the concepts in question. We will see that 'alienation' as the failure of the worker to recognise her/himself in her/his product, no longer carries the weight it once did, and now has much more to do with the ubiquity of the image and the decline of imaginary capacities; other concepts, such as 'fractal' and 'clone', which are well out of the range of Williams's lexicon, evoke contemporary experience and so are included in this collection.

STYLE OF APPROACH

There are many ways in which a reference book such as this can be written and organised. Some adopt the assiduous approach, including an entry on every important concept or term in a given subject or discipline. The model here is the lexicologist's language dictionary, even if the result is more circumscribed. Here the aim is breadth. At the other end of the scale, still in the assiduous realm, is the approach that aims for depth. Articles are long, but impeccably chosen in order to be representative of a given field. There is no question of self-indulgence in the choices made. This type of work models itself on the encyclopedia, even if, once again, the result is more limited. A third approach, I call the whimsical reference approach. As an example, we can point to Jacques Attali's *Dictionnaire du XXIe siècle* (Dictionary of the XXIst century) (1998). Attali retains, as he says, a nucleus of traditional concepts, but also indulges himself. Thus we find an entry for '*Adolécran*' (*écran* = screen) (a young person whose world revolves around television, film, computer games, the internet, etc.), and '*nanotechnologie*': 'marriage between physics and information technology'. Entries for numerous terms (e.g. love) are aphoristic and humorous, rather than serious and scholarly.

'Style of approach', then, boils down to the kind of terms chosen, to the nature of the explanations given, and to how these are presented. Unlike Attali, I have avoided the appearance of using terms that *predict*. I have avoided assuming, for example, that the world faces a population crisis in the twenty-first century, and that, *therefore*, we need to understand the rudiments of human sexuality and reproduction. Similarly, I have not made the twenty-first century the object of speculation, as is sometimes done in the media and science fiction. My approach is rather to offer a selection of concepts which relate to life as we find it now, at the start of the twenty-first century. And my argument is that if we do not 'catch up on' the terminology of our own time, we will be unprepared for the new era. In effect, the present work's *raison d'être* is the current 'disjuncture' between understanding and reality.

Although I shy away from the whimsical approach this does not mean that I am offering a work only for specialists. For while specialists – in philosophy, for example – might find entries which seem to be written just for them, my aim is both to explain concepts which have a profound relevance for a wide variety of readers, and to provide the basis for the interested reader to do more research on his or her own behalf. I hope, indeed, that the reader's appetite for learning in the broadest sense will be stimulated. To enable learning is a goal to which Heidegger aspired. Why not all of us?

My style is to engage with each of the concepts explained and analysed. In effect, I attempt to draw out the real and possible implications that seem to derive from the subject area that the concept opens up. If, for instance, 'cyberspace' has no centre, is a non-totalising multiplicity of endless connections and is not owned by anyone – if it allows the complete anonymity of participants who take on a 'virtual' rather than an 'actual' identity, in what sense does this spell a loss or gain for human freedom and interaction? Maybe virtual reality is a *reality*. For, indeed, society as a totality is virtual, while localised instances of it are actual. Does it matter that the technology that makes virtual cyberspace possible is digital (and therefore entirely formal, based as it is on a system of differences)? These are some of the questions that arise regarding cyberspace; to answer them definitively is impossible.

AN AGE OF CYBERSPACE?

In many ways the evolution of photography mirrors the changes that have occurred over the last century with regard to the relationship between reality and processes of reproduction and representation. Or at least the changes that have occurred in photography give us an insight into a world many see as nothing but a simulacrum* (a representation which ultimately refers only to itself). Photo- graphy was once entirely dependent on the analogical process of exterior light hitting an interior photosensitive surface, with the effect that the image produced could not but be believed in: the photo of the man falling from the building was thus a true event because the analogical photographic image did not lie. Even the techniques of photographic trickery performed with the analog- ical technique were in the main equivalent to a *trompe-l'oeil*: that is, a true appreciation derived from the tell-tale give-away sign (a seam, a suture, a discontinuity) that revealed the image as a fake. With digital technology, by contrast, a fabricated photographic image is now 'almost impossible to detect' (Mitchell 1994: 164). If we have now tumbled to the air-brush that aimed to wipe Trotsky from the stage of history, it is also arguable that

> [a]n interlude of false innocence has passed. Today, as we enter the post-photographic era, we must face once again the ineradicable fragility of our onto-logical distinctions between the imaginary and the real, and the tragic elusive-ness of the Cartesian dream. We have indeed learned to fix shadows, but not to secure their meanings or to stabilize their truth values; they still flicker on the walls of Plato's cave. (Mitchell 1994: 225)

'Ontological' (to do with the study of being) is indeed the term I would use, after Mitchell, to describe the field where we encounter the dilemma that the digital construction of images raises. Like Plato's cave, digital photography (and perhaps digital technology in general) forces a rethink of the relation-ship between the image and what is imaged – between the representation and what is represented. After nearly two centuries of stability, the status of the human capacity to know and to represent is again in question.

One tendency, in vogue today, urges us to solve the problem by giving it up. Accept, this view says, that there is only hyperreality, the reality of the techniques of reproduction itself. There is no longer any 'real' to which representations in general, and images in particular, refer. Or again, if we must wander around in Plato's cave once again, we should now accept the shadows on the wall as (a) reality and not be fussed, as we once were, by the difference between shadow and sunlit truth, between appearance and reality, image and simulacrum or semblance, or between true reality and false image. Even more radically, it is sometimes argued that it is not even a question of accepting the shadow, semblance or appearance as the (good-enough) reality or truth, but of disengaging altogether from this terminology and philosophical problematic. Even to plump for the shadow or the simulacrum, against the idea of a true and authentic image, is to remain caught in Plato's web – as the West has been for more than two millennia. And some (perhaps I am one of them) say that we will remain beholden to Plato on this issue well into the third millennium.

The vicissitudes of representation and the philosophical framework that sustains it are thus at the heart of issues that key concepts invoke for us at the end of the twentieth century. This is part of our ineradicable environment, as it were: the air we breathe.

Not only philosophy but changes in science have contributed to the intellectual and cultural environment of the last century. In particular, thermodynamics* and theories of chance* have set up paradigms. Here, the dynamic of order and chaos comes to the fore, and time* is seen as essentially irreversible, unrepeatable, once and for all. This is interpreted as a result of the second law of theormodynamics, which says that in the spontaneous movements of energy, the molecules involved break down into random distributions (disorder or chaos). This breakdown makes processes irreversible. The idea of randomness as the emergence of disor-der seems to have spilled over into many different areas. Thus, entirely in keeping with this logic, history, we say, never repeats itself; it is irre-versible, and the measurement of time is serial rather than cyclical. In other respects, the irreversibility (the fact of disorder) of time seems to imply that punctual death is our lot as humans. Perhaps none have put it better than the French philosopher of science, Michel Serres, when he says: 'Order is only a rarity where disorder is the norm' (Serres 1977:10). And Serres elaborates: 'Disorder is almost always there. That is to say: cloud or sea, storm or wind, mélange and throng, chaos and tumult' (ibid.). Disorder (therefore death) is the most probable thing in this world. Life is order; life is rare and fragile.

After thermodynamics comes complexity theory, where disorder begins to throw up a hitherto invisible order, an order manifest in fractal geometry, if we take chaos theory into account. The concepts presented here attempt to mirror this change.

We should note, however, that the foregoing depends on a scientific and wholly secular view. Religions of all denominations and cultures have invested as much in the idea of an afterlife as they have in the things of this world. The afterlife, then, would be a supplementary *order*: it is death brought to order, as it were. Of course, science as we generally understand it in the West is essentially unable to support this view. For science, unpredictable death becomes chaos – the most probable outcome, if we wish to make predictions. What science tells us regarding chance is that it is not on our side; it is not on the side of life, or order. The (scientific) theory of probability, then, will tell us that there is no point buying a ticket in the million dollar lottery because, objectively, the chances of winning, if there are millions of other contestants, are minuscule. How much more so is the chance that someone might live for ever? Objectively, the lottery is chaos. Hence the saying of the disillusioned: 'life's a lottery'. At the beginning of the new millennium we are challenged to consider whether this is so. We are challenged to recall what religion and the imaginary capacities which underpinned it once were. It is not a question of saying that science is wrong, but of pointing out that there may be something more which science needs to take into account. If I believe in *fortuna*, I might intuit that luck is on my side. I will win the lottery! The religious person, for his or her part, says: I believe that I will have eternal life. I will live again; I will live a second time.

Irreversible time and imaginary repetition (the same returning) – these notions confront us, now, at the beginning of the century. Certain concepts in this anthology allude to this relation and the issues it raises. Concepts such as: 'imaginary', 'image', 'imagination', 'sacred–profane', 'identification', 'love', '*logos–mythos*', along with other concepts which, initially, may seem to have little to do with the play between science and the imaginary, concepts such as 'eros-eroticism', 'community', 'communication', and 'transcendence'.

The emergence of virtual technologies – in biology as much as in information science – opens up the possibility that, if reality (nature) is fundamentally code-like, or based in patterns of chaos, radical disorder will progressively be on the retreat. For, in what now seems to many to be a bizarre conflation, virtual, cyber- reality would also be part of reality. If we were to discover that order was in fact at the heart of all apparent disorder – if the most recalcitrant (scientifically speaking) aspects of nature were patterned and ordered – this would seem to imply that rather than order being a rarity, disorder – the unpredictable – would every-where and at every time be the most improbable. But because this order is always invisible, as a species, humanity would still have something more to know. It does not mean either that a spiritual or religious longing would in any way be assuaged. However, without having some insight into and knowledge about these kinds of developments and the issues that come in their wake, it will be impossible for people to participate in their own destiny. Concepts relating to virtual technologies are therefore included here: 'analogue', 'clone', 'complexity', 'cyberspace', 'digital', 'frac-tal', 'fuzzy logic', 'virus'. These are concepts that call on us to think.

INTERPRETATION

In this collection of concepts, there are terms from the social sciences, phi-losophy, information science, music and even from physics ('quantum') and biology ('clone'). While I speak as a social theorist and philosopher, I do not pretend to speak as musician or biologist. What justification can there be for me to explain concepts in music and physics? The question is worth posing in light of a recent controversy in France concerning the appropriation by philosophers and others of concepts originating in physics and mathematics (see Sokal and Bricmont 1998). My task is not to present nuclear physics's version of 'quantum', or the biological version of 'clone', but to explain how such concepts have been used in non-biological contexts and with what effect. It is my further task to assist the reader in deciding whether greater insight has been facilitated or impeded by such borrowings. In total, such concepts would not number more than two or three; I therefore consider my approach completely legitimate.

Many of the concepts included here derive from my own experience of what has become important in contemporary thought and culture. To some extent, the collection is bound to reflect my own conscious and unconscious predilections. Does this matter? I think not. For to recognise this, readers must begin to come to grips with their own predilections, a fact that I take to be the first step on the path to realising the Oracle's call to 'know thyself', a call that is surely fundamental to thought itself.

Attali, Jacques (1998) *Dictionnaire du XXIe siècle*, Paris: Fayard.
Lechte, John (1994) *Fifty Key Contemporary Thinkers: From Structrualism to Postmodernity*, London: Routledge.
Mitchell, William J. (1994) *The Reconfigured Eye: Visual Truth in the Post-Photographic Era*, Cambridge, MA and London: MIT Press.
Serres, Michel (1977) *Hermes IV: La Distribution*, Paris: Minuit.
Sokal, Alan and Bricmont, Jean (1998) *Intellectual Impostures: Postmodern Philosophers' Abuse of Science*, trans. from the French, London: Profile Books.
Williams, Raymond (1976) *Key Words. A Vocabulary of Culture and Society*, Glasgow: Fontana.

ABJECTION

Among the earlier meanings of abjection are 'wretchedness' and extreme debasement.

This term would not, in all probability, have become popular in art and psychoanalytic circles, were it not for the publication of *Powers of Horror* by Julia Kristeva in 1982. In that work, Kristeva outlines a psychoanalytic theory of the subject where there is a pre-symbolic phase characterised by strong feelings of horror and revulsion in relation to certain objects, people and situations. What is abject is decidedly not desired; it thus has a strongly negative status attached to it. It is what an identity rejects because it instils horror. And yet this rejection of the abject thing is, Kristeva suggests, formative of the ego, if we accept with her that abjection characterises the elementary ego struggling for autonomy. For abjection is also the means through which the child separates from the mother, as it is also the first intimation of the interdiction against incest.

Above all, abjection is a dimension of human experience that is based in affect, rather than reason. It is a negative *feeling*, not a rational law. An individual's dislikes in food will have an abject basis. For some, rancid butter induces the revulsion of abjection. Who one is can be partly defined by such dislikes (and corresponding likes). Such then is the psychoanalytical meaning of abjection.

On a socio-cultural level, feelings of horror can be evoked in purification rituals, rituals which are enacted so as to avoid defilement, and which are intricately tied to the sacred. In other words, abjection is at play when a Jew feels revulsion for pork, or a Hindu for killing a sacred cow. Prohibition and transgression – pollution and purification – are, then, tied to abjection. The one who commits an act of defilement feels wretched and worthless; that is, he or she will feel they are nothing. And they may be seen to be so by others.

In studying the sacred in non-state societies, or in societies with a weak state, Mary Douglas (1969) found that those things which were sacred and the subject of an interdiction or taboo were also things that were essentially ambiguous because they were on the border between different states or processes. Thus nail clippings, hair, faeces, tears and menstrual blood, often deemed to be polluting and subject to taboos, all invoke the borders of the body: they are neither wholly inside nor outside. Our feeling of revulsion when we come into contact with the said objects (except under specially defined circumstances) keeps taboos in place.

Cadavers, because they also have an ambiguous status, being neither the dead person nor not the dead person, are subject to some of the severest taboos, as are sexual practices. In the latter situation, the borders of the body of another may only be violated, and the prevailing taboo on sexual activity transgressed, under special conditions, such as marriage or during fertility rites. To transgress a taboo produces revulsion and a feeling of abjection.

While some feminists have reservations about the viability of abjection as a term for describing psychological development (Kristeva talks about the negative feelings of daughters for their mothers as an aspect of separation, and mentions symbolic 'matricide'), others have welcomed it as a way of showing, after the predominance of Cartesianism, that the body is a fundamental element in human relations, including the area of thought. The idea that humans also think with their bodies is one implication of the study of abjection.

During the last decade of the twentieth century, artists began eliciting feelings of revulsion by presenting base objects as a way of making a statement. A number of works are composed wholly or partially of faeces, both human and animal. In other cases, graphic portrayals of internal bodily organs feature in the work of these artists of abjection. The intended effect, we can assume, is to provoke horror and thus regenerate an affective relation to art in place of a relation that had become too cerebral.

Abjection also shows its face in public in the moral domain, or rather, in the domain of amorality as seen in various forms of corruption. To the extent that corruption is abject, it is a betrayal of trust. When a judge in the legal system secretly engages in criminal behaviour, this is abject in a way in which a known criminal's criminal behaviour is not. For the judge has betrayed the trust that makes him or her 'above suspicion'. All secret, corrupt behaviour is abject, whereas open defiance is not. Hypocrisy, therefore, is a manifestation of abjection.

Within the moral frame, a friend who stabs you in the back, science (which is supposed to save life) producing weapons of mass destruction, a politician on the take, all exemplify abjection, and we ask ourselves whether, in the present age, abjection is more prevalent in the moral sphere than previously, and if it is, what can be done about it. The implication deriving from Kristeva's work is that there are two kinds of strategy: one is to strengthen the symbolic order, so that a moral and political framework is clear and unambiguous – in some cases this may entail a more active state; the other strategy is to bring about a revivified order of ritual, in order that ambiguity in social life might be reduced.

Douglas, Mary (1969) *Purity and Danger*, London, Boston and Henley: Routledge & Kegan Paul.
Kristeva, Julia (1982) *Powers of Horror: An Essay on Abjection*, trans. Leon S. Roudiez, New York: Columbia University Press.

See BODY; SACRED–PROFANE

AESTHETICS

Aesthetics, or aesthetic, is often used as a synonym for art in general. But then we might ask what art is. The origin of the word is helpful here. In ancient Greek, *aisthesis* (the root of 'aesthetic') means 'feeling' and corresponds to the German, *Gefühl*, a term which Immanuel Kant (1724–1804) used to evoke the idea of inner feeling. Art would then be the sphere where inner feeling is evoked, rather than being the sensations evoked by an external source.

The modern conception of aesthetics, originating in the eighteenth century, had an empiricist version, as exemplified by Edmund Burke (1729–97) in England (although Burke never used the term), and a rationalist strand, as exemplified in Germany by Alexander Baumgarten (1714–62), in whose work the term 'aesthetics' appeared for the first time. In the empiricist version, aesthetics is the sensation of perfection experienced before an ostensibly beautiful object. Although individual experiences of beauty are very likely to differ, it is possible that there will be common empirical qualities of the object which evoke the sensation of beauty. Whether or not taste remains a private and subjective matter, not open to universalisation or consensus, is an open question.

The rationalist view sees beauty as being located in the abstract concept, or representation, of perfection, whether real or imagined. In all probability, a real object will only approximate the ideal perfection that the concept makes communicable. The rationalist aesthetic approach is thus conceptual – that is, cognitivist. A consequence of this – still evident today – is that beauty, or what is aesthetically perfect, would conform to a norm represented by an ideal (if conventional) model, often featuring symmetry, that one strives to imitate. Advertising uses just such a notion in its presentations of the ideal body, the ideal holiday location, the ideal face, the ideal house, etc.

In the work of Kant, an attempt is made to improve on the two approaches outlined. Instead of accepting the individualist and relativist approach of empiricism, which can never produce a consensus about beauty, Kant argues that beauty, rather than being a sensation directly perceived by the senses, is essentially a subjective, interior feeling. He famously says that this feeling evoked by beauty, in principle, will be shared by everybody: beauty is the 'object of universal delight'. Moreover, against the rationalist view, Kant says that the aesthetic faculty is not cognitive: beauty, then, has no concept, or prior model; this is entailed in its being a feeling. Indeed, in terms of an ideal model of perfection, beauty might even be characterised by imperfection. Beauty is its *own* model.

Against the notion of aesthetics is Heidegger's (1889–1976) view that it stems from the humanist metaphysic of modernity. It thus becomes too subjectivist, too audience focused at the expense of the work (cf. Heidegger 1982: 43–44). The latter raises questions of truth and Being*. In so doing, the work of art reveals a world that would otherwise remain concealed.

Sociologically, much has been made of the Kantian language of aesthetics which suggests there are people of refined taste and that they have the right to demand that others will delight in the same objects of beauty that they do. Furthermore, as the beautiful object, qua beautiful object, should have no end other than its own existence (it should not be a commodity or something that is merely useful, or functional, which contributes to physical survival), beauty cannot usually be found – good taste cannot be found – in crafts, or in pleasures of the flesh.

There is of course much more to Kantian philosophy than this. However what has been said should indicate how the realm of aesthetics has often been construed in class terms, where the wealthy, who constitute the élite of society, would also have good taste and refinement and, what is more, because of their wealth, can impose their notion of what is aesthetically pleasing. The working, or middle class, by contrast, reveal their inferior class position partly by the 'bad' or 'vulgar' taste that they exhibit, especially through their preference for pleasures of the flesh, and through their functionalist approach to life. 'High' and 'popular' are current terms in relation to culture which attempt to capture this class difference.

Aesthetics has often been viewed as a sphere that has very little to do with real life, and more to do with mere decoration and the rarefied existence of connoisseurs. To take a purely aesthetic approach to something can be seen as tantamount to rejecting life as it is actually lived, especially in a highly secular society.

For certain cultural critics, the final decades of the twentieth century saw the collapse of the distinction between high and popular culture, so that, in music for instance, classical and popular genres become intermixed, while in Pop Art, classical allusions appear in works featuring objects from consumer society. This collapse was seen to be democratic, and thus highly desirable. It was embraced in particular because the whole idea of a 'judgement of taste' (Kant), which enabled the discernment of beauty, was deemed to be anachronistic and élitist. Such judgements, far from being universal, were said to be always the taste of some particular person or class. And at the everyday, psychological level, many people have come to subscribe much more readily to the empiricist creed of *chacun à son goût*. Art works in

such an environment become highly personalised and idiosyncratic, having meaning for the producer, but being inaccessible to a wider public. The wider public is included on the basis that, in principle, no one is excluded from putting work on public display, if they work at it hard enough and for long enough.

Against this tendency, is the idea that aesthetic concerns now attract a wide public because life has ceased to be a matter of satisfying utilitarian needs, and has become a matter of 'life-style', in which the way one lives becomes an end in itself. Life becomes art, in effect.

Heidegger, Martin (1982 [1959]) *On the Way to Language*, trans. Peter D. Hertz, New York: Harper & Row.
Kant, Immanuel (1978 [1790]) *The Critique of Judgement*, trans. James Creed Meredith, Oxford: Oxford University Press.

See BEAUTY

ALIENATION

In his book on games, Roger Caillois (1962) speaks of alienation as a corrupt form of mimicry where the simulator, instead of maintaining a distance between the character and the self merges completely with the character, or 'other'. In other words, alienation occurs when there is no longer a distinction 'between fantasy and reality'. No doubt it is in this sense that it used to be said that mad people were 'alienated'.

For Marx (1818–83) there is link between commodification and alienation (Marx 1967). This gives us one of the dominant social meanings of the term today. Before elaborating, we should recall that alienation also means foreignness: that which is other and strange. The alien is foreign to identity. What is alien relates to difference. A desert can be very alien. In the immigration context, an alien is someone who is not a citizen or a national of a given country. During a war all aliens might be interned or even deported. To be seen as alien, as the Nazis claimed Jews were in Germany, can be enough to evoke the wrath of popular hatred. A so-called alien often has to cope with prejudice.

It is, however, commonly said that one feels alienated from something (a work of art, sexual mores, form of employment, etc.), which means that one feels estranged, or removed from the reality concerned. In short, it is impossible to identify with this reality because it is other, and does not belong to what is familiar.

Marx, who made labour the key to human existence, gave a much more socio-economic and political meaning to alienation. At the time of cottage industry, before the division of labour had developed in industrial society, it was possible, Marx said, for man to feel a strong link with the product of his labour. The producer could identify with the product and thus know himself as the author of such products, which, because they expressed the author (as in a work of art) played an important part in creating the producer's identity. This, then, is unalienated labour. Certain people today (for example those with lifestyles inspired by the counter-culture of the 1960s) sometimes yearn for the putative 'golden age' of unalienated labour – an age before industrialisation, and before modern technology displaced the labourer, as occurs with the new computer technologies.

To the young Marx, modern labourers did not know themselves as the authors of products made for the market, because the division of labour separated the worker from the final product of labour. Objectively speaking, however, workers, whether they know it or not, are the authors of market products, or commodities. The point is to enable workers to become conscious of this.

Another way of conceiving this alienation is to say that, originally, a single worker, or craftsman, was united with the product of their labour. Consciousness was thus in harmony with reality. With the emergence of the commodity under capitalism, labour–power* is alienated from the labourer, because it is a collective reality that individual consciousness has been unable to grasp. Individual consciousness is fragmented by the modern labour process and cannot see itself as part of a collective spirit. The individual labourer cannot identify with the labour process as a whole. Hence, the resultant sense of alienation.

But even if the worker(s) were able to identity with the labour process as a whole, there is, in Marx's view, another obstacle preventing the elimination of alienation. Quite simply, it is that the end product of labour does not belong, formally or substantively, to the labourers. It belongs to the private capitalist who sells it on the open market in order to make a profit (what Marx calls the 'surplus value' produced by the worker). Alienation here arises from the fact of having to work for someone else or at least of having to endure the feeling that the other's success (profit) is not *my* success. Indeed, although Marx argues that labour-power objectively made the workers the collective authors of the commodity, and that it was a fragmented consciousness which stood in the way of them appreciating this collective authorship, it is not possible, under capitalism, for workers to identify with the success of the capitalist. For profits accrue only to the capitalist. The only way to overcome this form of alienation is to change the role and status of profit: namely, to make it accrue to the people in common instead of to a minority of capitalists. Such is – or was – the hope of communism. It entails creating conditions whereby the people receive the profits of their labour (the collectivisation of profits).

Although Marx's theory remains predominant because it is an explicit theory of alienation, the reality of alienation is also to be observed elsewhere. Modern bureaucracies are often experienced as alienating because they are essentially rule-based and formalistic (hence the significance of the 'office'). The implicit motto of the bureaucracy is: 'without regard for persons'. This phrase is supposed to signal that, in the social and political worlds, equality (each person is treated the same) is the key element of bureaucratic domination. Consequently, the individual who is looking for special treatment should look elsewhere. But alienation is even more marked here because those who genuinely *need* special treatment might also look elsewhere. Often a person, looking for a kindly word and a friendly gesture, goes to a bureaucrat. And such a person might well be lucky. However, the bureaucrat qua bureaucrat, is not *obliged* to dispense personalised service.

The market-place can work in a similar way. As department stores and business enterprises get ever larger, they begin to acquire the impersonality of any bureaucracy. Moreover, banks, airlines, credit card agencies and even hotels and other private utilities, apart from being large and making profits the size of which the individual consumer cannot comprehend, have now instituted a range of answering services so that person to person contact is reduced to a bare minimum. Many people find these developments quite alienating, and dehumanising. They have a strong sense of being outcasts in relation to the logic of the inner workings of these vast institutions. Least of all can they feel they know who is responsible for errors. Who is responsible, for example, when an error occurs on a credit card? Indeed, who, in the vastness of these organisations, can be persuaded that there *is* a mistake?

Against the idea that the bureaucracy is *only* impersonal, is Michael Hertzfelt's thesis that bureaucracy is *also* often 'unhelpful, interest-directed, buckpassing' (Hertzfelt 1992: 18), and that there is a symbolic (ritual) element present which runs parallel with the efficient, rationalist element. Needless to say, being the victim of bureaucratic self-interest and inefficiency is also likely to be alienating. Kafka's *The Trial* (1968) is perhaps the most profound and deepest expression of this form of alienation.

Caillois, Roger (1962) *Man, Play and Games*, trans. Meyer Barash, London: Thames & Hudson.

Hertzfelt, Michael (1992) *The Social Production of Indifference: Exploring the Symbolic Roots of Western Bureaucracy*, New York and Oxford: Berg.

Kafka, Franz (1968 [1925]) *The Trial*, trans. Willa and Edwin Muir, New York: Schocken Books.

Marx, Karl (1967) 'Except Notes of 1844' and 'Economic and Philosophic Manuscripts (1844)', in *Writings of the Young Marx on Philosophy and Society*, trans. and ed. Loyd D. Easton and Kurt H. Guddat, New York: Anchor Books.

See ECONOMY; EXCHANGE; LABOUR-POWER; MONEY; RESPONSIBILITY

ALLEGORY

With the move away from mimesis* and the rise in the interest in the notion of representation and the 'inexpressible', an interest has come in the once outmoded device of allegory. For, it would seem, allegory is a representation which points to a proper, or literal, meaning. 'Allegory' derives from the Greek, *allegoria*, which literally means 'to speak otherwise' (from *allos*, other, and *agoria*, speaking).

In Medieval times, allegory was a story used to render visible what would otherwise remain invisible. Passion, for example, as an inner feeling is invisible, but can be rendered visible, not only through the words of a story, but in the facts of the story which, in themselves are not passion, but make passion communicable. As Eco points out, for medieval exegesis, allegory is not only *in verbis* but also *in factis* (in the facts as well as the words) (Eco 1984: 151).

During the Romantic period around the start of the nineteenth century, allegory came to be linked, especially by Goethe, to a series of characteristics that contrasted with those of the symbol. Allegory was said to be 'transitive', while the symbol was intransitive; allegory designated things indirectly, the symbol directly; allegory was conventional (that is, the relation between word and thing was arbitrary*), while the symbol was iconic (see icon); allegory was intelligible, the symbol sensible and, finally, allegory expressed the particular through the general, while the symbol was a particular item which gave rise to the general only retrospectively.

In the most thorough modern study, Angus Fletcher simplifies the literal-figural description of allegory by saying that 'allegory says one thing and means another' (Fletcher 1967: 2). In this light, Franz Kafka's *The Castle*, first published in 1926, is a modern-day allegory of a society bereft of final truths even though, at a literal level (the level of what it says), it simply describes how Joseph K. cannot gain admittance to the castle. John Bunyan's *The Pilgrim's Progress*, the first part of which was published in London in 1678, is an earlier example of a story couched within an other-worldly, Christian framework, but which recounts events in this world. More generally, the fields of power and religion have provided the most fertile ground for allegorical texts: from Thomas More's *Utopia* of 1516, to George Orwell's *Nineteen Eighty-Four*, first published at the beginning of the Cold War in 1949. Allegory has often been employed as a way of circumventing political censorship: those to whom a message is directed will know how to read between the lines, as occurred with texts of resistance written during Nazism and Stalinism.

Any action, or series of actions, can take on an allegorical aspect – that is, can evoke something more than the fact of the action itself. Most ritualised behaviour is of this order (cf. religious ceremonies), as is action that has a magical or therapeutic intent (Fletcher 1967: 181–219).

The force of allegory today is no longer exhausted by the significance (or the notoriety) which it has often been given in literary studies. Since the 1980s philosophers and artists have become intrigued by what we can call the play of allegory. At one level, realist literary works are read in order to reveal another, figurative – that is allegorical – meaning. In this situation, reading creates the allegory, rather than the allegory being an essential part of the text, or object, being read. So while, in a previous era, allegory opened the way to a real truth, now a literal truth can give way to a profound poetic truth. In light of the latter possibility, the American literary theorist, Paul de Man, spoke of 'allegories of reading', and showed that the line, 'How can we know the dancer from the dance?', from W.B. Yeats's poem, 'Among School Children', can also be read literally, despite the received reading which assumes the question to be purely rhetorical (see de Man 1979: 11–12). And Walter Benjamin said that, within allegory, 'any person, any object, any relationship can mean absolutely anything else' (Benjamin 1992: 175, cited by Owens 1988: 216).

As a result, commentators such as Craig Owens have suggested that during the postmodern era (see postmodernity*), allegory tends to describe the structure of texts or art works, so that within the same work there is simultaneously a literal and figural dimension. Robert Rauchenberg's painting, *Allegory* (1959–60) is a visual exemplification of this.

Also characteristic of the postmodern approach to allegory is the appropriation of a range of different texts and images to form another whole which gives a new meaning to the elements so appropriated. Or again, other works simply become collections of items without any clear relation between them. Rauchenberg's and Sigma Polka's paintings, amongst others, exemplify this tendency, and Walter Benjamin, a key thinker in the allegory revival, dreamed of producing a book made up entirely of quotations. The result is that the spectator or

reader is challenged to provide his or her own interpretation of the images or texts for there is no generally available explanation, no original context or source, for the would-be interpreter to hang on to. Just as Freud said that a collection of dream images had to be read as a rebus, where the paradigmatic axis of association takes precedence over the manifest whole, so that individual images could give rise to insights often far removed from the initial whole, so modern-day texts are read with ever increasing frequency as though each element in the text came from elsewhere. Here allegory describes a process of decontextualisation and recontextualisation: elements from one context are evoked in another, the clearest example of this being a quotation, where a passage from one text is inserted into another and so acquires a new meaning.

Postmodern allegory also refers to a notion of writing* as a trace that renders identity impure, impurity being the other element always more or less hidden in any given text, discourse or artifice, in the mode of a palimpsest, or what can be deciphered underneath the manifest text. The point often made here is that there is no entirely homogeneous, enclosed and pure entity, as a book originally was thought to be. There are always echoes – traces – from elsewhere. The pun form is thus closely tied to allegory. James Joyce's *Finnegans Wake* would be nothing, if not allegorical.

Allegory has come to challenge approaches to language and society that are founded on (an ideology* of) identity* as something that is self-enclosed, homogeneous, pure and the same as itself (without otherness, difference or impurity). Identity, in short, is not 'other speaking' (allegorical). Whether this is an entirely positive development needs to be weighed against the importance of context in situations such as that of Australian Aboriginal art, where context also constitutes a community identity. The decontextualisation that allegory implies must also mean the loss of community. We are still waiting to see what the political and cultural fallout from this loss will be.

Benjamin, Walter (1992) *The Origin of German Tragic Drama*, trans. John Osborne, London: Verso.

de Man, Paul (1979) *Allegories of Reading. Figural Language in Rousseau, Nietzsche, Rilke, and Proust*, New Haven and London: Yale University Press.

Eco, Umberto (1984) *Semiotics and the Philosophy of Language*, London: Macmillian.

Fletcher, Angus (1967 [1964]) *Allegory: The Theory of a Symbolic Mode*, Ithaca, NY: Cornell University Press.

Owens, Craig (1988) 'The Allegorical Impulse: Toward a Theory of Postmodernism', in *Art After Modernism: Rethinking Representation*, ed. Brian Wallis, New York: The New Museum of Contemporary Art.

See ARBITRARY; DIFFERENCE-INDIVIDUALITY; METAPHOR; UNCONSCIOUS

ANALOGUE

Information technology and computing are mainly based on digital* technology, which is the product of the 'either/or' principle. Analogue procedures and phenomena, by contrast, are based on the principle of 'both . . . and'.

Many concrete, physical operations are analogical. These include aspects of communication that relate directly to context, such as inflection, rhythm and cadence as well as all non-conventionalised. (i.e. non-linguistic) gestures: facial expression and arm movements, posture and demeanour (cf. Wilden 1980: 163). Similarly, the senses, and thus human perception, are analogical, in so far as there is a direct, continuous connection between the senses and the external environment. In order to see and to feel the sun setting on a tropical island, one must be there. As a result, analogically based communication, unlike digital communication, cannot be understood outside the context in which it is articulated. The analogical is connected to context as the digital is connected to decontextualisation. This implies that no context-bound, analogical utterance can be exactly repeated.

Being part of, or continuous with, the world that they represent, analogical phenomena are thus 'iconic' (see icon). Translating iconic phenomena into another medium or representation is difficult, if not impossible: meaning in iconic phenomena, as analogical, is well nigh inexhaustible. As Wilden explains: 'the analog [*sic*] is pregnant with MEANING whereas the digital domain of SIGNIFICATION is, relatively speaking, somewhat barren' (1980: 163). The analogical may possess an essential complexity that has not yet been fully appreciated due to the dominance of digital processes. The example of photography gives us a further insight into this.

As certain commentators have pointed out, analogue photography (which derives its name from being based on the real physical process of light coming into contact with a light-sensitive surface) can allow the discovery of elements that were not initially visible in a photograph. As the information contained in an analogue photograph is almost inexhaustible, enlargement can produce new elements: e.g. the emergence of new details (a mole on a chin, a scar on a face).

With digital photography, this is not possible.

In the analogue domain there is no negation, a characteristic Freud also observed in the unconscious. Nor is there any equivalent of zero. For zero is the ultimate abstraction, while analogical phenomena are concrete. It follows from this that an analogue feature is not conventional, but real. So the notion of no-thing (zero) is foreign to it, as are the synonyms of negation like denial.

Emotions tend to be analogical in character because they are linked to real processes: changes in drive energy levels, sweating, shaking, dilation of the pupils, etc. Analogical processes are thus characterised by flows and the absence of borders. Linked to this is the idea that emotions tend be 'phatic', by which is meant that the actual expression of an emotion can constitute a link with others, quite independently of the reason for the emotion. Or, as Wilden puts it: 'The analog would cover the emotive, the phatic and the poetic' (1980: 166). The sounds of speech and the disposition of marks on the page are also analogical, even if the alphabet is not.

Analogical forms are not always different from others; instead they may entail a specific kind of relation to things. Analogically, pain is pain while, for a doctor, pain can be a symptom which then becomes a sign* of something else. Or again, the sound of a voice experienced as a (beautiful) sound, as compared to the same sound as a phoneme or a letter of the alphabet. A similar situation pertains with poetry when one hears and is moved by the poetic word, as opposed to studying the nature and form of poetic devices.

While there is now a tendency to see analogical forms and processes as a valid and necessary part of the world, this occurred only after an attempt was made by the structuralist movement to see all analogical forms linguistically and as the products of differential relations, that is, as being digital.

Wilden, Anthony (1980) *System and Structure: Essays in Communication and Exchange*, 2nd edn, London: Tavistock.

ANALYTIC–SYNTHETIC

The origin of the word 'analytic' is the Greek *analutikos*, meaning to dissolve into constituent parts. The opposite is 'synthetic', from the Greek *sunthetikos*, meaning to build up from a given starting point. An analytical whole, or totality, is one already present in an ideal form and can be examined as such. The notion of 'blueprint' also evokes the notion of analytic here. A synthetic whole, by contrast, is one that is essentially open and always available to accept new elements. Gilles Deleuze has said that the totality of shots in a film in cinema participate, through montage, in an open whole, and that the film whole cannot be understood as an ideal (i.e. analytic) totality (Deleuze 1986: 27).

In Western philosophy, inspired by classical Greek philosophy, the tendency has always been to take an analytical approach by asking questions, such as: What is truth? What is virtue? What is justice? What is man? This presupposes that the entity about which one is asking the question already exists, and that it is then a matter of coming to know the nature of the entity through a knowledge of its parts, or its qualities. All rationalist philosophies exhibit this tendency, as do philosophical orientations that explicitly call themselves 'analytic'.

Although the distinction between analytic and synthetic was foreshadowed by Locke (1632–1704) and Leibniz (1646–1716) in the seventeenth century, it was Kant (1724–1804) who really brought these terms to prominence. For Kant, an analytical proposition is one in which the meaning of the statement is implied in the statement itself – famously: a bachelor is an unmarried man. In other words, a truly analytical statement is tautological. It cannot be denied without contradiction. A synthetic statement, such as: it is raining today, or: all lemons are yellow, by contrast, does not contain the meaning in its terms. The synthetic has to do with contingency, while analytic reveals what is eternally, or essentially the case.

It is worthy of note that the distinction, analytic–synthetic, is itself analytical, a fact that can serve as further confirmation of the dominance still evident today in the academic domain of the analytic mode of thought.

Given a certain kind of society – a society of the book – the precedence of the analytic approach is the order of the day. This stems from the innovations of Peter Ramus (1515–72) who went against the old 'scholasticism' by inventing 'tree diagrams' and schemata as a way of organising knowledge. The model of the tree moves from the general, or most comprehensive, unit to the particular. This is an analytical procedure. To proceed synthetically, one goes in the opposite direction: from the particular to the general, with the proviso that the range of particulars will always ensure that there is never a category which is quite general enough to cover all the particulars.

Alphabetic literacy is also analytical. It makes possible a different approach to criticism because writing lays out the argument, or text to be considered, before one's very eyes. An oral rendition, by contrast, is ephemeral, indicative of the irreversibility of time. It is, in this sense synthetic. With a written text it is at all times possible to scrutinise what is already there, or at least to proceed as though the meaning were already there, with analytical work doing the revealing.

Looked at another way, this relation is the one presented by the history of cybernetics* and the movement from artificial intelligence (AI) to artificial life (AL). AI attempts to replicate human consciousness and intelligence by establishing what intelligence and consciousness is in the first place. AI researchers have tried to program machines to anticipate all the possible situations that might be encountered in given contexts. An ideal model of likely experience, based on the presumed nature of consciousness, is first formulated, then the machine is put to work. This analytic approach contrasts with AL which, using a computer, constructs a relatively simply program which is geared to reproduce itself. In the manner of fractal* behaviour, very small changes after each generation of reproduction have been seen to produce significant and entirely unanticipated long-term changes in the program. This is thus an exemplary synthetic phenomenon.

A final question arises as to whether art is analytical or synthetic. If it were exclusively analytical it would follow the model of what good, or even great, art should be. This is academicism at its purest, and of course led (and perhaps still leads in certain ways) to the exclusion of many art works from the so-called pantheon of art. Extreme academicism is breaking down in the art world, with works that, as if in a dream, are synthetic in that they bear the model of their perfection within them, much as Kant's notion of artistic genius points to its own model of perfection – this being the criterion that marks out the genius.

In the early 1950s, the philosopher, W.v.O. Quine challenged the distinction between analytic and synthetic, saying that in practice it is impossible to separate the two dimensions, and that the concepts should be abandoned. Yet Quine fails to recognise the extent to which his own inquiry is indebted to the analytical mode, and to see that it, like the majority of academic papers, is distinguished by the absence of a synthetic element. This is so, even if, in practice, it might not be easy, or even possible, to distinguish the analytic from the synthetic. There is, after all a fluidity between synthetic creativeness and the analytic discourse that enables us to become fully aware of this, apart, that is, from the fact that such creativeness is a pure experience.

Deleuze, Gilles (1986 [1983]) *Cinema 1: The Movement Image*, trans. Hugh Tomlinson and Barbara Haberjam, Minneapolis: University of Minnesota Press.

See ANALOGUE; COMPLEXITY; DIGITAL

ARBITRARY

While 'arbiter' – one in a position to exercise discretion – and 'arbitrate' are connected to 'arbitrary', the term has come to take on a more technical meaning in social science. 'Arbitrary' is often used to point up an injustice of some kind. In political terms, it might be said that a dissident's imprisonment was quite arbitrary, meaning that there was no obvious legal or *de facto* justification for it. In this usage an injustice is frequently claimed because some substantive quality is lacking, whether evidence, reasoning or some kind of foundation. Or it might be said that the choice of one term rather than another to describe a state of affairs seems quite arbitrary, that driving on the left is arbitrary: it could have been otherwise. The relatively recent, structuralist use of 'arbitrary' is connected to the absence of a substantive quality, and the idea of injustice, which depends on a notion of substance, is muted there, if it is present at all.

In linguistics, the term appears in the theory first proposed by Ferdinand de Saussure (1983) to the effect that the relationship between word and meaning – or, more rigorously, between signifier and signified – is arbitrary. That is, there is no substantive reason why one word rather than another should be used to refer to a given thing, or be the bearer of a specific meaning. The only requirement is that once a word is chosen it should be used consistently. On this basis, a given word's identity is established negatively and relationally; for language is a system of differences, even if a dictionary definition often belies this by proposing a fixed relation between a word and what it signifies.

Etymology is an important factor in confirming the dictionary's assumption of a substantive relation, and implies that, at any given moment in the use of a natural language, the relationship between word and thing is stable. Were this relation to be absolutely arbitrary, there would be no basis for attaching a given meaning to a word. Like Humpty Dumpty (and perhaps certain writers and politicians), it would merely be a matter of who is the master – or the arbiter – of a word at any given moment. Be this as it may, the idea that there is no essential foundation for the relation between word and thing (or meaning), other than that deriving from the system of relationships between words, negatively established, is opposed to the nineteenth century's search, through etymological research in the discipline of historical linguistics, for the original meaning of words, where the nature of Sanskrit, deemed to be the origin of all Indo-European languages, is of paramount importance.

The principle of the arbitrary nature of the sign is also opposed to the usual approach of a given user of language, who acts as though there were a fixed relation between word and meaning. This is because language use entails an imaginary relation between a speaker and words. Words become a transparent vehicle of meaning, or even of truth. At a conscious level at least, communication seems to depend on the permanence of the relationship between word and meaning. In understanding the significance of 'arbitrary', it is therefore necessary to distinguish between a systemic and executive perspective. At the level of the system, the belief that the relationship between words and things is permanent or essential is an illusion, if a necessary one. Such is implied by the notion of the imaginary*. To some extent, then, the principle of the arbitrary relation between signifier and signified is a linguistic, or metatheoretical view; it is not the view from the executive, or user's, side of language.

In light of the etymological approach taken by the German philosopher, Martin Heidegger (1889–1976), interest in a more essentialist view of language is now re-emerging. Poetry, or even art in general, cannot be arbitrary if by this we mean that there is no reason for the work of art to take one form rather than another. And despite Marcel Duchamp (whose work is now highly prized by art galleries the world over), a stone, or whatever else happens by chance to be lying on the side of the road, is not something that can be arbitrarily designated a work of art. A work of art, therefore, is the limit of the arbitrary.

From a sociological point of view, we find a strong adherence to the arbitrary in the work of Pierre Bourdieu (1930–2002) and Jean-Claude Passeron (1977) in the field of educational research. In this work, reference is made to the 'cultural arbitrary': the idea that the founding principles of good education are established through a given system of cultural values, a system which serves to reproduce relations of dominance and subordination of a given set of class relations, and which, as arbitrary, could have been otherwise.

Finally, the significance of the arbitrary in relation to information* science cannot be overestimated. The digital* nature of the operation of computers fits in well with the structuralist definition of language as a system of differences without positive terms. Whether we speak about '0–1', 'yes–no' or 'on–off', the principle is that the content of the operation is arbitrary because the differential aspect of the units alone is pertinent.

Saussure, Ferdinand de (1983 [1916]) *Course in General Linguistics*, trans. Roy Harris, London: Duckworth.

Bourdieu, Pierre and Passeron, Jean-Claude (1977 [1970]) *Reproduction in Society and Culture*, trans. Richard Nice, London: Sage.

See CODE; COMMUNICATION; DIGITAL; SIGN: SIGNIFIER/SIGNIFIED

ATONALITY

Atonal literally means 'without tone'. If the voice is said to be tonal, and thus able to express emotion, writing* seems to be atonal and conventional: a kind of formal algebra bereft of expressivity. On this basis, tonality is analogical*, and atonality digital*.

Quite against this way of proceeding is the notion of atonality in music, and in the music of Arnold Schoenberg (1874–1951) in particular. Here, atonality has expressive power. To understand the full import of the innovation Schoenberg's work represents, we need to look as some aspects of the history of music – specifically, the development of the diatonic scale and Schoenberg's challenge to it.

The diatonic scale sounds good to a Western ear, even though it only fully became the basis of Western music in the eighteenth century. It is the 'do, re, mi' scale of eight notes ('do' to 'do') every child used to learn at school. The physical sounds of the scale were famously systematised as 'equal temperament' by J.S. Bach in his series of works known as the *Well Tempered Clavier* (1721), although Bach was not the first to do this. There are thus two aspects of the scale, one physical (the sounds that are heard), the other relational. Tonality occurs when music is composed in a certain key of the diatonic scale, the key (or tonic) being the note to which the music 'returns'. The key, therefore, constitutes the tonality of the music in question. Music composed without a tonic, or return note, is said to be 'atonal'. As the music theorist, Robert Erickson says: 'The great forming power of tonality rests on these simple ideas: (1) a home base; (2) harmonic movement to areas within a key or even to new keys, in order to express harmonic tension, which (3) is finally resolved by a return to home base' (Erickson 1977: 83).

From a psycho-social point of view, tonality was music in the modern European West. It thus came as a shock when Schoenberg, building on the works of Wagner and Debussy, presented musical works that owed more to what is called the chromatic scale than to the diatonic scale. Chromaticism is the use of twelve half-steps (there are two half-steps, or semitones, in the diatonic scale) and no full steps to create 'altered chords': chords that alter the interior relationship between intervals, thus disturbing the familiar diatonic scale. Each note has equality in the open whole, rather than key organising notes existing within a closed whole. There are no cadences (chords of rest) enabling a return to the 'home', or tonic note; instead there are unresolved discords. In short, a new kind of complex harmony is created, one that produces a sensation of decentring that challenges the homogenising, 'homing' tendencies of the modern ego.

In a further development, attention came to be focused by Schoenberg's students, Webern and Berg, on the materiality of the notes, or the timbre of the musical sounds. A new melody called in German, *Klangfarbenmelodie** (sound-colour melody), emerged to augment Schoenberg's chromaticism.

Overall, the non-musically-trained can come to appreciate that, just as James Joyce revamped the form, or 'grammar', of the novel, Schoenberg and atonal music brought into being a new musical 'grammar'. Both in their own way have enriched the European emotional and imaginary capacities. Both have also given rise to new artistic possibilities for greater individuality of expression and for the expression of more complex forms of individuality.

Erickson, Robert (1977 [1955]) *The Structure of Music: A Listener's Guide*, Westport, CT: Greenwood Press.

See ANALOGUE

BEAUTY

Beauty has not had, over the last decades or so, a good press. Once, when the link between beauty and truth seemed unproblematic (cf. Keats), beauty itself seemed unproblematic. Nietzsche's claim that truth is ugly was symptomatic of the deep distrust that the idea of beauty had begun to arouse. Was it not really the case, critics began to wonder, that beauty simply hid more deep-seated and sometimes quite unpalatable realities – the reality of sexual desire, implying violation, not purity? If beauty was a pure front hiding an impure truth, what value could it really have?

For the Classical Greeks, beauty is the perfection of form. It is unity, order, good proportion, symmetry and balance. It is, in short, perfection itself: that which is conceived as being without flaw. For Augustine (354–430) near the beginning of the first millennium and Thomas Aquinas (c. 1225–74) towards the beginning of the second, and for the Middle Ages generally, beauty is connected to God's creation of man and nature. Here again, the idea of perfection dominates. For Augustine, beauty is based in geometrical regularity, with the circle its epitome. Aquinas saw beauty as incarnated in perfection, proportion and clarity. Clarity emerges as what is apprehended by the intellect, or

through a cognitive process; it is not simply a physical relation. Overall, beauty is the embodiment of a rational order created by God. It thus exists objectively and not in the fine arts, as a later era would come to believe. God, then, is the author of the perfect order of the universe; man, by contrast, sullies the universe, at least in an external, physical sense, even if his soul is ultimately perfect, i.e. beautiful. No doubt the unworldly nature of beauty here entails its decline in the wake of a secular age.

In the twenty-first century, beauty is making a comeback – not in the sense of displacing all the approaches to art that have become current, but in the sense that it is being recognised that beauty still has a place in artistic endeavour and, in a more banal sense, in advertising.

Even if the reinventers of beauty are unaware of it, the real thinker of beauty was, for the modern era, Immanuel Kant (1724–1804). To understand Kant's approach here, we need to turn to the nature of taste in the *Critique of Judgement* (1978), first published in 1790.

To begin with, Kant says, an aesthetic object of taste, an object able to communicate beauty, can never be distinguished simply by its existence or context. Existence is not part of aesthetics*. Recalling Rousseau, Kant points out that whether or not the palaces of the rich are indicative of the exploitation of the poor is irrelevant to the beauty of an object. Similarly, to cite paintings of nude women as being indicative of the objectification of women (or of woman) is irrelevant to the judgement of taste. In terms of beauty, therefore, a political or moral approach is entirely beside the point from a Kantian perspective. For beauty and political correctness do not mix – which is not to deny a possible political reading of art. What it *is* to say is that it is not the political tenor of the work that makes it beautiful or ugly.

A judgement of taste, therefore, is essentially 'disinterested'. Yet it is not an objective judgement. Aesthetic judgement, which reveals beauty, is essentially subjective and universal. It is indeed a feeling – an *immediate* feeling (*Gefühl*) based in pleasure. And yet, this immediate feeling of pleasure is not linked to emotion. Emotion, like sensation, taints beauty. And so, with the appreciation of beauty, there is subjectivity, but no emotion. However, emotion is always linked to a specific context: that this is why emotion falls outside aesthetic judgement. With the latter we have a feeling of emotionless pleasure, which is subjective and immediate, as well as universal. But unlike the Thomist approach to beauty, there is no concept by which beauty can be communicated. Beauty for Kant is not an intellectual thing. The beauty of any object is marred if it is conceptualised in terms of its use; use mars beauty; it also 'mars its purity'. Tattoo designs can be beautiful in themselves, but when they are transferred to the human body, the beauty is lost. That is, the beauty of the design is independent of its context. By implication, a truly beautiful tattoo design is a

museum piece, or what is shown in a gallery: that place which is a non-place for the object, that place which enables the beauty of the object to shine forth in all its purity and autonomy – in all its beauty. When speaking of the beautiful, Kant uses the term, 'finality', and not 'end', even though beauty is an end in itself. And the true finality of beauty is form: 'what pleases by its form … is the fundamental prerequisite for taste' (Kant 1978: 67).

In contrast to a previous tradition, beauty is not flawless, because the very notion of a flaw presupposes an existing conception of perfection, and beauty is not perfection. Even so, beauty is a form of purity. Against Alexander Baumgarten (1714–62), Kant argues that beauty and the 'flaw' go together, if we mean by this that the beautiful object, through its distinctiveness and singularity, has no model. The kind of perfection that beauty implies is an inimitable perfection: a beauty that is its own model. Against Augustine, beauty cannot be geometrical. Beauty is, instead, its *own* context. Its context is its (relative) 'imperfection', or (relative) 'irregularity': that which is the mark of its specificity, or singularity. Beauty is the embodiment of a universally specific object: one that will be immediately and universally recognised as beautiful through the faculty of judgement.

With the agreeable there is no universality. The agreeable depends on sensation, and can be verified empirically, just as the good depends on its concept, while beauty alone is autonomous: a 'universal delight'. This is the famous community of feeling, or sense: a *sensus communis*, of which beauty has no object or referent; but if there is a *sensus communis* it is not based on knowledge, or intelligence, but on the imagination stimulated by feeling, by a form of harmony: an interior music. As with the *Khora* as vehicle of the semiotic*, this music has an order, but is not subject to any extant harmonic rules. This music does not consist of the proportion of architectural harmony, but is a music of timbres, of chromaticisms.

On a more contemporary front, beauty is making a comeback in two further ways – through a revival of the subject–object framework. The first, represented by James Kirwan (1999), accepts that there is a relativity about what is beautiful, but that there is an objectivity in the feeling of beauty. Thus, when someone says that the painting is beautiful and the sculpture ugly, and another says that the sculpture is beautiful and the painting ugly, there is nevertheless a common feeling of beauty. To take this approach to the topic is to give credence to the level at which beauty is actually experienced and to take the question away from the dominance of philosophical aesthetics. In this approach, then, the fact that beauty is subjective does not constitute an insuperable problem.

From a different perspective, Jeremy Gilbert-Rolfe (1999) looks for the beautiful, not in high culture and seriousness, but in vernacular forms and in frivolousness. Frivolousness has no end other than itself. Beauty as an end in itself can be present provided it is appreciated in relation to changing circumstances where high culture no longer has the imprimatur it once did. Indeed, drawing's link with reason, and therefore with seriousness, means that it is no longer the vehicle of beauty. The colour photograph – in advertising in particular – becomes the source of beauty in a postmodern age. Through the colour photograph, beauty becomes glamour and frivolousness 'as the attractively unproductive' (Gilbert-Rolfe 1999: 80). In effect, beauty is brought out into the open, is popularised and seen as broadly accessible, as it must be in an era dominated by the growing democratisation of culture.

Gilbert-Rolfe, Jeremy (1999) *Beauty and the Contemporary Sublime*, New York: Allworth Press.

Kant, Immanuel (1978 [1790]) *The Critique of Judgement*, trans. James Creed Meredith, Oxford: Oxford University Press.

Kirwan, James (1999) *Beauty*, Manchester and New York: Manchester University Press.

BEING

Being is the guiding motif of the thought of the philosopher, Martin Heidegger (1889–1976). It means for him more than being alive – more than being there as *Dasein* (existence) – which has become the object of scientific theory and research. Being is also linked to truth as *Aletheia*: as that which comes into unconcealment. Thus truth here is much more synthetic*, than analytical*. Analytical truth is truth as correspondence, or as adequation, where word (concept) and thing are deemed to be in harmony with each other because the word is supposed to be determined by the thing existing prior to it. Heidegger's thought breaks with this common conception of things. Most of all it breaks with the calculating, instrumental rationality of late modernity* and postmodernity*. It is thought which places all the weight on thinking as action, as an end in itself. It does not deny mean–ends rationality, and thus the work of science, but it wants Being as thought to be given its due. Because of the dominance of instrumentalism, we are not yet thinking, and Being remains concealed.

Through what avenues is it possible to hear the call of Being – the call to thought? The Greeks experienced this call through a sense of wonder in face of the world. Equally relevant today is the work of language and art. Language, for Heidegger, is always more than communication in the everyday sense. It is also the history – time – which speaks in language, as it is the plain song which sings the impossibility of ever finding the word for language as such. In other words, understanding language through the science of linguistics will never enable Being to come into unconcealment. For Heidegger, 'language is the house of Being' (Heidegger 1993: 217). And: '[T]here is a thinking more rigorous than the conceptual' (1993: 258).

In this vein, the work of art enables us to sense Being when, as in Van Gogh's *Pair of Boots*, a world is opened up to us, a world otherwise closed as everydayness conceals it through causing it to be taken for granted. Art brings forth Being into unconcealment; it is poiesis as a form of knowing that is different from scientific knowing (in Aristotle, Poiesis means 'making'). Scientific knowing is technical, founded on *causa efficiens* (efficient cause), and is concerned with knowing beings, or particular entities, characteristic of *Dasein*. It is the field of the subject–object relation. In this context, it finds and names the origin of things, so that this origin can then be represented. Being, in contrast, is founded on the difference* between Being (*Sein*) and *Dasein*. For *Dasein* – as the notion of origin indicates – there are concepts and representations; Being, on the other hand, is not open to any concept. This is why it is such a powerful call to thought. For it sets an almost impossible task, yet one that cannot be avoided; being human is to be called upon to

think, but not just in the sense of propositions. The thinking which Heidegger has in mind goes beyond propositional thought and links up with poetry – with language speaking Being.

A difficulty often noted by Heidegger is the conflation of Being with human being. In other words, there is a risk of anthropocentrism, a risk all the greater with humanist philosophies such as existentialism. In his 'Letter on Humanism', first published in 1947, and written in response to Jean-Paul Sartre, Heidegger points out that Christianity is a humanism in that in it 'everything depends on man's salvation (*salus aeterna*); the history of man appears in the context of the history of redemption' (1993: 225). Every humanism takes us further away from Being because it is ultimately metaphysical – it is already known in advance; it does not say anything new, only repeats what has already been established in notions of 'nature, history, world, and the ground of the world, that is, of beings as a whole' (ibid.). In this sense, metaphysical thinking is not original as Being is original. In original thinking which takes us to the heart of Being, Being is not prior to thought, but is constituted by thought and language itself. So thought, language and Being go together and cannot be separated. Truly original thinking, is not thought which returns to reveal an origin, as is the case with the representational view of thought – a view characteristic of science. Instead, such thinking, *as* thinking, is itself the origin. Being does speak, therefore, but only as non-representational, non-metaphysical thought. Being speaks in language prior to all subjectivity – hence Heidegger's search of language for 'original' meanings of terms. He finds, for instance, that the word 'thought' is linked to Old English word *thanc*, 'a grateful thought' (Heidegger 1968: 139) – that thinking is therefore linked to thanking, to the gift of thought as the gift of Being. As this gift, Being is, in a sense, the speech of difference, a speech that can never really ever be anticipated.

Through this conception of thought, language and Being, Heidegger's philosophy challenges the way things are done in the calculating world of capitalist economic and social relations. As such, this philosophy is a force to be reckoned with – even if one must ultimately disagree with it, and even if one must retain severe reservations about it because of Heidegger's political and moral failures.

Heidegger, Martin (1968 [1954]) *What is Called Thinking?*, trans. J. Glenn Gray, New York: Harper & Row.
Heidegger, Martin (1993 [1947]) 'Letter on Humanism' in *Basic Writings* ed. David Farrell Krell, London: Routledge.

See ANALYTIC-SYNTHETIC; DIFFERENCE-INDIVIDUALITY; KNOWLEDGE; METAPHYSICS; OBJECT; ONTOLOGY; SUBJECT

BIOTECHNOLOGY

The term 'biotechnology' derives from the Greek *bios*, meaning life* as a specific way of life; *tekhnē*, meaning art as production; and *logos*, meaning the word (see *Logos–Mythos*); and scientific discourse. Technology and life thus come together in biotechnology.

In the wild – a state of nature where the principle of natural selection operates – biodiversity is the norm. The gene pool is extremely complex because plants and animals have had to adapt to a large range of different conditions over very long periods of time. If, for example, apples grown in the wild from seed (as opposed to being cultivated through grafting) are studied, it is found that there is an enormous variation in the genetic contents of these seeds, with the effect that each generation of tree will be different from the previous one. Each generation of apples will also be different, quite unlike the product of cloned, or grafted stock. The latter are characterised by genetic uniformity, or homozygosity: each new generation of trees contains exactly the same genetic information as its predecessor, a fact which enables the production of the same desirable fruit.

Modern agriculture is based on cloning – on reducing genetic material to its simplest form. Allowing genetic diversity – heterozygosity – to flourish would result in products that the modern consumer would find imperfect, if not unpalatable. The modern consumer, so the marketeers say, wants an apple with unblemished, red skin, firm and sweet flesh. Oranges must be juicy and sweet and without pips, tomatoes should be red, firm and sweet, with a good shape, etc. Desirable qualities also pertain for most fruit, vegetables and meat.

Over the last two centuries in Europe, modern agricultural techniques have narrowed the range of produce available through the introduction of monoculture, apparently in the interest of producing more perfect specimens. Indeed, the ideal of perfection dominates food production. As one observer has said in speaking about the exclusive cultivation of Russet Burbank potatoes for the French fries market: 'they're Platonic ideals of french fries, the image and the food rolled into one' (Pollan 2002: 244). Why and how has all this come about?

Part of the explanation is economic. The monocultural food chain is more productive because plants (and animals) can be cultivated more efficiently due to economies of scale, more prolific growth, and minimal wastage. On the other hand, monocultural plants are the outcome of genetic modification, and are therefore homozygotic. Since their resistance to predators and disease is vastly reduced, huge amounts of fertiliser must be applied prior to every harvest. Apples, in their genetically modified form, now require more fertiliser than almost any other food crop. Increasingly, the exorbitant financial cost of fertiliser and the danger to human health of using it has led to the search for an alternative in the form of genetically modified plants which are resistant to pests and diseases. Such is the project at the heart of biotechnology. It holds out the possibility of 'made to order' characteristics in produce: everything from reducing fat absorption to delivering vaccines (Pollan 2002: 202).

In contradistinction to the use of cloning within species varieties biotechnology engages in intra-species genetic modification, within the genome of the plants themselves (that is, within the total genetic structure of the plant or animal world). Whether or not this is a good and desirable thing is still unclear. Some argue that species barriers have acted as safeguards to prevent a disease, which wipes out one species, from wiping out all species, and that playing around with the genome is to put the whole of the plant kingdom at risk. For example, a superbug that became resistant to the potato toxin of a genetically engineered potato might then be capable of challenging all plant species. Others have said that the production of such radically new kinds of plants allows

them to be patented, and be classified as intellectual property, so that a whole domain of 'nature' would effectively become privatised. Under such circumstances, farmers could be policed to see whether they are using products without permission, and be penalised accordingly. It is hardly necessary to say that this is a gigantic change in what was thought to be a natural process.

The alternative to conventional monoculture farming and to biotechnology is organic farming. Here the aim is to construct a self-sustaining ecosystem which, through biodiversity, is able to withstand attacks by pests and radical changes in natural conditions. Sometimes the products of organic farming may not measure up to the Platonic ideal of current desire, but they do express the infinite potential contained in the complex genetic inheritance that comes from produce grown in the wild. With heterozygotic products, land is opened up that was previously unable to sustain agriculture. The Incas have shown the way here. 'Instead of attempting, as most farmers do, to change the environment to suit a single optimal spud – the Russet Burbank, say – the Incas developed a different spud for every environment' (Pollan 2002: 207). Through encouraging heterozygosity, the Incas had food for every contingency. Inca food production contained a philosophy, just as cloning does.

With the Irish potato blight of the 1840s, a whole monoculture was wiped out at a single stroke. While in other places, substitute foods could be called upon, in Ireland, for various historical reasons (endemic poverty and harsh Poor Laws, poor soil, harsh English colonialism), a single variety of potato – the Lumper – had become the staple of agriculture. When the potato crop was ruined, so were the people. Over one million died of starvation. This was monoculture at its worst.

The contrast could not be starker: on the one hand, the development, through biotechnology, of a single fruit or vegetable to withstand all environmental changes – in which case the complexity of the genetic pool is drastically reduced; on the other hand, the development of a multiplicity of fruits and vegetables to fit into a multiplicity of different environments. The choice is ours. Do we have a choice?

Pollan, Michael (2002) *The Botany of Desire*, London: Bloomsbury.

See CLONE

BLASÉ As the form of the word indicates, 'blasé' is of French derivation, from the verb, *blaser*, which came into currency in the eighteenth century to refer to the loss of sensations due to alcohol abuse. In the twentieth century the term, through the work of Georg Simmel (1858–1918), has become known as referring to the attenuated sensations and emotions of modern city dwellers. According to Simmel, life in dynamic urban environments brings with it such an intense range and speed of potential sensations and impressions that, in order to maintain equilibrium, mind and body filter out all but a consciously manageable quantity. This process produces a distancing, or detachment, from things themselves; for the idea is to control experience through conscious manipulation, not be controlled by it. The blasé attitude is also tied to the intellectualisation of

life Simmel claims characterises modernity in the city.

Rural and small town life, by contrast, was marked by a 'slower, more habitual, more smoothly flowing rhythm of the sensory-mental phase' (Simmel 1971: 325), which entailed embracing the sensory flow rather than filtering it, so that emotion and affect would have free rein. It was as though one freely gave oneself to emotion rather than trying to organise and control it.

This idea of the blasé attitude as a trait of individuality in city life is part of early sociology. Defining it as the analysis of, and response to, modernity, the early sociologists (Marx, Durkheim, Tönnies, Weber, Simmel) saw rural life as essentially simple, based in community and affective ties, with a minimal money economy, while urban industrial life was seen to be complex, abstract, formal and based on individuality and exchange. The idea is, then, that the blasé attitude emerges in an environment dominated by a well-developed money economy, where commercial operations become highly formal and impersonal, and where ties of association (citizenship, corporate membership, workplace relations) are also essentially formal rather than personal and affective. By implication, the blasé attitude of the large city is a psychological trait instilled by social conditions. Indeed, it must be this for otherwise the formalism of modern industrial life would be experienced as an unbearable yoke on emotion. The early Marx's theory of alienation* tends exactly in this direction, as does Freud's theory of civilisation.

Here, then, is where the question rests: on the one hand, there is the idea that the blasé attitude is the unavoidable outcome of a specific type of society – industrial society as it is manifest in large cities – and that fundamental psychological dispositions are ultimately the outcome of social conditions while, on the other hand, there is the idea that the formalism and intellectualism of modern city life unnaturally stultify the universal human need both to form a community based in affective ties and to express emotion publicly as well as privately. On this basis the blasé attitude becomes the outcome of an alienating form of society.

Finally, we no doubt need to recognise that many societies today are multicultural, with a range of communities cohabiting under the umbrella of a single state apparatus and/or geographical location. In such societies, hitherto rural people rub shoulders with, as it were, urban sophisticates, with the result that a new form of the social bond is in the process of formation, one that would be neither essentially affective nor formal in nature, but rather a new synthesis of both dimensions.

Simmel, Georg (1971) 'The Metropolis and Mental Life', trans. Edward A. Shils, in *On Individuality and Social Forms: Selected Writings*, Georg Simmel, Chicago and London: University of Chicago Press.

See MODERNITY

BODY

'Body' is a term with a very heterogeneous history. It has figured largely in relation to: the bodies of the planets; the biological, or animal body; the body of Christ in Christianity – both through the crucifixion and through the Church as the body of Christ. More metaphorically, 'body' can refer to a body of work (corpus); to institutions (e.g. regulating body); to the *corps de ballet* (body of dancers). The 'body politic' is the totality of members of political society. Overall, though, two key tendencies are manifest with regard to 'body' in the West, which are of interest to us here: these are the body in Christianity as flesh and as a source of pleasure and lust, and as the origin of sin. For ancient – and not so ancient – Christianity, 'woman', as in the figure of Eve, would be the primary incarnation of this body as flesh. The other key tendency is the body as the source of secular deviation in the mind–body dichotomy, where the body and its passions constitute an obstacle to the objectivity sought by the mind of the philosopher.

In Christian-religious conception of the body as flesh, the issue turns around the idea of the body as a vehicle of temptations, temptations that turn the believer away from the spiritual world of God towards the material world of carnal desire. The soul, in such circumstances, needs to escape from the material, finite body (from the body as flesh), in order to find the infinite in the next world. As the perceived object of concupiscence, and of reproduction, the female body is the body as such. Even in modern psychoanalysis, the body, as the mother's body – the child's first object – is essentially female.

The latter half of the twentieth century saw fundamental reversals of these two tendencies. In the first place, the disenchantment (= secularisation) of the world brought with it the idea (Mauss, Merleau-Ponty, Foucault, feminism) that the body is an entity of primary, and not secondary importance.

Philosophically, attention to the body derived from the work of phenomenology, particularly as found in the thought of Maurice Merleau-Ponty (1907–1961). Rather than accepting the body as an object like other objects in the world, or as a representation, which, in sum, implies grasping the body from the outside, Merleau-Ponty argued for the 'lived' or immanent status of the body. The body is the key part of my being-in-the-world, which means that I inhabit my body – but not like an external shell; rather, my body is connected to me as the most intimate part of my being. In this sense I can say quite authentically that I *am* my body: I live it, even as I think it (cf. 1992: 96). In this sense, too, the body, as something lived, is phenomenal, not objective. The objective body is in time and in space; the phenomenal body *inhabits* time and space (1992: 139). In contrast to idealism and the *cogito* (the 'I think'), the phenomenal body is not the result of a universal constituting consciousness, and therefore the same for everyone. Instead, the lived body is the specific, contingent body – the singular, concrete body, not the abstract, ideal body.

What of the other's body? Again, the other's body is not accessed through the objectified body any more than is my own. Others become accessible because we all inhabit the same world. Here, it is language which prevents a complete solipsism. In language, intersubjectivity becomes possible, so that the other comes to inhabit the self, and reciprocally: the self inhabits the other – in the thoughts the other's question shows me I have, in the anger the other's gesture provokes, in the sadness the other's grief evokes in me.

This general development, begun by phenomenology, to see the body as a lived experience and not only as an object of knowledge (as in physiology) has prompted thinkers such as Julia Kristeva (b. 1941) to highlight ways in which the body is also present in language and modes of signification. Thus, in poetic language, the rhythm and song of words evoke bodily drive energy, a phenomenon Kristeva calls the semiotic*. The latter could be seen as the material basis of poetry. Even in supposedly non-poetic forms, such as prose and everyday speech, rhythmic patterns are always discernible, implying that the body is imbricated in areas where it is not always visible.

Moreover, as the mother's body is a crucial stimulus to bodily drives, Kristeva's work has inspired a wide range of feminist research into the ways in which the body is present in every aspect of human life.

Through psychoanalytic theory, the body has been seen to be on the side of the woman, with the man, under the auspices of the father, occupying the place of the symbolic (that is, all forms of language and representation). Philosophy and its distinction between mind and body (cf. Descartes) would exemplify this division. Now, however, feminist and other research has been able to show that men and women incarnate a lived experience in the world and that, as a result, the body is *in* the symbolic as well as inevitably coming to have symbolic significance.

The concept of the 'body without organs' was made famous, after Antonin Artaud (inventor of the Theatre of Cruelty), by the French thinkers, Gilles Deleuze and Felix Guattari. The 'body without organs', these authors say, is a body 'without an image' (Deleuze and Guattari 1977: 14), an 'unproductive' body. Unlike labour, capital, for instance, is a body without organs. The body without organs is an open flexibility that can be compared with a solid, closed material body; it 'neither unifies nor totalises' (1977: 51–52). Such a body then is an open system which thrives and is enriched by difference. It is radically inclusive, not exclusive. It is as much a way of thinking about the relationship between parts and whole as it is an actual entity. And yet Deleuze and Guattari speak about a body without organs which can be mine – but as a multiplicity and open system, not as a closed body. Indeed, the body without organs is never conventional, never predictable, never coded. It is not a fantasy, but an unformed, material space of pure intensities. It turns out that the body without organs is less opposed to organs as such, than to a specific organisation of organs which constitutes an organism. Clearly, the body without organs is a form of resistance to programmes, or to 'God-given' ways of organising people; it implies that we do not have to be as we are: we can be different; we can create differences; we can resist enslaving forms of subjectivation articulated through psychoanalytic and other frameworks. From so-called patho-logical states – like schizophrenia – a creative spark can come, new connec-tions can be made. The diagram – which is liberating – can take over from the program – which is enslaving. The risk is that this clearly anti-para-noid view of the self and social life might itself be a bit paranoid. Is it really true that conventional subjectiv-ity is *essentially* enslaving?

Deleuze, Gilles and Guattari, Félix (1977 [1972]) *Anti-Oedipus: Capitalism and Schizophrenia*, trans. Robert Hurley, M. Seem and H.R. Lane, New York: Columbia University Press.
Merleau-Ponty, Maurice (1992 [1945]) *Phenomenology of Perception*, trans. Colin Smith, London and Atlantic Highlands, NJ: Routledge and Humanities Press.

See DIFFERENCE–INDIVIDUALITY

C

CHANCE Etymologically, 'chance' derives from the Latin, *cadere*, meaning to fall. From *cadere* also comes 'cadence' in music, which is a fall in pitch. 'Cadaver' derives from the same root. It evolved in Middle English into 'chea(u)nce', and in Old French *chéance*. This echoes the origin of the French, *échéance*, meaning the date something falls due.

It does not take a great deal of imagination to see that chance might also be connected to the Fall – fall from grace – in Christianity, as a fall from perfection and the advent of contingency in human affairs. And indeed, chance and contingency go together; death and contingency go together.

Chance has of course been studied in relation to the idea of probability. Probability theory goes back to the middle of the seventeenth century and was first developed in relation to gambling and the work of Blaise Pascal (1623–62). Basically, Pascal investigated the laws governing random events and showed that the probability of throwing a double six in dice in 25 throws was 0.505 (Hacking 1984: 60). Pascal thus contributed to the 'art of conjecture'.

In the nineteenth century, with the interest in the natural sciences and business, the theory of probability was extended beyond the framework of games of chance; it was taken up in relation to thermodynamics*, with its theory of entropy, and invoked for the calculation of insurance premiums and annuities.

Entropy*, the breakdown of order in molecular activity, could be countered, it was thought, if molecular behaviour could be controlled. To do this, the physicist James Clerk Maxwell (1831–79) imagined a 'demon' able to prevent disorder (energy loss) occurring in a system by separating out the faster molecules from the slower ones. In the age of steam this was a dream that many hoped would be realised.

Stochastics, or the study of randomness, also came into being in the nineteenth century. In this regard, Michel Serres (1982) links paintings by J.M.W. Turner to the age of steam – steam being an exemplary instance of randomness. As a forerunner of Impressionism, Turner, by comparison with the realist volume and form painting of the mechanical age of Newton, paints chance. That is, he paints steam, fire and smoke, clouds, water and ice. He paints the irreversible time of the industrial age.

Chance, in the nineteenth century, was located in a wider ambit than that of science and probability. It evokes two aspects of thought of this time: freedom* and necessity*, or caused and uncaused events. For the nineteenth century and its search for causes, chance existed by default, not in its own right. As every event was deemed to have a cause, so-called chance simply marked the limitation of human knowledge and understanding. For God, chance does not exist. On this reasoning, we think that an earthquake occurs suddenly, and inexplicably, because we have inadequate knowledge. With complete information about the state of the earth's crust, it would be possible to predict exactly the time and the severity of the quake. In fact, a perfect scientific description of a state of affairs at a specific moment in time would give not only perfect powers of prediction but also the capacity to bring about a reversal of time itself, including the events with which it was inextricably entwined. As such information is unobtainable, chance appears to have its day. Chance, however, was still to be an illusion in the nineteenth century: a true, objective cause was at the heart of things, but it was often hidden by chance. Appearances were thought to be deceptive.

Subsequently, chance has come to be understood as an autonomous force in nature and society. In Mallarmé's poem, *Un coup de dés* ('A Throw of the Dice'), there is an endeavour to imitate chance. As Mallarmé says, the whites of the page, 'the "blanks" in fact assume a striking importance' (Mallarmé 1945: 455). The poem assumes an importance as a physical entity. As Fraenkel has shown with a number of designs (1960: 24–28), the disposition of the words on the paper (first published in *Cosmopolis* in 1897, where the page was not an issue) evokes the waves of the sea and thus has the qualities of a calligram (words representing an object).

Chance is being imitated here in and through Mallarmé's poem. The poem is surreal. Always evolving, it generates effects; it thus ceases to be a unique harbinger of meanings that can be discovered through deduction.

Georges Bataille also addresses chance, recognising that it puts analytical thought into question. For him, analytical thought supports the restricted economy of balanced books and instrumental rationality. It is always a matter of suppressing chance, for '[c]hance represents a way of going beyond when life reaches the outer limits of the possible and gives up' (Bataille 1992: xxv). For Bataille, chance moves us inexorably into the world of ecstatic states, to what Roger Caillois, in his book on games, would call, *ilinx* (possession and vertigo) – 'a state of dizziness and disorder' (Callois 1962: 12).

Caillois reserves the term, *aléa* (literally: destiny, but more colloquially, the fall of the dice), for the key meaning of chance. Only in Bataille do we find chance integrated into 'inner experience' (Bataille 1988: 72), and thus into the manifestation of *ecstasies* – of communication. How does this come about? It is, Bataille tells us, a play between 'dizziness' and 'harmony' – *'the giddy seductiveness of chance'* (ibid.), or between being controlled by chance (giving in to it) and controlling it: 'Two opposing impulses seek out chance. One of these is predatory, inducing dizziness; the other promotes harmony' (Bataille 1988: 73). Chance, therefore, is not disguised necessity, and in this Bataille absolutely opposes the nineteenth-century view of the phenomenon. For him, chance is not an indication of limit to human intellectual capacities. It exists in its own right. Chance bursts through in laughter. Bataille evokes the Freud of

On Jokes, although Freud himself did not believe in chance.

Chance also provokes anguish. It is integral to a work of art if apprehension – a symptom of anguish – possesses the artist, poised before the blank page, before the empty canvas, before the sculptor's material. Creation implies chance. Beauty*, says Bataille, 'derives its sparkle from chance'. Imitating chance in art takes one into a never-never land of impossible thought. Yet, chance gives rise to productive mimesis. It is the synthetic mode *par excellence*. Which implies that it is also at the limits of analysis. Freud's hesitant writing on art confirms this.

Chance, as what cannot be predicted, as the unassimlable element for rationalism, turns the work of art into the richness that it is. As the most impoverished notion, because of its abstract nature, Being, from which contingency has been excluded, cannot compete with the richness of chance.

An event will not be repeated, but chance will come again. It always returns, and in so doing it remains one of the most mysterious paradoxes of human existence.

Bataille, Georges (1988) *Guilty*, trans. Bruce Boone, Venice, CA: The Lapsis Press.

Bataille, Georges (1992) *On Nietzsche*, trans. Bruce Boone, New York: Paragon House.

Caillois, Roger (1962) *Man, Play and Games*, trans. Meyer Barash, London: Thames & Hudson.

Fraenkel, Ernest (1960) *Les dessins de Stéphane Mallarmé à propos de la typographie de Un coup de dés*, Paris: Nizet, 24–28.

Hacking, Ian (1984) *The Emergence of Probability*, Cambridge: Cambridge University Press.

Mallarmé, Stéphane (1945) *Un coup de dés* in *Oeuvres Completes*, Paris: Gallimard, 'Bibliothèque de la Pléiade'.

Serres, Michel (1982) 'Turner Translates Carnot', trans. Mike Shortland, *Block*, 6: 46–55.

See ANALYTIC–SYNTHETIC

CLONE

Clone, etymologically, is an adaptation of the Greek word, *klon*, meaning, twig, slip. This evokes the idea of a small piece of material coming from a parent source of the same quality.

Botanically, a clone is a group of cultivated plants, the individuals of which are transplanted parts of one original stock, propagated by grafts, cuttings, bulbs, etc. In its wider botanical usage, a clone is any group of cells or organisms produced asexually from a single sexually produced ancestor. During the twentieth century techniques have been devised for producing 'clone cultures' from single cells.

From the 1970s onwards, the above meaning is used most often to refer to the cloning of humans or animals. Technically, cloning is growing a complete organism from the genetic material (DNA) of a single cell, so that the new organism is identical to the one from which the cell is taken. Simple organisms, such as plants, have what are called undifferentiated cells because a completely new organism can be produced from single cells, which have all the necessary genetic information to enable the propagation of a complete specimen. Humans and other mammals, by contrast, have differentiated cells, which means that single cells contain only specialised genetic material, relating to one specific function of the organism. Consequently, cloning a new human being is immensely complex. Yet, the technology exists for doing precisely this. Theoretically, it would be possible to remove the nucleus of a certain type of reproductive cell equipped with a full complement of genetic material and exchange it for the nucleus of an egg cell. From this a human embryo could be implanted into a uterus and birth given to a new human being with genes identical to those of the original reproductive cell.

Generally, cloning has the effect of reducing genetic diversity – as has occurred in agriculture. Biotechnology* looks set to increase the tendency towards greater homogenisation.

Apart from a loss of diversity in gene stock and the huge cost of developing clone technology to produce a complete human being, there are moral and political objections. The moral objections centre on whether humanity has the right to manipulate events to such an extent that humans can be 'made to order'. Homogeneity – at least in certain areas – might be the order of the day as individuals order children with the most sought after and desirable features. Some might call this the ultimate in human narcissism, typical of a particular kind of society, where the dream of the rich and powerful is to reproduce themselves. This raises acute political questions about equality. The French philosopher and psychoanalyst, Julia Kristeva (b. 1941), has protested that, instead of being a subject with a moral and intellectual disposition in the classical, idealist sense, the individual is becoming simply the owner of his or her 'genetic inheritance or organo-physiology' (Kristeva 1996: 18). In Kristeva's terms, there is a psychological and cultural loss when individuals are defined exclusively as genetic maps, and as bundles of organs – organs that can be transplanted and even sold throughout the world. Cloning, then, would be part of this process of the exclusive biologisation of the human being.

Opposing these fears are those who say that the genetic engineering does not erase subjectivity or uniqueness. Cloning, for instance, despite uninformed views to the contrary, cannot reproduce memory, experience, knowledge or symbolic activity, such as art. So the idea that cloning might result in indistinguishable replicas of the worst possible human types, or that it might be the way to produce a team of Einsteins, would seem to be misplaced.

Nonetheless, one could respond by pointing out that the very presence in a growing proportion of Western societies of the desire to circumvent contingency, and, ultimately, physical death, through techniques like cloning – even if doomed to failure in practice – is a sign of a deep psychological and cultural malaise, which needs to be addressed if the richness of our symbolic and imaginary life is not to suffer irrevocably.

Kristeva, Julia (1996) *Sens et non-sens de la révolte. Pouvoirs et limites de la psychanalyse*, Paris: Fayard.

CODE

Code in linguistics can be distinguished from two other forms: code as cipher, and code as a system of information. Both of these meanings will be discussed, but first we briefly look at the origin of the term.

Code derives from the French, *code*, and the Latin, *codex*, a block of wood split into leaves or tablets. Codex now refers exclusively to the manuscript volume of a work. Code can also refer to a systematic body of rules or laws, as in the moral, or legal, code.

Code as a cipher refers to the translation of one set of symbols, words or letters by others – hence Morse code, or the secret code used in military intelligence, such as the German Enigma code broken by British military intelligence in the Second World War.

Code is also important in the domains of:

- reproduction, where the code is a formula for simulation and dissimulation (here we see the emergence of simulacra (see simulacrum), where the code produces its own object);
- cloning (see clone), where the genetic code is involved;
- reversible time, where the code would enable the actual replication of events in time, and contingency becomes ambiguous;
- cybernetics*, where nature and machine become one;
- fractal* techniques (repetition of the same shapes);
- the observation of simulated worlds with the use of massive supercomputers, where cyberspace* allows a completely virtual world to be experienced as if it were real;
- the structural theory of language, where difference is critical, and not what the differences signify in themselves;
- dissimulation and lying: here learning the meaning of things – of life – is no longer transparent; the possibility of deception is great; learning is necessary (e.g. as to what things mean); social identity now entails using the available codes in order to signify who one is. Realism in cinema (use of effects) becomes

possible due to this aspect of the code. In photography, the faked photograph becomes an issue.

More generally, a society of the code supplants a society of myth. Myth is the imaginary truth of things. Religiously oriented (fundamentalist) societies are not societies of the code – although the code (potentially) exists in all societies, and, conversely, all societies need an imaginary basis (a truth). In fact, the code is never absolute, even if there is a desire to make it so. Computer technology is exemplary of the desire to make the code dominant. This desire is not always expressed in a conscious way; it can be expressed in the way people live their lives in light of this technology.

Umberto Eco's theory of a code starts from the structural model of language – language understood as a system of differences. There are two aspects to this: language as a given speech act, and language as grammar, syntax and existing vocabulary. Linguists have always been fascinated by the question of why one form of a language prevails rather than another: why this word rather than that? The structuralist answer is that, globally, there is no answer; or rather, the answer is that words have an arbitrary* relation to what they signify. There is no essential reason why this word is used rather than that. All that matters is the relation. Interestingly, writing* is a better guide than speech for pointing to the structure of language. Writing exemplifies more features of the code.

To say something is to say something new, and also something that is ephemeral. The code, by contrast, represents the permanent, institutional form of language. Without this, no speech is possible. The code also represents language as a system; speech represents the imaginary side of language because a speaker always speaks as though words have a direct and essential link with meaning or with the world of objects.

The code, as a permanent structure without content, opens up possibilities of imitation (forging handwriting, paintings, etc.). So, Eco argues, the actual presence or absence of an existing state of the world is not necessary for the semiotic model of communication to function. *'Every time there is possibility* [sic] *of lying, there is a sign-function*: which is to signify (and then to communicate) something to which no real state of things corresponds. A theory of the code must study every thing that can be used in order to lie' (Eco 1979: 58–59. Eco's emphasis). The essential feature of the code, then, is that it is the very precondition of reproduction. But the capacity to lie and the signs related to this must be distinguished from a signalling system. Bees' signalling system and the rabbit's false tracks are not part of a code in the strict sense because they cannot be used in order to lie.

It is not just a question of what makes communication possible, but a question of how it works.

The non-essentialist character of the code enables it to make inroads into a society for which reality as such is no longer seen as material, or even as needing incarnation. This implies that the ultimate reality is virtual and that it will, *ipso facto*, be found to be reproducible within cybernetics. It is precisely this cybernetic view of language that certain thinkers have argued does not entirely explain the working of natural language. For the rhythms, laughter and timbre of language – the elements of the semiotic*, in short – are beyond the confines of the code, as understood within digital* formats.

Eco, Umberto (1979) *A Theory of Semiotics*, Bloomington: Indiana University Press.

See DIGITAL; SEMIOTIC

COMMUNICATION

The word 'communication' has its origin in the Latin *communicare* meaning 'to share', or 'to be in relation with'. This links the term to community*. A disease can be communicated: that is, it can be transmitted. This sense came into being in the early nineteenth century. Communication referring to sexual intercourse is now a largely obsolete eighteenth-century meaning of the term.

Of relevance to long-established meanings is the notion of the religious community and the idea of communing with God. And of the communicant in Holy Communion receiving the blood and flesh of Christ as a confirmation of the community that is the Christian Church. The sender and receiver of the 'message' in the communion are, by that very fact, at one with each other: complete communication creates a single entity. Only in situations where there is 'failure' of communication are there individuals (see difference–individuality).

The religious meaning of communication has given way to the secular sense of the term. In the environment of the twenty-first century, the colloquial sense of communication evokes the idea of sending and receiving information over a distance using a form of media technology (telephone, internet, television, radio, newspaper).

The context can be domestic and private, as when friends and family contact each other, or public, as when politicians and advertisers communicate messages, or when messages are communicated (or at least sent) in times of war. Again, and more directly: individuals might say that they have something that they want to communicate to each other. Or the members of a couple might say that they are just not communicating, meaning that they are not getting along very well.

'Communication theory' is about the communication of information* understood as a statistical entity. In this context, communication could be a signalling system, or a variant of a stimulus response system. Information here is understood in a purely physical sense.

As a development on this, we can refer to Michel Serres's work, where communication is studied as the translation between order and chaos. Chaos also means noise in Serres's terminology, and communication takes place when noise is overcome. For Serres, the overcoming of noise or chaos is essential to human life. Noise, in short, is the raw material for communication. Noise (chaos) must be translated into a message (order). It is a 'joker' necessary to the communication system itself (Serres 1982: 66).

Certainly, in an age of information technology, communication is so frequently invoked that it has become a cliché. Modernity itself was, for early sociologists such as Durkheim and Tönnies, a product of a communications revolution, in which the telephone, the telegraph and radio changed society's relation to space and to time. An event occurring in one part of the world could be known in other parts in a dramatically shorter time than in the eighteenth century.

Compared to the months the first Europeans settlers in Australia in the eighteenth century had to wait for news of events from 'home', the instantaneous (at the speed of light) communication of events to, or from, anywhere in the world in the twenty-first century has made place increasingly irrelevant in informational terms, and thus in terms of the commonly understood sense of communication.

With potentially instant, worldwide communication speculators are no longer able to take advantage of price differentials in national or international markets. Bernard Stiegler relates that, in 1836, the Bordeaux Stock Exchange still followed the prices of the Paris exchange, but with a certain delay, due to the later arrival of information. As a result, the Bordeaux exchange became the object of speculators when the new telegraphic technology enabled information about changing prices in Paris to be communicated to Bordeaux before the official change in prices had occurred. In short, because of the telegraph (which was not yet officially in use), some speculators knew in advance what the changes in the Bordeaux stock market prices would be (see Stiegler 1996: 124).

Stiegler uses this example to claim that information exists only when there is a differential in the possession of it: when some people are 'in the know' and others are not. If so, the information society becomes a misnomer, for the electronic means now exist for an instantaneous knowledge of events in any place on earth. In practice, this state of affairs has not yet arrived, with certain locales not yet being part of the 'global village', for political or for cultural reasons. The point, though, is that, in principle, all locales can now be included in

41

instantaneous information networks, where information travels. Distance has ceased to be a factor with regard to information.

Part of the communications revolution is the now widespread use of personal computers, allowing access to the internet wherever there is a telephone line. Messages can be sent instantaneously through the internet – even to Antarctica. Communication has become decontextualised. And the question arises as to whether it is still communication in anything but the minimalist sense of making contact. To throw some light on this, we need to return to the eighteenth-century letter writer and the materiality of writing, which is relevant to communication.

In the first place, the material incarnation of the message will be in the handwriting of the author, something that can only be imitated with difficulty. The signature is another material reminder of the author's presence. There might also be some idiosyncratic features, such as writing from right to left on the page, as Leonardo da Vinci did, or the leaving of wide but irregular margins. Or, the author might characteristically leave no margin and write some lines vertically as well as horizontally. Of course there might be tell-tale ink blots, which suggests carelessness about the amount of ink on the quill. Or maybe the letter is written in blood. A political protest, as well as a love letter, could conceivably be written thus. The features referred to here can be called semiotic*, as opposed to purely semantic features, the latter being easily communicated electronically. They are also very contextual, as opposed to the decontextualising force of electronic technology typical of the information society, and are difficult to reproduce.

It is possible to argue that there is a loss of communication in electronic formats because of the loss of certain semiotic features. Decontextualisation seems to bring with it depersonalisation – the personal dimension being articulated by the semiotic dimension of the communication medium.

Of course, it might be argued that, as far as personal communication is concerned, there is no imperative to allow letter writing to disappear or, for that matter, other, older forms of media. Mail services still exist along side the internet, and in any case the dominance of one media format does not necessarily entail the demise of the other. Furthermore, would not the claim that the existence of the electronic technologies leads to the loss of letter writing amount to a form of technological determinism?

The answer to this question must be in the affirmative. And yet sociological observation would suggest that personal letter writing is a dying activity, if not a dying art. Part of the reason for this might be that people do not want to reveal personal semiotic indicators, which are only partially consciously produced. In societies which are becoming even more highly differentiated, individuality seems to demand more anonymity at the semiotic level. Spelling and grammar, once semiotic markers, no longer apply in electronic communication. The goal seems to be the complete instrumentalisation of the message, which implies its complete decontextualisation. This, in turn, implies the possibility of adopting a range of personas to ensure anonymity. The often-heard claim that people feel freer to express themselves on the 'net', should perhaps be tempered by the insight that this 'freedom' is the result of finding the means of hiding ever more surely.

Serres, Michel (1982) *The Parasite*, trans. Lawrence R. Schehr, Baltimore: Johns Hopkins University Press.

Stiegler, Bernard (1996) *La Technique et le temps 2: La désorintation*, Paris: Galilée.

COMMUNITY

Sociologically, community is often spoken of as having receded into marginal areas of society, such as the family, if it has not entirely disappeared. From the Latin meaning of this word, evoking 'fellowship', we get the sense of community as the incarnation of a common feeling, or spirit, where differences become imperceptible. Those in the community are at one with the community. In medieval Latin, 'community' referred to an actual body of fellows or fellow-townspeople, and this was also the meaning in the Middle English use (especially 1300–1400).

Another sense of community links it with the notion of 'common' (as opposed to unique), especially in relation to ownership, for example common ownership of land. Or the sense of common that refers to the well-being of all, as in commonwealth. The idea of owning things in common is of course central to the political ideology of communism; however, communality can evoke a common language (a language used by all or most people), and can also connote broad agreement or understanding, as in the phrase, 'common sense'.

Historically, community embraced those having common or equal rights or rank, as distinguished from the privileged classes. These people were known as the body of commons. This usage is now obsolete, except in the name of the House of Commons, in the English parliament, as opposed to the House of Lords. Even in this meaning, however, 'common' refers to the most prevalent, the most homogeneous, as opposed to the exceptional and rare. Democracy sees a certain rarity in everyone, without exception; or at least there is the sense that each has a worth.

Community as oneness also implies certain conditions relating to communication. Communication takes place in language, for example, when the message sent is the same as the message received. At the level of the message, the sender becomes the receiver, the receiver the sender. This is why linguists talk about a 'community of speakers'. Noise, on the other hand, is the gap between sender and receiver at the level of the message. A similar point is made when it is said that a message is quite transparent: its meaning is clear to everyone.

Misunderstanding, in the context of communication, is outside community. The mad person – mad, because incomprehensible to members of the community – is thus excluded from the community of speakers. Poets and artists too have been excluded, particularly those of the modernist avant-garde, who might have obscurity, not immediate transparency, as their goal. In this context community has been formed through those who are excluded, rather through those who are included.

The one who says things that the community does not want to hear might also be excluded from the community. This is particularly true in the political sphere where corruption or prejudice might be exposed – as occurred in the Dreyfus affair in France in the late nineteenth century. Community in language, the arts and politics can be a mixed blessing. Socially, too, community has been seen as problematic when, according to liberal principles, it restricts the freedoms of individuals, as can happen in very strict religious communities. In such cases, the rights of the individual must be weighed against communal rights.

So, despite the nostalgia of certain critics of modernity, community can have negative aspects. These same critics sometimes point to the alienation* experienced by people when community breaks down, or when it gives way completely to individuality. People in large cities, living cheek by jowl with others, but without knowing them, come to feel isolated and lonely. The transformation of the family into a highly mobile and changing unit seems to reinforce this tendency. On the other hand, it is also possible that individuals now seek a certain solitude because they recoil from the responsibilities a communal life (including the life of the family) often entails.

Community in the deepest sense borders on a religious, if not on a mystical experience. Christian communion – imbibing the body and blood of Christ – is a way of constituting community through Christ as the body of the Church itself.

Christianity does not, of course, have a monopoly on this type of communal experience. Many cultures, through experiences close to the mystical, reinforce the oneness of community by using rituals of various kinds. In a more secular context, the French thinker, Georges Bataille, coined the phrase 'inner experience' to refer to 'the states of ecstasy, rapture' and anguish, where the boundaries between self and other become blurred (Bataille 1988: 3). Emotional excess drives the self beyond itself so that it overflows the limits of the civil individual and opens up the possibility, through the

loss of self, of contact with the other. Eroticism is such a mode of inner experience; it makes possible a oneness between those so affected. Inner experience, therefore, is the basis of a certain kind of community. More precisely, inner experience erases boundaries, particularly boundaries established analytically on the basis of intellectual work. Inner experience challenges reason without simply being irrational.

At another level, inner experience constitutes a specific form of communication – not the communication of words, but the communication of anguished bodies, of 'non knowledge' – in a community (hence the added significance here of lovers and eroticism). Inner experience is the non knowledge induced through the loss of self in a desire to communicate (Bataille 1988: 53). In effect, inner experience in eroticism or rapture has a phatic aspect: it constitutes communication, and thus community, in its enactment rather than through what it intelligibly signifies.

There is one final point. We should note that inner experience opens the subject to the outside; this is the force of a 'loss of self'. All those experiences (ecstasies) which we might have thought were absolutely private, personal, intimate and internal – experiences founded on a high emotional charge – turn out, with inner experience, to be an opening up to the other – to the outside – and become the basis of a oneness constitutive of community.

Bataille, Georges (1988) *Inner Experience*, trans. Leslie Anne Bolt, Albany, NY: State University of New York Press.

See COMMUNICATION; DIFFER-
ENCE–INDIVIDUALITY

COMPLEXITY

Complexity theory can be briefly summarised in seven key points:

1 Complexity deals with unpredictable, or non-linear, aspects of the world/universe. Non-linear equations can now be written to map these unpredictable chaotic formations using powerful computers. To describe the world as 'non-linear' means, in part, that everything is connected to everything else, that small events can, in the manner of fractals in chaos theory, have large cumulative effects.
2 Indeterminacy becomes a feature of events, as instanced in the phenomenon of increasing returns in economics, which are particularly noticeable in high-tech activities requiring a large resource base to get set up. Increasing returns are to be compared to the idea of diminishing returns favoured by the abstract, a priori, economic model, which says that, inevitably, an enterprise will cease to be cost effective. Historically, this has not always proved to be the case because historical accident can change the situation, something all the more likely with very complex, high impact domains such as information technology.
3 Complexity theory moves in the direction of showing a necessary connection between the disciplines and the external world, and that, if philosophy is complex, it is non-linear and connected to the world willy-nilly; were it to be linear – like light – it would be isolated in itself and have no impact.
4 With complexity, the whole is never reducible to the sum, or nature, of its parts (a molecule of water does not have the quality of liquidity): the nature of the whole is thus 'emergent'; as complex, life is an 'emergent', not an inherent property.
5 Complexity is always in the organisation, not in the elements or principles (which might be simple), and organisation is interaction.
6 Economic modelling based on complexity takes account of increasing returns, or the effect of history, whereas abstract modelling of the classical kind assumes that equilibrium is the normal state (with only decreasing returns).
7 Because complex systems are unpredictable (although ordered), the emphasis is on self-organisation prompted by new knowledge or information. This is the real consequence of irreversible time. In a Newtonian mechanical system, time is reversible and events are, in principle, entirely predictable.

See ANALYTIC–SYNTHETIC; CYBER-NETICS; FRACTAL

CULTURE

The word 'culture' derives from the word for the cultivation of the soil. A spin-off from this is 'cultivated', referring to someone with a broad knowledge of the arts and sciences. Public debates can only really take place, some would say, between cultivated individuals, between individuals with an appreciation of what is happening across a wide range of endeavours and fields of inquiry.

Culture today has both an anthropological and a sociological significance.

From an anthropological perspective, culture designates the way of life of a certain people or group. This is reflected in all areas: language, religion; the presence or absence in varying degrees of a sexual division of labour; a system of marriage rules; cuisine (including forms of cooking); taboo rituals; a common history known through oral performance or writing; forms of dress and clothing; a system of manners; informal or formal education, initiation or instruction; a view of knowledge as sacred or instrumental; modes of agriculture and/or industry; the use of, and place in, space and time (including forms of travel); arts activities and forms of knowledge; conceptions of youth and old age; the presence or absence of a social hierarchy; ways of birthing and child rearing; mourning and interment rituals, and a relation to the dead; forms of medicine and ways of dealing with illness; a system of government and division of power; a mode, or modes, of celebration and sports; style of music; notions of community and individuality; modes of architecture and housing; interactions with, or withdrawal from, nature; rules of war and hospitality; forms of friendship and personal relations; degrees of hierarchy or equality in relation to wealth; forms of giving and receiving; a division between private and public domains; and forms of technology. Into all these levels, the anthropologist would say, the individual is born, or, as the phenomenologist would say: culture is a world human beings inhabit – at least initially. People are formed by their culture.

More importantly, this thoroughgoing and modern anthropological view of culture comes as a challenge to the idea of culture as something somehow added on to a human condition of brute survival, or to *zoë* as bare life* in the classical Greek sense. Even the most abject poverty (as in India or the Sudan) can take a cultural form within this idea of culture. It is a notion that refers to something deep seated.

Modernity*, and the capitalist economic system which accompanies it, on the other hand, often sees culture as a domain of human experience that becomes possible only after a certain surplus value enables a choice of ways of life. For modernity and capitalism, human life is first of all a struggle for material survival before it is a *way* of life, and such a struggle is an entirely instrumental affair – a means to an end. On this view, subsistence implies that the hunter and gatherer in desperate straits after a drought (which is most of the time) simply grabs what food is available unconcerned about *how* it is consumed. And so the capitalist sense of things is that only after the basic struggle for survival has been won can cultural practices be developed.

The anthropologist will retort that the struggle for survival – the condition of bare life – is exceptional and contingent, and anything but the norm, and that there has never been a stage prior to culture any more than one can say that there was a human society prior to language. The satisfaction of basic needs will vary from region to region and from historical era to historical era, even to the point where cultural practices will be engaged in even if they hasten death. This is because, for human beings, culture means the precedence of a *way* of life over mere life, and thus over physical survival.

From culture as a way of life we have to consider, too, the idea of culture as a separate set of attainments – as in high culture: a knowledge of the canon in philosophy, music (including opera), ancient and modern history, the fine arts, classical languages, literature, ancient and modern sciences. High culture is, in short, academic rather than practical, even though the artists in the canon – those who are revered, such as Picasso – are also, or maybe even essentially, great craftspeople. Popular culture (entertainment) – within which the electronic media (television, cinema) are included – is not high culture, because the latter is more than entertainment.

For a number of commentators the difference between high and popular culture arose with the Enlightenment and formal, secular education. The latter separated itself from the traditional, peasant culture of the people. To be someone in society was therefore to be able to separate oneself from popular culture embedded in rural habits and practices. Culture came to mean refinement in all things. Peasant dances were supplanted in importance by ballet; the fine arts took the place of peasant crafts; architecture replaced traditional building and materials; literacy and literature took over from the oral tradition of the people.

As Rousseau was quick to note, there is a political issue here: some have (high) culture, while others do not. The Enlightenment remedy is to universalise education, to give everyone access to literacy and other cultural goods. Has it been successful? The answer given is frequently in the negative because working-class culture – for one thing – seems like an oxymoron. In the work of a sociologist like Pierre Bourdieu, high culture is the way the dominant class retains political ascendancy. High culture is a part of symbolic and cultural capital, which objective indices show is differentially possessed.

The professionalisation of cultural attainment – the struggle required to develop a high level of expertise and knowledge – means that culture is acquired; it is not a given in society, as the anthropological account suggests. This view of culture evokes the idea of decontextualisation. Instead of being tied to place, culture is now mobile and flexible. In his justly famous semi-autobiographical work, *Tristes tropiques* (1974), Claude Lévi-Strauss ponders what it means to be an anthropologist and to travel the world, living within other cultures. Does it mean that one absorbs the way of life being studied as it unfolds in context? The anthropologist says: 'Through a remarkable paradox, my life of adventure, instead of opening up a new world to me, had the effect rather of bringing me back to the old one, and the world I had been looking for disintegrated in my grasp' (1974: 376). There are two ways of understanding this: one is to say that away from home the voyager's imagination is saturated with home; or, one could say that when the European is away from home he or she is never really away because European, Enlightenment culture is the culture, not of practices and ritual, not of context, but of the virtual images one carries in one's head irrespective of place – irrespective of context. Unlike the traditions it has superseded, European culture is mobile and decontextual in its essence. Writing and the book and, subsequently, other technologies of symbolism, are its true emblems. Such a culture certainly cannot be destroyed from within, but neither is it easy to destroy it from without; for the uprooting of symbols and peoples that has had such a devastating effect on colonised peoples is not what makes European culture what it is. What might really destroy such a culture is closure, a return to tradition. For such a return would mean that context would once again assume the greatest importance, even as it confirmed the reality of the culture's very finitude.

Lévi-Strauss, Claude (1974) *Tristes tropiques*, trans. John and Doreen Weightman, New York: Atheneum.

CYBERNETICS

Norbert Wiener, who founded cybernetics in 1947, pointed out that the term itself orginates in the Greek work for 'steersman' (*kubernētēs*) (Wiener 1973: 11). (Most English language dictionaries give this etymology.) This implies that the broadest definition of cybernetics is something like the study of 'control using feedback information', or the study of 'information feedback systems'. Or, more succinctly: 'the science of control and communication' (Porter 1969: 19) in relation to modes of organisation. It is in the quest for control over environments that mathematics and computer technology have been brought to the fore. But unlike the control of nature envisaged by a thermodynamic paradigm, where the behaviour of energy is the point of departure, cybernetics is based in patterns of organisation and feedback. Cybernetics is an informational phenomenon. If energy has to do with heat and its loss from the system (entropy*), information systems are cool, based in codes (see code). The steam engine gives way to the computer.

'The method of control by information feedback' involves the correction of a system, set to perform in a given way, in light of information which indicates that the system is moving away from the desired state (homeostasis). Examples include: steering systems of all kinds (boats, cars, planes), response mechanisms (firing at a target, or walking on ice), sporting activity (where to miss a goal by centimetres calls for corrective action), playing a musical instrument – in fact, all forms of 'learning by experience' involve control by feedback. Illness, and the maintenance of good health, also involves the use of feedback control. Changes in body temperature and blood pressure can result in significant changes to the 'homeostasis' necessary for maintaining good health. In sum, as Wiener points out, all homeostatic processes exemplify control by information feedback.

THE EVOLUTION OF CYBERNETICS

The history of cybernetics has given rise to three stages: (1) the period of the dominance of **homeostasis,** where the emphasis is on the self-regulating stability of a system that is relatively separate from its environment, even if it necessarily interacts with the latter. The question: 'what is the status of the observer?' of the system gives rise to, (2) the period of **reflexivity,** or auto-poiesis, which emphasises the control of the system through feedback; it presupposes that the observer is part of the system and that, as a result, systems are 'informationally closed' (Hayles 1999: 10). Autopoiesis also implies that the world is not external, but is internal to the cybernetic system itself, and that this system is composed of multiple visions of reality. If everything is information*, as cybernetics leads one to believe, then the body, as a physical entity, becomes redundant; (3) **virtuality** emerges as the most recent phase, where 'pattern and randomness' (of information) overtakes 'presence or absence' (of physical bodies) as the key epistemological framework. But, we might ask, are physical, biological and intellectual systems compatible? Is the computer an adequate model of the brain or of consciousness? Such questions have accompanied cybernetics right from the outset.

At a still broader historical level, cybernetics corresponds to the third age in the emergence of three stages of systems of control: (1) the mechanical stage (example: clock); (2) the thermodynamic stage (example: steam engine); and (3) the informational stage (example: computer). In the information age, 'mechanisms of all kinds, from computers to the hypothalamus [are] understood in cybernetic terms' (Hayles 1999: 90).

CYBERNETICS AS ARTIFICIAL INTELLIGENCE

As scholars such as N. Katherine Hayles (1999) have pointed out, Norbert Wiener's work can be seen to mark the artificial intelligence phase of cybernetics, otherwise known as AI. AI proponents, of which Wiener was the leader, not only view human and other living beings as systems, but are interested in replicating human intelligence using the digital* technology of computing. Even more: as well as wanting to replicate human intelligence, so that machines could do most tasks that humans do, AI advocates see the human as essentially intelligence – as mind. Classically Cartesian, AI separates mind from body and then links the human exclusively to mind, the latter conceived as a high-powered computer.

The halcyon years of AI (1950–65) were also those when the human mind as computer gave rise to 'intelligent' robots, and other machines, programmed to imitate human thought processes, processes assumed to be exclusively digital and informational. Of course, if mind were a computer, it could be replicated, almost by definition. For digital codes are essentially codes of reproduction.

For AI, then, human intelligence, or consciousness, is the model for machine intelligence. Machine intelligence entails the attempt to replicate human intelligence, an intelligence that is already there prior to its activation. Thus AI robots 'act' in light of a prior model which gives rise to a centralised representation of reality derived from external data. They only 'learn' in a very convoluted way, and often break down when confronted with information for which they are not already programmed.

FROM AI TO AL

During the 1980s, AI, which had continued during the 1960s, was overtaken by a new field of research: artificial life (AL). In contrast to AI, 'the goal of AL is to evolve intelligence within the machine through pathways found by the "creatures" themselves' (Hayles 1999: 239). AL, in short, does not depend on a prior representation of the world, but is an 'emergent' process, whereby intelligence and other qualities emerge through activation. According to Margaret Wertheim, with *emergent* life 'the properties transcend the sum of its component parts' (Wertheim 1999: 41). The component parts interact with other parts of the machine itself. There is no overall central representation that is taken as a given. Emergence takes precedence over predictability.

With the creation of artificial life, two contrasting approaches are in evidence: (1) the **analytical**, simplicity approach, which seeks to move from complexity back to the simplest elements (the Cartesian approach), so that models of biological life can then be constructed (this is the simulationist approach); (2) the **synthetic***, complexity* approach, where 'complexities emerge spontaneously as a result of the system's operation' (Hayles 1999: 234). (See analytic–synthetic.) Here, there is no distinction between model and life. Rather, artificial life is seen as 'alive', in the sense that it evolves through contact with the environment, or through activation, which is a kind of learning. Like the icon* which is what it symbolises, this approach to artificial life means that it *is* the life it replicates. Carbon-based life forms coalesce with silicon-based life forms. Carbon-based life is no longer seen to be life *per se*.

CYBERNETICS PROBLEMATISES THE BOUNDARIES OF THE SYSTEM

Humberto Maturana, along with his partner, Francisco Varela, was the principal exponent of the implications of reflexivity (acknowledgement of the observer) in phase two of the development of cybernetics (Maturana and Varela 1980). The term that expresses this development most succinctly is 'autopoiesis'. It refers to a system's self-organisation through self-awareness.

Another term, also developed by Maturana, 'allopoiesis' refers to systems which have as their goal 'something other than producing their organization' (Hayles 1999: 141). This is a 'cog in a wheel' situation.

The key question here is: 'Is the claim that autopoietic closure is *intrinsically* a feature of living systems, or is it how a human observer *perceives*

living systems, including itself?' (Hayles 1999: 145. Hayles emphasis). What might thus have seemed like a progression in cybernetics, through the inclusion of something equivalent to subjectivity, itself comes up against a seemingly insoluble conundrum.

In addition, as Hayles again points out, autopoiesis describes autism, not interactive social relations.

A number of researchers have suggested that the cybernetic age leads to the 'posthuman age' (i.e. a post-liberal humanism age), where: (1) information is privileged over 'material instantiation'; (2) access (to information) comes to take precedence over property or ownership; (3) consciousness becomes an epiphenomenon; (4) the body becomes a prosthesis; (5) the human being is so formed as to be 'seamlessly articulated with intelligent machines' (cf. the cyborg*).

In the end, the most testing issue of cybernetics is entailed in Hayles's claim that: 'human being is first of all embodied being' (1999: 283).

In keeping with the downgrading of the importance of the body as a material entity, typical of the whole field of cybernetics, AL advocates also assume that the 'logical form' of an organism can be separated from its material base (see Langton quoted by Hayles 1999: 231). It is the treatment of the body as a dispensable container which is the most challenging and, for many, most unsatisfactory, aspect of this region of scientific endeavour.

Hayles, N. Katherine (1999) *How We Became Posthuman: Virtual Bodies in Cybernetics, Literature and Informatics*, Chicago: University of Chicago Press.

Maturana, Humberto R. and Varela, Franciso J. (1980) *Autopoiesis and Cognition: The Realization of the Living*, Dordrecht: D. Reidel.

Porter, Arthur (1969) *Cybernetics Simplified*, London: English Universities Press.

Wertheim, Margaret (1999) *The Pearly Gates of Cyberspace: A History of Space from Dante to the Internet*, Sydney: Doubleday.

Wiener, Norbert (1973 [1948, 1961]) *Cybernetics, or Control and Communication in the Animal and the Machine*, Cambridge, Mass.: MIT Press.

See CODE; CYBERSPACE; THERMO-DYNAMICS

CYBERSPACE

'Cyberspace' is a term coined prophetically in 1984 by William Gibson in his novel, *Neuromancer* (1995 [1984]), where it referred to a realm created by computer technology, a virtual realm that became detached from the physical, carbon world of the body and nature, as these had been known hitherto. Cyberspace, as evoked by the novel, is a realm of 'disembodied consciousness' and of 'bodiless' experience (Gibson 1995: 12). For Case, the cybercowboy hero, the 'body was meat' a 'prison' of 'flesh'.

In *Neuromancer*, cyberspace is another virtual world within the world, a world governed by the matrix: the synthesis of the data banks of every existing computer 'in the human system'. It is a 'consensual hallucination experienced daily by billions of legitimate operators, in every nation, by children being taught mathematical concepts' (Gibson 1995: 67). On this reading, cyberspace is the realisation of the ultimate dream of artificial intelligence (AI) advocates: a world beyond the physical world that is the creation of pure consciousness, that is, of pure intelligence. By implication, this is a universal, abstract world removed from the materiality of existing everyday life. Indeed, once intelligence is all there is, there is nothing to prevent this intelligence from existing for ever; only carbon-based life dies, is unique and irreplaceable.

From another angle, cyberspace is a virtual milieu in which and through which people can communicate with each other and have certain kinds of experience, such as cybersex. But whatever we might say, cyberspace involves contact at a distance. The limitation of physical space seems to be overcome. While it might have taken eight to twelve weeks for a letter to travel from Australia to England in 1800, communication over the same distance can, in the twenty-first century, occur at the speed of light. This is the key feature of the information age: speed overcoming distance.

It would be misleading to think that the digital technology that underpins cyberspace and facilitates contact at distance is unrelated to past forms of communication, particularly phonetic, alphabetic writing: writing as it has commonly been understood. Writing has always been a way of communicating at a distance. The modern nation state, is unthinkable without writing as a way of keeping citizens in touch with the state, with the law, and with each other. Writing is what makes representation possible. This is despite Rousseau's warning that any society that extends beyond the range of the human voice is alienating (see alienation). Writing, in the Rousseauesque sense, implies a complete loss of original intimacy, if not of innocence.

To the extent that intimacy is connected with physical proximity, the internet, as the most obvious manifestation of cyberspace, confirms this loss. For cyberspace is a virtual space 'beyond' the physical world. It is digital, while the physical world is analogical (see analogue). Sociologically, the debate about the effect of the internet has turned around whether or not the loss of physical intimacy is equivalent to absolute loss in human terms. Some people argue that it is more than compensated for by a gain in virtual contact with others. The sociologist, Sherry Turkle (1997), gives examples in her research of individuals who live in physical isolation and find, as they see it, a virtual community, where they can form relationships with others and assume a persona of their own choosing. Turkle suggests that we are now in the era of simulation, where we 'come to question simple distinctions between real and artificial' (1997: 23). Others, such as Margaret Wertheim, point out that cyberspace is not automatically accessible. Or if it is accessible – to women, for example – it is not always welcoming. 'Behind the utopian rhetoric, the bits can still pack a hefty sexist bite' (Wertheim 1999: 293). Instead of allowing a flowering of individuality, cyberspace can demand a very traditional conformity, the breaking of which may result in the transgressor left to talk to him- or herself.

This 'new realm of the self' is also a realm of a loss of roots. Such is implied by the loss of the distinction between appearance and reality. In cyberspace, in multi-user domains (or dungeons) (MUDs), who someone really is – what his or her origin, or true identity, might be – is irrelevant. To all intents and purposes, identity *is* the chosen persona. What worries commentators like Margaret Wertheim is that the 'game' of the MUD is becoming equivalent for many to 'true' life. Simulation, within and without cyberspace, is becoming 'reality'.

Another approach to the issue is to see cyberspace as neither an entirely positive nor negative domain, but a domain above all that is beginning to affect human experience at the most profound level, much as the print revolution has done. Michael Heim puts it better than most when he says, in an appeal to move beyond the utopian–dystopian opposition in relation to technology, that, 'as we deepen our understanding of computer interaction, we will also increase our self-understanding' (Heim 1993: 70).

Gibson, William (1995 [1984]) *Neuromancer*, London: HarperCollins.
Heim, Michael (1993) *The Metaphysics of Virtual Reality*, New York and Oxford: Oxford University Press.
Turkle, Sherry (1997 [1995]) *Life on the Screen: Identity in the Age of the Internet*, London: Phoenix.
Wertheim, Margaret (1999) *The Pearly Gates of Cyberspace: A History of Space from Dante to the Internet*, Sydney: Doubleday.

See CODE; COMMUNITY; COMPLEXITY; CYBERNETICS; CYBORG

CYBORG

This term is a blend of 'cyber'(netic) and 'org' (anism). In an everyday sense, a cyborg is a person whose physical tolerance or capabilities are extended beyond normal human limitations by a machine or other external agency that modifies the body's functioning so that it becomes an integrated human–machine system.

In 1960, a report in *the New York Times* (31 May) stated that: 'A cyborg is essentially a man–machine system in which the control mechanisms of the human portion are modified externally by drugs or regulatory devices so that the being can live in an environment different from the normal one'. At the same time, one could occasionally read in scientific magazines that the 'Cyborg' was an entity of complex (see complexity) functioning which incorporated external components in order to extend its capacity to adapt to new environments.

Despite these early examples of its use, the term really came into prominence in the 1980s and early 1990s outside specialised cybernetics after the publication of Donna Haraway's essay, 'A Cyborg Manifesto' (1990), in which the author argues that the cyborg is a conjunction of technology and discourse. So the cyborg is more than the technologies which have produced artificial hearts and hips, electronic pacemakers, and a range of prostheses; but it is more, too, than the power of the imagination to posit a human–machine entity. The cyborg is as real as it is imaginary, and includes the connection of people to virtual worlds, whether in the neurosurgeon, who uses fibre-optic microscopy, or the player of video games. The argument is that a new form of subjectivity comes into being once information circuits become an extension of the brain and perception itself.

At a more basic level, a prosthesis becomes a cyborg element when it is integrated into the identity of the individual to whom it is attached. Woody Allen's black-rimmed glasses, or George Shearing's dark glasses; Captain Hook's hook, or the cowboy's pistol; 'Babe' Ruth's baseball bat, or the conductor's baton – these prosthetic devices, in becoming an extension of the (organic) person, also become part of the identity of a person, an identity which transcends the purely organic dimension.

There is, though, a wider meaning to cyborg implicit in the examples just given. And it is that an actual (as opposed to analytic: see analytic–synthetic) distinction between the organic and technological domains is increasingly difficult, if not impossible, to sustain. There is perhaps little reason to be surprised at this because the human body – as a key instance of the organic – has often been spoken of as an 'instrument', both in terms of its individual features (as in 'the human voice is a wonderful instrument'), and as a totality, where the body becomes a site of techniques. This becomes even more pronounced when learning and techniques are identified as inseparable. The human as such is essentially, if not exclusively, a site of learning. Thinking (ideas) and grasping (objects) are the outcome of learning – of technique(s).

In one sense, to posit the body as instrument and technique (see technics) is to move away from the intention behind Haraway's use of 'cyborg', given that she is primarily concerned to mount an argument that technology can be claimed as a feminist domain – that feminists do not have to shy away from the technological, and that through cyborg configurations, or connections, new hybrid identities are there waiting to be constructed. In another sense, though, the body as instrument and technique is also a celebration of the very 'confusion of boundaries' that is also integral to Haraway's project. Included in this boundary confusion that can be seen to define the cyborg entity is the line between exogenous and endogenous, which is often invoked in order to explain the meaning of cyborg. Analytically, the distinction might remain. However, practically, it is becoming increasingly difficult to mark out this difference objectively. As such, 'cyborg' is still another indicator of the movement away from identity as original, having roots extending back into the past (the family tree) and towards identity as a weave of connections.

Haraway, Donna J. (1990) *Simians, Cyborgs, and Women: The Reinvention of Nature*, New York: Routledge.

See CYBERNETICS; CYBERSPACE

DECONSTRUCTION

The term, 'deconstruction' derives from the French philosopher, Jacques Derrida's reworking of Martin Heidegger's German term, *Destrüction*, meaning breaking down, analysing. Generally speaking, 'deconstruction' has been popular in literary theory in America and Australasia. It does not simply mean analysis (as it has come to signify in common parlance and the media), but stands for the methodological arm of Derrida's grammatology*.

The deconstructive method highlights the inevitable point of duplicity in every text and, possibly, in every image, in relation to its system of concepts or terminology, whether at the level of argument, presentation, or mode of articulation. If, in light of the structure of writing* as double (as pun-like), as grammatology says, there must be a flagrant break with univocity in every text, and/or image*, deconstruction refers to the effort to find this break-point.

In Paul de Man's work, deconstruction examines the play between the 'figural' and the 'literal' (de Man 1979), neither term providing an exclusively rigorous insight into the way a text works. In an attempt to relate deconstruction to the everyday, de Man cites the comic strip character, Archie Bunker, who, when asked by his wife whether he wants his bowling shoes laced over or laced under, replies by saying 'What's the difference?', to which his wife responds literally by beginning to explain the difference, whereas Archie can be read as saying, rhetorically, that he could not care less what the difference was. De Man argues that such a case is emblematic of the ambiguous (pun-like) structure of all texts. There is always a point at which the literal and the figural cannot be distinguished (de Man 1979: 9–10).

Sometimes the break-point of an ostensibly univocal text can be an apparently incidental detail (the frame of a painting in aesthetics*, rather than the (mimetic) content), or an unassimilable, contradictory element – an incompatible element of duplicity in a concept or word. The word, 'supplement', for instance, can mean both something extra (a supplementary exam) and something needed to fill a lack (a vitamin supplement). The pun and the rebus also evoke the plurality of meaning in words and images (think of James Joyce's *Finnegans Wake* and Salvador Dalí's surrealist paintings). Having once identified the break-point, the deconstructionist can then push it further until the mimetic viability of the text (its univocity) collapses.

Is deconstruction thus an essentially negative strategy? This depends on the point of view adopted. It is negative if a univocal text is prized above all else; but not if the generation of a plurality of meanings is seen as an enrichment of philosophy and communication*. Deconstruction also might be found wanting when attempting to cope with the sacred text as the key instance of unique meaning. For here is a text which is what it is *in* its univocity, even if those who are sceptical about the relevance of the sacred (see sacred-profane) in today's secular society will claim that there is no univocal text; rather, it is proposed, every text qua text, is plurivocal.

Beyond this, there is a tendency to avoid defining deconstruction for the very reason that it bypasses traditional philosophical prescriptions and definitions. Indeed, prescriptions and definitions are ripe for deconstruction, which all goes to confirm that, as someone once said, 'Deconstruction is not what you think' (meaning, too, that you don't 'think it' because it is a mode of thinking).

De Man, Paul (1979) *Allegories of Reading: Figural Language in Rousseau, Nietzsche, Rilke, and Proust*, New Haven and London: Yale University Press.

See MIMESIS

DICTIONARY –ENCYCLOPEDIA

'Dictionary' comes from the medieval Latin, *dictionarium*, meaning manual, and *dictio*, to speak, enunciate – hence, 'diction'. 'Encyclopedia' derives from the Greek, *egkuklios paideia*, meaning all-round education.

Generally speaking, both dictionaries and encyclopedias – which are now being produced at an ever greater rate as classical liberal education declines – are books defining, or giving interpretations of, various vocabularies: the most common for the dictionary being of natural languages, and the most common for encyclopedias being general knowledge. In both genres there is now an increasing number of specialist volumes, such as dictionaries of sociology or philosophy, and encyclopedias of the social sciences. It has to be acknowledged that an additional reason for the prevalence of dictionaries and encyclopedias is commercial success. This is no doubt partly due to the broadening of the educational base and a consequent demand for reference materials. This fact partly evokes the purpose of the two kinds of reference book when they first appeared in the eighteenth century – two famous examples being Diderot and D'Alembert's *Encyclopédie*, which began appearing in 1751, and Dr Johnson's *Dictionary of the English Language*, which first appeared in 1755.

Eco (1984) has found a broader significance in the relationship between dictionary and encyclopedia, which broadly echoes the distinction between analytical and synthetic*. Eco's model of a dictionary is the linguistic one. And so we shall stick to this because it provides a model of language and thought. A dictionary, in its structure, is 'tree-like' and closed, with each word ultimately linked to every other word. Or rather: a dictionary is closed because, in principle, all meanings of a word can be given; all contexts can be considered. Thus when I say that the *end* of the film was sad, I realise, upon looking in the dictionary that 'end' as a noun in fact has at least 10 different levels of meaning, which includes the figurative sense as in, 'no problem, my *end*' (= everything is fine).

From this we do not yet have the sense that a dictionary is hierarchically structured. But according to Eco, this is indeed the case, since definitions go from the general to the particular. Thus, the first meaning of 'end' is 'extreme limit'. 'Extreme' is first defined as 'reaching a high or the highest degree'. 'Limit' is defined as 'a point, line or level beyond which something does not or may not extend or pass'. This illustrates Eco's point that in the conventional dictionary there is no exact reciprocity or equality between the *definiens* and *definiendum*. For while an end is a limit, a limit is not just an end. In fact, 'end' does not even appear anywhere in the entry for 'limit'.

Although the dictionary is structured around a hierarchy of meanings, where the most inclusive are the most important, to fulfil its task properly, a dictionary has to be open to new meanings arising, as it has to be open to further interpretations of existing lexical items. In other words, a dictionary – or the dictionary form – has to become encyclopedic. According to Eco, a dictionary is, in principle, '*a disguised encyclopedia*' (Eco 1984: 68. Eco's emphasis).

In contrast to the dictionary 'as a regulative idea', the encyclopedia is horizontally organised and contains broad-ranging explanations. The area of the encyclopedia is, in principle, unlimited. It is an open whole, in which new connections can be made. The images Eco invokes here in an effort to specify the structure of the encyclopedia are: net, rhizome*, map and labyrinth. Unlike the dictionary structure, there is no necessary or essential connection between the subjects dealt with, although connections can be made. There is no end to the encyclopedia since there is no end to knowledge. An encyclopedia is thus a vast labyrinth 'with no centre'; it is an 'inconceivable globality' (Eco 1984: 83), in relation to which maps will be drawn up according to the interests and resources of the inquirer. The encyclopedia is clearly a synthetic phenomenon.

Interestingly, the fact of being unable to represent the whole – the fact of the openness of the labyrinth, or net – means that every approach to knowledge will be locally inflected. If we take the internet as a possible example of the encyclopedia as a regulative idea, we see that, in its encyclopedic aspect, no single position can englobe the whole, for the latter is essentially open. Consequently, the local view assumes greater importance, for better or for worse. For better, perhaps, in that the locality (whether a particular cultural, philosophical, social or gendered position) can come into focus without being submerged by a greater whole; for worse, in that the place and significance of the universal becomes uncertain. Maybe the liberty opened up by the encyclopedic labyrinth has to be tempered by a respect for the pre-existing universal values which derive from a centre.

No doubt societies of the modern world influenced by Western-style democracy are becoming more encyclopedic, with local values coming to dominate over universal values. Eco's response to this is to turn the dictionary's regulative idea of a closed totality, which informs the idea of universal values, into a pragmatic device to be used 'when one needs it'. It is, however, difficult to imagine exactly what this would mean. Does it mean that we support human rights when we need to and not at other times? Or that we invoke the dictionary when we need to support human rights and other ideas about which there can be no compromise? The problem here is that it seems unlikely that the latter position could be supported without a less pragmatic status being given to the dictionary as such. No doubt this points to precisely a dilemma of our times.

Eco, Umberto (1984) *Semiotics and the Philosophy of Language*, London: Macmillan.

See ANALYTIC–SYNTHETIC

DIEGESIS
Adopted from the Greek, *diēgēsis*, narration as spoken (what happens, or the stating of the case), this may be contrasted with *mimēsis** meaning, 'to show' (see Genette 1969: 50).

Diegesis is possibly used most often in film theory to refer to the setting in which events unfold, rather than to the events themselves. To show the struggle for survival of a group of people, the film-maker might choose a desert island in the eighteenth century, as the key time and place situation – or 'scene' – for the narrative; or a remote beach in Australia in the 1950s might be chosen; or a large city after a bomb attack in 2220. The diegesis will become prominent to the extent that the setting for what happens also impinges on the *way* that events unfold, rather than on the nature of the events themselves. For instance, the isolation of suburban life in the 1980s will have a different effect on a struggle for survival to the isolation of a prison.

This cinematic use of the term is preceded by a more literary critical meaning, where diegesis refers, after

Plato, to the third person narrative, and is distinguished from dialogue, monologue or 'stream of consciousness' formats. In other words, the narrative dimension (diegesis) is to be distinguished from the dramatic dimension (mimesis*).

The real significance of the term, diegesis, however, arose with the structuralist and semiological study of cinema in the 1970s – specifically with the work of Christian Metz. As with other arts like literature, the semiologist was keen to show how, despite its apparent realism, cinema was also riven by conventional procedures, to the point, Metz speculated, where it could even be grasped as a kind of language. Here then is a popular and realist art form, which will be shown by the semiologist to be anything but realist in an objective sense. In short, films are open to analysis, and the idea of diegesis became the key to such analysis: 'The notion of *diegesis* is as important for film semiology as the idea of art' (Metz 1978: 100). For Metz, diegesis includes the whole of the denotative dimension of the film, including all aspects of the narrative, aspects that entail the temporal and spatial context, the characters, landscapes, events, and all other narrative elements. Diegesis becomes, as it were, the very condition of possibility of a given film. The elements making up the diegesis go to make up the whole which is the film.

Perhaps the clearest way to present the idea of diegesis is to image* a story line (a man loses all because of his greed), then image how this story line is to be realised (a young man speculates on the New York stock market in the 1980s and loses all because, driven to accumulate still more wealth, he takes ever greater risks). The diegesis would be the specific realisation of the story in a feature film. As a result, we see that cinema can tell the same story over and over again; it is the diegesis which makes each telling a unique event. In this sense, although diegesis does not include an analysis of stylistics, for many film theorists it includes the essential elements of the cinematic experience itself.

And yet Metz and others speak, too, about a 'non-diegetic' image. What would this be? An example given by Metz is that of an image which has 'purely comparative value*, and presenting an object external to the action' (Metz 1978: 126). There are also, according to Metz, displaced diegetic images: images taken out of their expected sequence and inserted elsewhere for emphasis. Some images of the heroine, Lola, running in the 1998 German film, *Run Lola Run*, might exemplify this type of image.

Overall, it is the diegesis of a film which can enable a heightened awareness of the way the action is presented in its setting. Finally, if the screen is equivalent to the signifier, the diegesis is the equivalent of the signified (Metz 1978: 129).

Genette, Gérard (1969) *Figures II*, Paris: Seuil.
Metz, Christian (1978) *Essais sur la signification du cinéma*, Paris: Klincksieck.

DIFFÉRANCE

Différance is a neologism coined by the French philosopher, Jacques Derrida (b. 1930), in the context of grammatology* and deconstruction* in order to indicate that writing* comes out of non-presence. Différance echoes the French word, *différer*, which means both to defer (a temporalisation), and to differ (a spatialisation). According to Derrida, we are dealing neither with a word nor a concept. Instead, différance is the inexpressible plurality that is always at work in language understood, as Ferdinand de Saussure (1857–1913) said, as a system of differences. This implies that each element in language, understood as a sign* system, echoes other elements, making language an intertextual weaving of voices, much as one finds in James Joyce's *Finnegans Wake*.

Another aspect of différance is that it problematises the commonly accepted secondary status of writing in relation to speech. For it is impossible to hear the difference between difference and différance, with the silent 'a'; one can only see it, thus confirming that many essential diacritical marks are visual, not auditory, and so are a distancing from the immediate presence emblematised in the voice.

Différance does not evoke identity (which is a pure entity), and thus does not evoke presence (= immediacy): for, as writing, it is a mediation that is simultaneously one and other. In sum, if identity is the presence of the selfsame, différance stands for non-presence as a temporal and spatial distancing. If truth and Being since the Greeks have been understood in the West as presence, différance must bring a different notion of truth* and of Being as différance. It thus claims to bring into question the tradition of philosophy, indebted to Plato and Aristotle, called metaphysics (or 'logocentrism', to use Derrida's term), where identity and non-contradiction are privileged.

Différance, then, is the impurity of things which, as impure, cannot be shown or demonstrated. As such, différance cannot be conceptualised because concepts are concepts of pure entities – of identities (see identity), not of differences. Hence, differences are impurities which cannot be shown under an identity.

Should we say, finally, that this is all philosopher's talk, talk for the specialists and not of concern to non-philosophers, just as a common response to Freud's theory of the unconscious was to say that it was of concern only to (some) psychoanalysts? To take a cue from différance, it could be said in response that there is always a trace of philosophy in non-philosophy, that the ideas of common sense are invariably founded in certain philosophical assumptions, whether or not people are aware of this. Thus, it might well be that the thinking behind différance could itself one day be close to common sense, and that a new era of thought could come into place, one that would also be indebted to information* technology.

Or perhaps différance is, despite itself, indicative of the dominance of analytical thinking to the detriment of experience, the latter being equivalent to full presence, even if this is essentially imaginary*. We are most often caught in the position of trying to determine what différance is exactly – an entirely analytical strategy – when the real point is that différance is a complexity which gives rise to things without itself being revealed. As such, it connects with the spirit driving the development of artificial life (see cybernetics).

Derrida, Jacques (1982 [1972]) 'Différance', in *Margins of Philosophy*, trans. Alan Bass, Chicago: University of Chicago Press.

See DIFFERENCE– INDIVIDUALITY;

DIFFERENCE–INDIVIDUALITY

Difference is related to identity*, to that which is the same as itself. There can be a relationship between two identities, which are separated by difference. Difference here is the third term which enables the two identities, but is itself without identity. Difference cannot, therefore, be represented: it is impossible to give an instance of difference in itself.

Difference as an impossible representation has led to much confusion in social and political life. Often it is claimed that society is a kind of unity in difference in the sense that there are many different identities which make up society. On the basis of our earlier distinction it is clear that identities are united by at least one common feature: in order to be identities they are all the same as themselves, and as identities they can be represented. Even more: from identity comes the model (of society, of the economy, etc.), or the typical figure. If we take the identity of a person, we might be able to say that: this is male (and thus has the characteristics of all males as a male), is a young male (and thus has the characteristic of all young males as a young male), is tall, of medium build, of fair complexion, has blue eyes, a round head, long hair, is wealthy, comes from a middle-class family, is university educated, is intelligent, plays tennis, is heterosexual, is conservative, has travelled to Rome, is Protestant, likes Van Gogh, fell off his bicycle at the age of three, etc. In effect, identity does not lead to the *differentia specifica* of this person. Identity easily leads to generalities through the fact that characteristics are in fact categories, and so have the effect of making people the same. In order that there can be an identity, there must be a representation of it.

Difference, by comparison, has no common quality to which we can refer in order to distinguish it. Even though difference is at the other pole from identity, were difference to be removed, identity would disappear also – first, as what sustains individual identities; then, when identity became a single entity – oneness – this would disappear as well because a single entity is unimaginable without otherness (= difference).

All this might seem very abstract and the result of an excessive concern for logical correctness, but it does have practical import. First of all, without difference, there would only be sameness; it is not in terms of our identity that we are unique, but in terms of difference. Second, were it not for difference, there would be no distinctions. Similarly, if it was not for the devil there would be no God; for to say that God is everything is to say that He is nothing. This is simply to remind us that difference has been important in sacred as well as mundane affairs.

Difference is crucial for understanding individuality. It is here in particular that the social domain is of great importance. If we imagine a very traditional family unit where the individual is submerged in the solidarity and loyalty of the group, we can see that this entails the merging of difference (individuality) into identity. Traditionalist and, even more, fundamentalist groups valorise group solidarity above difference. Not to follow custom, not to follow the legitimised authority, is to put the solidarity of the group at risk. In certain circumstances perhaps, even the group's very survival as a group could be put at risk by individual actions.

It seems that all entities which value solidarity devalue individuality – as least they devalue the kind of individuality which puts individual rights on a par with group rights. All modern political parties which, *as* parties, have been set up on the basis of group solidarity, find it difficult to deal with individuality. The latter, as difference, infects identity as group solidarity.

The way things are often seen, however, is in terms of one identity (an individual) opposing the power of the group. And so the son opposes the father in the family, and the dissident opposes the leadership in the political party. 'Ego against ego', as they say, or identity against identity. But in opposing authority as an individual, one rather becomes the unassimilable element (hence expulsion from the party) – the singularity as difference – that threatens the very being of the group. Let us be clear here: not another identity, but difference as revolt threatens the group.

It is often said, by psychologists as well as by common sense, that a true individual is someone who has a strong identity: that individuality implies being identical with oneself, being a unity. A counter-view is that individuality is not identity, but difference, that individuality as such cannot therefore be represented. Identity is always derived from the solidarity of the group, while individuality derives from being the difference that challenges all solidarity. The link between identity and the group becomes clear when we are reminded that identity goes together with identification – that is, it entails the uniting with a dimension external to the ego.

It is no doubt a truism to say that, in terms of well-being, extreme forms of identity (loss of individuality) or of individuality (loss of identity) are difficult, if not impossible, to bear. Each person strives for a certain equilibrium. The question for an information* society, which increasingly devalues all forms of solidarity, is whether persons in such an environment can support the intensely virtual experience a life of individuality entails. Even more: can there really be individuality without solidarity? These questions remain to be answered, and perhaps must be answered if life is to evolve.

In biology, the ideas of August Weismann (1834–1914) have been influential and have a bearing on the notion of individuality. Weismann distinguished two types of cell in the human body: germ cells, responsible for the transmission of inherited qualities, and soma cells, the contingent cells of the human body which are mortal and die when the human body dies. The unique cells, or soma (also called the phenotype), are the basis of physical individuality, while germ cells (also approximating the genotype) are common to the species. As individuals who cannot be replicated, humans are soma; no two soma are alike; as soma humans are also mortal; hence the link, in biological terms, between individuality and death. This is difference as physical being, not as abstraction.

Again, in relation to the 'rules of the game' in society, improvisation, occurring outside the model, and constituting a unique way of doing things, is also the point of individuality and difference. Jazz, as a musical genre based in improvisation, evokes, *ipso facto*, difference and individuality.

Finally, difference (if not individuality) is fundamental to the philosophy of two important thinkers of the twentieth century. In the thought of Martin Heidegger (1969), ontological difference is the difference between Being* and existence (the realm of beings).

Existentialism, as well as modern science, views existence as the object and subject of thought and discovery. Difference, in Gilles Deleuze's (1994) thought, takes the form at one point of the simulacrum* – the figure which contributes to the overturning of the Platonic framework, where the model takes primacy over the copy. The simulacrum is difference to the extent that it is autonomous *vis-à-vis* the model; indeed, it is something new, something individual that cannot be given an identity.

With the influence of Heidegger and Deleuze, the idea of difference has reached a new phase, one that links it to Being in the former thinker, and to repetition in the latter. Through their thought, practical problems relating to the multicultural and to sexual difference are being thought in a way that leads to difference freeing itself from any prior model. Here, difference becomes synthetic invention (see analytic–synthetic).

Deleuze, Gilles (1994) *Difference and Repetition*, trans. Paul Patton, New York: Columbia University Press.
Heidegger, Martin (1969) *Identity and Difference*, trans. Joan Stambaugh, New York: Harper & Row.

See ANALYTIC–SYNTHETIC

DIFFEREND
The term, 'differend' is specific to the thought of the French philosopher, Jean-François Lyotard (1924–99). Although the word is an adaptation from the French, *différend*, meaning dispute, Lyotard (1988) gives it a special inflection following the work of revisionist historians who deny the reality of the Holocaust, by denying

the reality of the Nazi gas chambers. Here the differend becomes a way of discrediting, or silencing, a player in the 'game' of knowledge production. This is often done with subtlety, by rigorously adhering to the rules of evidence. In order that there be proof that the gas chambers existed, there need to be witnesses who were there in the gas chamber. Of course anyone who was literally in the gas chamber would also have died, therefore there are no witnesses, therefore the evidence of the existence of gas chambers is subject to doubt. A differend exists because there can be no counter to the claim, given the definition of 'witness'. Only a victim can be a witness. Since a victim qua witness cannot speak, the case for the existence of gas chambers falls down. It is a perverse logic but, Lyotard argues, philosophical and scientific debate is vulnerable to it. Many historians have been justifiably outraged by this literal use of the rules of evidence and refer to the bad faith of the perpetrators.

While the differend exists as a political phenomenon, there is more to it than two sides battling for (political) supremacy, since the postmodern incredulity towards metanarratives renders irrelevant a battle between different worldviews. Instead, discourse, as a mosaic of very specific language games, is the site of the differend. The latter exists when there are no agreed procedures for allowing very different views to be presented in the current domain of discourse. The upshot of this is that a correspondence theory of truth* no longer works: the presence of an object or reality (referent) is no longer seen to be automatically reflected in a representation. Instead, a range of conditions must be satisfied before a statement is deemed to carry truth value. Any statement which claims to designate a whole universe can quickly be shown to be part of the very universe it claims to describe. In Lyotard's terms, then, a differend is essentially based in a language game made up of precise rules. A differend exists when the rules of a given language game do not allow a new statement to made (= do not allow a point of view or particular case to be heard). A classic instance of this is when non-European cultures can have their case heard only if it is phrased within a European legal framework.

Little purpose would be served by defining the differend were it not for the fact that its emergence is indicative of a growing frequency of situations where a victim's voice cannot be heard because the victim does not 'speak the right language', or follow the right procedures. Because the language game of science is essentially arbitrary* – that is, it is a discourse, not a reflection of reality – deciding between competing claimants, especially in the social sciences and humanities, is particularly open to contestation. Consequently, relativism is an ever-present risk, since there are no universal* principles which can be invoked and be accepted by everyone. Revisionist historians no doubt exploit the vulnerability of this liberal framework, which claims to give everyone the right to be heard. But who is to say – what authority is to say – whose evidence or view is or is not acceptable? Politically, liberalism knows no way of silencing the enemy of liberalism. But not only this: liberalism does not know either of a way, or of ways, of distinguishing convincingly between the quality of different positions and points of view. For it cannot decide beyond dispute who should judge. And, indeed, only an anti-liberal would claim to be able to judge without any problem – thus do we have another perverse illustration of the working of the differend. At one level liberalism is suspicious of universal claims. Lyotard seems to go along with this. Indeed, he advocates a regionalist approach to questions. At another level, all views are supposed to get a hearing. That this does not happen, and the reason for it, is one of the major insights claimed for the notion of the differend.

There is one further point. The differend is geared to highlighting the fact that no general idea can be made identical with a specific real instance (as Plato had wanted). Philosophers, social scientists and mathematicians now have come to recognise the paradoxes arising when a general statement about the world is forced to take its own place of enunciation into account. In fact, the differend is an antidote to the totalitarian obsession with reducing everything to a single genre, thereby stifling the voice of the victim. In short, the differend is an idea which points to questions of justice* precisely when pressure is brought to bear to silence those who would ask such questions.

Lyotard, Jean-François (1988) *The Differend: Phrases in Dispute*, trans. G. ven den Abeele, Manchester: Manchester University Press.

See VALUE

DIGITAL

The term 'digital' derives from the Latin, *digitus*, meaning finger. Fingers were originally used for counting and other arithmetical tasks. There has, then, always been a close connection between the digital and number. This is true in particular with regard to the notion of individual numbers being discrete, rather than continuous entities. The digital is thus to be distinguished from continuous, analogue* forms. It is based on the 'either/or', 'on/off' principle, which is the principle of non-contradiction.

Unlike analogue forms, negation and zero, which are abstract, are integral to digital processes. Furthermore, while there are no gaps in the analogue continuum of reality, digital forms depend on 'gaps' and 'absences' (the notion of no-thing). In structural linguistics, a sign* implies the absence of the thing signified, while in structural psychoanalysis, castration implies the absence of the penis. Both evoke the digital format. Because it can say 'not-A', in light of it having the capacity for negation, a digital computer can represent the 'truth functions of symbolic logic', a task not possible on an analogue computer (cf. Wilden 1980: 162).

Generally speaking, the digital corresponds to the level of 'signification' (the *fact* of the text or thing), rather than meaning (what the text itself says, or the thing symbolised). Even pain becomes a signifier from a digital perspective. Signification also implies the possibility of a metalanguage, or what Wilden calls higher 'logical typing' (1980: 170–172). An animal which sets a false trail is usually so immersed in its analogical world that it cannot envisage the trail as seen by another, and consequently continues to make the same false trail, even though its strategy has been discovered. In short, the animal has no metalanguage that would allow it to make the trail an object of reflection, as is the case with digital, human communication.

In light of the previous example, we can say, too, that digital forms always have borders. Without borders there could be no metalanguage, no basis for forms of classification, and no basis for separating 'on' from 'off', the latter feature being essential to digital computers.

Information* technology and the computer revolution that has accompanied it have of course made digital forms the most prevalent technical development of the last century. It would be wrong, however, to think that digitality is a relatively recent phenomenon. For although modern computers operate on the basis of a binary switching (0–1) governed by a set of instructions called a program, digital processes and phenomena have been formally present in Western culture at least since the time of the Phoenician alphabet (around the thirteenth to the eleventh centuries BC), the latter being considered the origin of today's phonetic script. (The Greeks in 500–400 BC refined the Phoenician system.)

The key feature of the phonetic alphabet as it is known in the West centres on the fact that it is a digital phenomenon. The 26 letters are conventional and assume their identity only in relation to the other letters in the series. That is, there is a differential relation between the letters, giving the alphabet features of a structure. As such, the letters of the alphabet form a digital code. Western literacy itself, then, is riven with digital features.

As a digital code, the alphabet is simple and abstract, not complex and concrete, as are many analogical phenomena. Crucially, the alphabet enables meaning to be communicated over time and space without that meaning having any essential relationship to the nature of the alphabet itself, just as the binary code* (0–1) in computing is not what is communicated. This is entailed in its being conventional and a code. Like phonetic writing* in general, the alphabet is a technology. It is a means to an end, not an end in itself.

When the Greeks developed the first truly phonetic alphabet they gained intellectual ascendancy. The difference between the Greek and what went before is that the Greek system of writing, based on the alphabet (which makes it phonetic), enabled the writing system to become autonomous. Writing alone could convey meaning, rather than 'non-textual', analogical elements based in the life-world, which were part of previous forms of writing. The Greek alphabet, Walter Ong notes, was democratising because it was easy to learn. It was 'internationalising' because it could be used as a basis for translating other languages. Moreover, writing favours left-hemisphere brain activity – i.e., 'abstract, analytical thought' (Ong 1997: 91). Analytical processes can thus be described as digital.

As also noted by Ong, the alphabet has lost all connection with things as things and instead has become a thing itself. This is the consequence of its being binary, differential and a code.

Given the dominance of phonetic writing and analytical thought in Western culture, the rise of digital technologies is hardly surprising. Such technologies have played an important role in the globalisation* of the world that has come in the wake of the development of media networks of all kinds. What does this mean? The short answer is that ever more analogical phenomena are being translated into digital format so that these phenomena can then be disseminated without any loss of meaning. The concomitant of this is that people now live in a world that has an ever-decreasing interest and investment in the origin of things, including the origin of communities. The things that matter can now be 'read' and appreciated independently of their original context. We do not need Shakespeare's autograph manuscript of *Hamlet* in order to understand the force of the play. Any good printed or electronic version will do. And, increasingly, a good reproduction of a work of art can suffice in lieu of the real thing, if the meaning and significance of the work are what matters. A digital photograph of a digital photograph (a work that quotes another) entails no loss in being reproduced. The sacred aspect, by contrast, is lost in the reproduction, because the sacred, ironically perhaps, is in the materiality (context) as originality of the work.

Or if the original nature of a work still captivates the buying public, so that the price of art works soars to ever greater heights, we should recall that money* is now a digital phenomenon *par excellence*. It is a form; it has no essential content; it is abstract; zero and negative quantities are also features of it. Moreover, money forms are infinitely translatable.

In sum, the key feature of the digital world seems to be found in the increasing speed at which everything is becoming, or is potentially, decontextualised.

Ong, Walter J. (1997 [1982]) *Orality and Literacy: The Technologizing of the Word*, London and New York: Routledge.
Wilden, Anthony (1980) *System and Structure: Essays in Communication and Exchange*, 2nd edn, London: Tavistock.

See ANALYTIC–SYNTHETIC; SACRED–PROFANE

ECONOMY

Economy derives from the Latin word *oeconomia*, adapted from the Greek *oikonomia*, from *oikonomos*: the one who manages a household (usually a steward).

Aspects of the economy of a society are studied by the discipline of economics. It is with the rise of economics in the eighteenth century (Adam Smith and J.B. Say) that the idea of scarcity, embodied in a consumption, or utility curve, comes to dominate political life. Economics assumes, in the spirit of nineteenth-century science, that society is a closed system and that, therefore, the more resources are allocated to one thing (guns) the less will be available for another (butter). Governments in the twenty-first century still largely adhere to this view to the extent that spending in one area necessitates a reduction of spending in another – deficits notwithstanding. Increases in economic growth have only led to modifications of the scarcity equation, not to its abolition. For no one can be sure that an increase in growth without negative effects (e.g. inflation) will continue into the future. Given that scarcity is at the heart of economic management, it is always better to be prudent. Growth in the economy and in the expansion of wealth, leading to higher living standards, do not change the fundamental role of scarcity in relation to the economy.

Political economy originally referred to the art, or pactical science, of managing the resources of a nation so as to increase its material prosperity; in more recent use, it is the theoretical science dealing with the laws that regulate the production and distribution of wealth. In modern Western economies this has meant ensuring that the market has the greatest role possible in resource allocation; governments only concern themselves with those who fall outside the market mechanism in the allocation of resources, such as the sick and the unemployed. If it is always a question of 'more or less', because of the underlying assumption of scarcity, it is also a matter, governments claim, of 'managing' resources, of allocating them efficiently.

No society committed to the efficient allocation of resources and to economic growth is going to accept waste other than as an unavoidable necessity. The idea that waste should always be avoided goes to the very heart of a key generic meaning of economy: namely, the achievement of maximum output with minimum input – the formula of efficiency. Waste and efficiency stand irrevocably opposed. The principle of utility is also there: that every means should realise a useful end. Nothing should be done for nothing. Or nothing (e.g. the pursuit of knowledge*) should be done for its own sake. Now that leisure, the arts, sport, and even key aspects of education have become industries, authorities can become more confident that fewer and fewer things are being done for their own sake in modern society. The market is deepening its hold on social life. The principle of efficiency – the input–output equation, or what Jean-François Lyotard (1924–99) calls the principle of performativity – is becoming increasingly hegemonic (Lyotard 1984: 41–53).

Economy, then, in a key generic sense, has been associated with making do with a small amount. To live frugally is to live economically. To live economically is based on the careful management of resources, to make them go as far as possible. With reference to money and material wealth, this has meant aiming for frugality, thrift, saving.

To do things with great economy has meant to achieve much with relatively little. And even though entrepreneurs in the twenty-first century will often say that to make money (wealth) it is necessary to spend money, the principle of efficiency is no less important; it is just that the stakes are higher. To spend a huge amount with the clear intention of getting no return is still unthinkable. In other words, an intended loss is unthinkable. From an accounting and thus financial management point of view, there is the 'bottom line': the relation of expenditure (input) to real, or estimated output. The 'left hand side' of the balance sheet must be brought into alignment with the 'right hand side'. Let us, after Georges Bataille, call this the 'restricted economy'.

What then of those activities which, precisely, fell, and still fall – if marginally – outside the restricted economy; activities with no obvious utility, activities like gift* giving, sacred (see sacred-profane) and religious activity, cooperative work, housework and gardening, home improvements done by the owner and therefore not included in national accounting, raising children, writing poetry, engaging in political activity as action as an end in itself. In almost all cases, the principle of performativity is enveloping each of these areas as they become part of national accounting, or as they cease to exist, as is happening with cooperative activity. Even churches now have to employ accountants and engage in efficient financial management and to become entrepreneurial if losses seem likely to continue (e.g. St Paul's in London). Children are increasingly in the care of paid nannies or professional child carers. Fewer people are doing their own home improvements and gardening; instead they pay others to do such work. Gift giving (Christmas, marriage, birthdays) is being taken over by consumerism. The restricted, money economy is becoming ever more hegemonic, pervasive and invasive.

The restricted economy of utility can be compared with another kind of economy, one that we can name, again after Bataille (1985), the 'general economy'. This is an economy of loss, disequilibrium and expenditure without the prospect of return. It is, furthermore, an economy of excess, heterogeneity and, ultimately, of disorder. Anthropologically, we can see, through the work of Marcel Mauss (1990), that the general economy is evident in the North American potlatch, or the 'big man' tradition in New Guinea, where giving not accumulating, establishes a reputation. An economy of the gift, then, still visible in a minor way in the interstices of the restricted economy, is the very foundation of certain forms of so-called traditional society. Such societies would tend towards a totalisation of life's activities, while the restricted economy, starting with the division of labour, tends towards ever more refined forms of differentiation.

It is evident that while the restricted economy is very much one of means without implying any judgement about a multiplicity of ends, the general economy can be understood to be the basis of ends – whether religious, political or cultural. Thus, the Aztecs offered human sacrifice in order that their sun god would continue to shine. Nothing else, in the end, really mattered. Could there be a greater distance than this between a secular society of the restricted economy and a general economy of sacrifice?

Bataille, Georges (1985) 'The Notion of Expenditure', in *Visions of Excess: Selected Writings*, trans. Allan Stoekl, Minneapolis: University of Minnesota Press.

Lyotard, Jean-François (1984[1979]) *The Postmodern Condition*, trans. G. Bennington and B. Massumi, Minneapolis: Minnesota University Press.

Mauss, Marcel (1990 [1923–24]) *The Gift: The Form and Reason for Exchange in Archaic Societies*, trans. W.D. Halls, London: Routledge.

See EXCHANGE; MONEY; SACRED-PROFANE

ENCYCLOPEDIA (see DIC-TIONARY–ENCYCLOPEDIA)

ENTROPY

Entropy comes from the Greek *tropé*, meaning transformation or, literally, 'turning', after the analogy of energy. The term was first proposed by Rudolph Clausius (1822–88) in 1865 in the German form, *Entropie*. Although he was not the first scientist to know of the second law of thermodynamics (others being Carnot, Joule, Kelvin and Maxwell), Clausius systematised the use of the term.

Assuming that the sense of energy is 'work-content', Clausius proposed 'entropy' as a corresponding designation for the transformation of the contents of a system. In Clausius's sense, the entropy of a system is the measure of the unavailability of its thermal energy for conversion into mechanical work. The term was first used in English in 1868.

Thermodynamics* has to do in effect with the order and disorder in heat energy. Order here corresponds to usable work energy (in a steam engine, for example), while disorder corresponds to the loss of usable heat energy from a work system. That a steam engine requires more fuel to keep it going is a result of entropy. That a projectile (cannonball, or bullet) cannot retrace the trajectory which it initially travelled is due to entropy, or to the breakdown into disorder, or randomness, of the energy molecules of a system. Entropy is what constitutes physical objects in irreversible time. In Newton's mechanical system, by contrast – a system in complete equilibrium – it was theoretically possible for a cannonball to retrace the path it initially travelled. Such an occurrence implies that time is, in principle, reversible. What Newton (1642–1727) did not recognise was that heat energy could be lost from the system.

As with chance*, a question arose in the mid-nineteenth century as to whether the break-up of energy into randomness and (unpredictable) disorder is a result of truly natural processes, or of the limitedness of the human intellect. Might it not be the case, William Clerk Maxwell wondered, that disorder is only apparent and that behind this appearance is to be found a more sophisticated order, but maybe one that only God can perceive? That is, maybe entropy was really subjective, and tied to the imperfection of human intelligence. In the twenty-first century, entropy, or randomness and disorder, is more readily accepted as part of natural processes and is not thought to be the result of inherent limitations to human knowing.

Further to this, though, there has always been a tension between the first law of thermodynamics, which states that energy always remains constant, and the second law referring to entropy, which states that usable energy is always lost from a given system. The first law thus refers to stability and equilibrium, while the second law evokes disorder and chaos. Gradually, different types of bodies (e.g. the human) and systems (e.g. society) began to be talked of in their relation to order and chaos.

In the economic sphere or, more precisely, in the sphere of economic logic, the relationship between input and output mirrors the law of entropy. For a greater output can be achieved, it is said, only from an increased input which always implies an increase in cost. Once the cost increases beyond what can be recouped from output, the system (company) begins to implode. It breaks down into disorder. This idea of performance (relationship between input and output) is derived from thermodynamics.

Lyotard goes further on this point when he says: 'The idea of performance implies a highly stable system because it is based on the principle of a relation, which is in theory always calculable, between heat and work, hot source and cold source, input and output. This idea comes from thermodynamics' (Lyotard 1988: 55). If all the variables could be known in advance, the behaviour of the system could theoretically be accurately predicted. Banks still operate in this way when trying to anticipate what effect a change in the interest rates will have on consumer demand. Governments want to know whether increased government expenditure will increase employment. Nobody knows for sure what will result because no one can know all the variables. Disorder is there at the heart of the system. In short, the control that can be exerted over random processes is essentially limited. What is more, the effort towards total control, observable in totalitarian political regimes, can cause such systems to implode. This happens because totalitarianism inhibits the process of renewal that every system needs to go through in order to continue.

We can see then that outside the specialist field of thermodynamics and physics, entropy has been used (without always being named) to explain that all existing systems are imperfect – whether they be political, economic or social. That a system in perfect equilibrium (without disorder of any kind) was the ideal to aim for is usually attributed to the eighteenth-century scientist, Laplace (1749–1827). But this ideal, impossible to realise, would be deleterious were it to be realised, because it could only be achieved at the cost of change and renewal. Generally, this is a typically deterministic explanation of society: once the initial conditions are known, the subsequent conditions can be manipulated.

In psychoanalytic thought, Freud, under the influence in his early work of thermodynamics, said explicitly that entropy was a term that was useful to the extent that it confirmed the irreversibility of time: 'In considering the conversion of psychical energy no less than of physical, we must make use of the concept of an entropy, which opposes the undoing of what has already occurred' (Freud 1981).

Since the advent of quantum* theory and atomic physics the relevance of the principle of entropy, especially in relation to understanding many important social and political systems, has had diminishing scientific importance, even if various public agencies still operate as if, on this front, science had stopped in the middle of the Industrial Revolution. For post-thermodynamic science, chance and complexity are at the origin of large systems like society, so it is in principle impossible to predict exactly the future of such systems.

With the information* age, entropy enters a new phase. For with the development of cybernetics* and systems theory, the question arises as to whether entropy, or disorder, is a negative or a positive force. Although Norbert Wiener, the founder of modern cybernetics, argued that information – equivalent to communication as opposed to noise – was the opposite of entropy, subsequent researchers in the field have suggested that as real information is a kind of unexpected disorder – or, in Bateson's terms, 'the difference that makes a difference' (cited in Hayles 1999: 51) – information has a kinship with noise. The more unexpected a message is, the more information it contains. In other words, information pertains more to what is out of the ordinary, to what, in everyday terms, is noticed, even if it is not understood. Randomness, in this sense, tends to be noticed much more than order, which passes unnoticed because it is taken for granted.

Within information theory, randomness, and thus entropy, is a factor that every discrete system has to overcome, but in overcoming it, the system becomes more complex. As such, entropy becomes a key element in a system's salvation, whereas, even in the decades after the Second World War, as in the nineteenth century, entropy was thought to be the bane of every system, whether macro or micro, human or animal.

Freud, Sigmund (1981 [1918]) 'From the History of an Infantile Neurosis', in *The Freud Pelican Library, Volume 9: Case Histories II*, Harmondsworth: Penguin.
Hayles, N. Katherine (1999) *How We Became Posthuman: Virtual Bodies in Cybernetics, Literature and Informatics*, Chicago: University of Chicago Press.
Lyotard, Jean-François (1984 [1979]) *The Postmodern Condition*, trans. Geoff Benington and Brian Massumi, Minneapolis: University of Minnesota Press.

See CHANCE

EPISTEMOLOGY

Epistemology comes from the Greek, *epistēmē*, meaning knowledge or science, and *logos*, meaning discourse. In Greek philosophy, *episteme* refers, as well as to knowledge, to the idea of 'approaching something, knowing one's way round it'.

More generally, modern epistemology is the theory of how knowledge is possible, and is especially important in the history of science, where different paradigms of knowledge (Kuhn 1970) correspond to different scientific epoques: the age of Newton, the age of Einstein and quantum mechanics.

In France, Gaston Bachelard (1884–1962), Jean Cavaillès (1903–44), Georges Canguilhem (1904–95), Louis Althusser (1918–90) and Michel Serres (b. 1930) constitute a tradition in studies in epistemology. Some of the questions they raise are: How is science possible? What is the relation between pure and applied scientific work? What is the difference between the normal and the pathological? What is the relationship between poetry and science? order and chance? noise and communication? For this group of thinkers, scientific knowledge is always mediated through a given framework of knowing; it is this framework which contains the real secret of knowledge. There is no such thing as a naïve form of scientific knowledge. The history of science is the living proof of this – if proof be needed.

Out of this school of epistemologists came another, even more controversial and celebrated thinker: Michel Foucault (1926–84). For Foucault, not only are epistemologists engaged in establishing the relationship between the knower and the known, but they are interested in studying the very conditions of possibility of scientific statements, statements which are part of a system of discursive practices. It is not a matter, then, of trying to discover how Newton (1642–1727) developed his physics, but of showing the discursive conditions which made Newton's work possible. It is not therefore to the history of ideas to which we should turn in order to understand the evolution of science, but to the documents existing at the 'archaeological' level of knowledge. In Foucault's hands, epistemology, and especially the term, *episteme*, have a far deeper meaning than conventional theories of knowledge

allow for – those, for example, which remain at the level of the subject–object relation.

Used in Foucault's sense, epistemology has a far deeper sense, too, than the idea of paradigm, developed by Thomas Kuhn. Paradigm still depends for its viability on the level of consciousness of the scientist involved in experimental research, whereas, for Foucault, it is a matter of making visible the epistemological configuration which places consciousness itself in the forefront of knowledge. The figure of man, as Foucault famously claimed – a figure leading to the privileging of consciousness in both science and philosophy – is of recent date and is due to disappear 'like a face drawn in sand at the edge of the sea' (Foucault 1974: 387).

The most ambitious, if not the most famous, work of modern epistemology, *The Order of Things* (Foucault 1974), uses the notion of *episteme* as its basic tool of analysis in order to examine the most seemingly self-evident and strongly held ideas about how humans know the world. The latter are radically challenged, if not completely overturned. For epistemological figures, not the human intellect linked to a worldview, organise knowledge, and these are revealed in discursive regularities, which are quite removed from consciousness. Thus there is the 'signature' as a series of signs in the Renaissance; botany and the 'table' in the classical age; life, labour and language in the modern age. In addition to this, Foucault, like Bachelard before him, uses the notion of 'epistemological break' to explain the movement of the history of science. As opposed to a logical and rational transition from one era to another, Foucault argues that there is no rational link between eras or, more precisely, between one epistemological figure and another. Such figures arise independently of the will of individual scientists. It is therefore pointless, if the serious work of epistemology is to be pursued, to invoke terms like 'ideology'* to explain the permutations and deviations of scientific work. Here it is certainly not a matter of the 'ruling ideas being the ideas of the ruling class' because, at an epistemological level, actors cannot be aware of what it is that fuels their search for truth and knowledge.

Through epistemology, Foucault recognises that history is also an intervention in what it studies. Historical writing cannot be totally external. Frameworks of knowledge are constantly changing; nothing stays the same. The dispute, in the eighteenth century, between Linnaeus's 'fixist' approach, and Buffon's more evolutionist approach to nature cannot be explained epistemologically by the truth of the one and the falsity of the other. Rather, it is necessary to show how the same epistemological conditions made both positions possible. Foucault writes that: 'Archaeology tries to show how the two affirmations, fixist and "evolutionist", share a common locus in a certain description of species and genera; this description takes as its object the visible structure of organs' (Foucault 1974: 152). Foucault is keen to emphasise that it is a matter of describing in an era the space of complex, 'multiple dissensions', rather than finding underlying epistemological continuities. In this way, an archaeological approach to epistemology differs markedly from the approach of the history of ideas and of the sociology of knowledge, which is often keen to give an ideological explanation for the presence of different epistemological frameworks.

The Marxist versus the liberal framework is but one example.

With Foucault, epistemology not only comes alive but appears for a moment to be the only truly profound basis upon which to write history. History thus becomes an 'archaeology of knowledge'. Like all good things perhaps, the archaeological approach has come if not to an end, at least to the point where it has been superseded in its turn – not least by Foucault's subsequent work. Nevertheless, were we to return to the field that Foucault opened up – which he left in haste – we might still find rich pickings and, in particular, a way of appreciating the way history as such is tied to the writing of it.

Foucault, Michel (1974 [1966]) *The Order of Things: An Archaeology of the Human Sciences*, Social Science Paperback edn, trans. from the French, London: Tavistock.
Kuhn, Thomas (1970 [1962]) *The Structure of Scientific Revolutions*, 2nd edn, Chicago: University of Chicago Press.

See KNOWLEDGE; TRUTH

EROS–EROTICISM

Eroticism comes from the Greek, *eros*, meaning love. The question here is: What does love mean? Perhaps the closest indication of the Greek sense of this term comes from Aristophanes's presentation in Plato's *Symposium*, where he relates the story of love's beginning. Originally, Aristophanes says, there were three sexes: male, female and hermaphrodite. The curious thing about these beings was that male and female were joined together in the same body, while the hermaphrodite was neither one nor other sex, as the moon is neither the sun nor the earth, but contains aspects of both.

Zeus, threatened by the power of these entirely self-contained creatures, but not wanting to kill them, cut them in half. As a result, each half – each sex – began an eternal striving to be reunited with its partner. Eros – love – thus comes to stand for this eternal urge to union with another. As for the hermaphrodite…all Aristophanes has to say is that this being is now forgotten.

Colloquially, eroticism refers to sexuality in the narrow sense of physical, genital sexuality. Nudity commonly figures here as the bearer of the erotic. So dominant in popular culture is this meaning of erotic, that Freud's more nuanced sense of sexuality as a life drive, along with the Ancient Greek meaning of eros as love, has all but disappeared from view. In his famous essay of 1920, *Beyond the Pleasure Principle* (1961), Freud acknowledges Plato's contribution to the issue, but also wants to go further than the Greek philosopher by looking at the implications of the idea of a life drive.

Thus Freud argues that beyond the search for pleasure – usually localised – in which humans, like many other creatures, participate, there is another principle, which he calls the 'reality principle'. Now, the reality principle is not just about the prudent preservation of life, in contrast to pleasure's drive to self destruction, but is about another kind of pleasure – what the modern French psychoanalytic tradition calls *jouissance* (bliss, enjoyment, ecstasy). This is potentially a higher, and different, form of pleasure to that apparently sought in genital sexuality, even if the latter, through orgasm, can also reach a certain level of *jouissance*, to the point where this can entail pain

of a certain sort. Certainly, *jouissance* is not entirely a stranger to pain, as can be seen in the lives of religious devotees and those who live life according to a strict moral code.

Anyway, for Freud, the life drives which entail a striving for union are of the order of the reality principle – the order of *jouissance*, as here outlined. They are then of the order of life. If Freud shows us that eros is tied more to *jouissance* than to pleasure, and if eros is therefore linked to a drive towards union with another at a spiritual as well as at a bodily level, and if, moreover, this implies a drive to life and is essentially what Freud intended by sexuality, it would imply that the claim that Freud's theory results in sexual determinism is based on interpreting sexuality far too narrowly.

As Freud also saw, were the life drives to obtain their goal of ultimate union, life itself would be at an end, in the sense that *jouissance* would have been overtaken by a return to a state of complete rest – a state of death, in fact. Thus do we have a life drive, the unconscious goal of which would seem to be death. This is what Freud came to call the death drive, which he described as the desire to return to an original state of things.

Whatever might be said about the plausibility or otherwise of Freud's speculations, it is clear that the Freudian approach to sexuality – to eros – involves profound philosophical issues that even now remain to be resolved.

There is another approach to eroticism. In some ways it deepens that of Freud and it is to be found in the writing of Georges Bataille. For Bataille human sexuality reaches its cultural perfection in eroticism as a regulated transgression of deep-seated taboos. More pointedly, eroticism here becomes a continuity of being even through death. The individual in everyday life is a discontinuous, symbolic identity, an identity to the extent that he or she is discontinuous with fellow beings. Eroticism, as the violation of boundaries (= transgression), changes all this, and remains a continual source of anguish. For violation implies the transgression of interdictions – the interdiction being made extant by the transgression itself. As the rupture of boundaries, eroticism leads to the (real or imagined) fusion of beings (is this an echo of Plato?). Fusion gives rise to the communication of anguish resulting from a loss of integrity. Contrary to what the doxa of everyday life might suggest, the erotic impulse has thus been appropriated in various cultures – including Christian culture – for religious ends. Instead of being the antithesis of the sacred, eroticism – as an opening up to the other – is its very foundation. Through tears, wounds and violation of boundaries, the possibility arises for human beings to become united. In eroticism I lose myself. The only problem is that, as Bataille says, this unity is the unity of death: 'This sacredness is the revelation of continuity through the death of a discontinuous being' (Bataille 1990: 22).

Through the prism of Bataille's analysis, we learn that the eroticism with which people are swamped in a mediatised and secularised culture is but one part of a very much larger picture of attitudes and rituals practised in light of life and death – rituals which are to be found in diversity of cultures throughout the world. The added sting of this comes when we realise that eroticism as Bataille outlines it is strictly non-utilitarian in character; it is not an eroticism which can be marketed (hence the importance of the religious aspect), but one which is

contrary to all rational economies. Eroticism is, in short, based on an economy of loss, not of equilibrium. As such it becomes the 'other' of every capitalist enterprise and for this reason, no doubt, remains the subject of extensive repression.

Bataille, Georges (1990 [1957]) *Eroticism*, trans. Mary Dalwood, London and New York: Marian Boyars.
Freud, Sigmund (1961 [1920]) *Beyond the Pleasure Principle*, trans. James Strachey, New York: Norton.

See DIFFERENCE–INDIVIDUALITY; SACRED–PROFANE

EVENT The word, 'event' was adopted from the Old French, *even* and adapted from Latin, *ēvent-us*, meaning occurrence, issue. It is formed also from *ēvenire*, meaning to come out, to happen, to result (*e-* out + *venir-e*, to come). Generally, an event is the (actual or contemplated) fact of anything happening; an occurrence; something that arrives, or happens (cf. Fr. *arriver*: to happen). People talk about the tragic *events* of 11 September 2001.

If *event* means that something has happened, is it not true that things are happening – throughout the world and in society – all the time? Here, everything that happens seems open to be defined as an event, and we are faced with a terrible lack of precision. Is it not also true that events happen in time, and in a given place? The philosopher, Willard van Orman Quine (b. 1908), argued indeed that an event was something that occurred in the same time and place – a view subsequently discredited because of the reality of simultaneous events in the same place.

A major difficulty with the concept of event is that the crispness of its analytical definition fails to do justice to the blurred nature of real, empirical events. To increase precision, a distinction is often made between happenings that count as events, where the effects and import of the happening are (judged to be) significant, and those everyday, ordinary happenings (getting out of bed in the morning), which are part of a repetitive routine, or habit. In effect, events are given the status of extraordinary occurrences, things that are in some sense remarkable. At least this is so if we are considering social or historical events.

In France, the historians belonging to the Annales school, developed a certain resistance to *l'histoire événementielle* – or the history of events. Events, in the eyes of a historian like Fernand Braudel (1902–85), were merely the micro, surface effects of history, the 'crests of foam that the tides of history carry on their strong backs'. The big structural changes that occur over centuries are what matter, and are the focus for 'profound' history, not events. For such historians all events are relatively trivial.

Maybe, however, what the Annales historian is looking for is not so far removed from a more common view of an event as something that is profound, not trivial. In this sense, when an event arrives it is often a shock, unpredictable and even traumatic. An event here makes an impact, has an effect, leaves a mark. War is an event in this sense. But so is success in a sporting event. Or it could be a work of art or a particular work of science or philosophy which becomes an event. The structuralist revolution in thought would be an event of this sort, as would be Picasso's painting, *Guernica*, or Einstein's theory of relativity in relation to space and time.

Scientifically, the notion of an event has been important in thermodynamics*. Here, events occur in irreversible time because of the effects of entropy*. That an event is irreversible gives it its status as an event. An event is unique and singular because it cannot be repeated. On this reading, an event would be something that is only so in light of the impossibility of its repetition. Getting up in the morning is thus decidedly not the model of event that we are looking for.

The philosopher, Jacques Derrida (1977), has provided another twist in the quest to understand the significance of 'event', when he examines language and writing in relation to repetition, or 'iteration'. On this view, were we to define repetition as inimical to an event, there would hardly be any events, least of all in language. This is explained by the fact that any speech act (written as well as spoken) enacted in one context, has, in principle, to be available to be reiterated in another. One standard convention of this reiteration is the quotation. Even a signature – unique and specific to the one who owns it – must be repeatable and be able to be inscribed in a wide range of contexts. Even though any particular enactment of the signature might have an inimitable and original aspect, the signature, to be what it is, possesses the quality of idealisation. This is what enables it to work as a signature, rather than as an entirely arbitrary and random mark.

Reference to language and the event brings us to the issue of an event and its representation. In this context, a key issue relates to the event as located in time – first, in relation to the events of history and, second, in relation to events in the life history of an individual.

Representing historical events has been an issue because: (1) these can only be represented retrospectively, from the position of the present; (2) these events might be appropriated by a particular ideology, so that the nature of the French Revolution differs according to whether one is a conservative or radical; and (3) the issue of representation arises in relation to history as the writing* of history*. From the last point has come the idea of historical discourse, as discussed in the essays of Roland Barthes, Hayden White and Michel Foucault. Rather than providing absolute access to the event itself, written history, so this argument would have it, instead gives us access to the event of writing, or to the event of discourse. Foucault writes in *The Archaeology of Knowledge* (1974) that a discursive event occurs when there are 'irruptions' in discourse, or 'discontinuities': these are events which challenge the usual idea of the 'infinite continuity of discourse' (Foucault 1974: 25) – or the idea that discourse and event are radically separate and different from one another. As presented here, there is no prior mute event which must then be represented and given a voice by writing. Events are always already speaking. There is no pre-discursive event.

Psychologically, an event occurring in the life of an individual can still be experienced after a lapse of time. In his early work, 'Project for a Scientific Psychology' of 1895, Freud (1966) tells the story of Emma who, after puberty developed a fear of going into shops. Subsequent analytic investigation showed that Emma's fear harked back to her being sexually molested at the age of eight inside a shop. At the time – time of innocence – Emma had not been traumatised by the experience because, being prepubescent, she did not experience its full impact. Only after the puberty did the trauma hit in the form of a fear of going into shops. From this Freud concludes that something which was not traumatic as an experience can be traumatic as a memory. As Jeffrey Melhman has succinctly said: 'Freud's (posthumously published) text plays havoc with the commonplace notion of the traumatic event' (Mehlman 1996: 52). What Emma's case shows is that, psychologically, an event might not only be in time, but also take time for its impact to be experienced as traumatic.

Derrida, Jacques (1977) 'Signature Event Context', trans. Samuel Weber and Jeffrey Melhman in *Glyph I*, Baltimore: Johns Hopkins University Press, 172–197.

Foucault, Michel (1974 [1969]) *The Archaeology of Knowledge*, Social Science Paperback edn, trans. A.M. Sheridan Smith, London: Tavistock.

Freud, Sigmund (1966) 'Project for a Scientific Psychology [1895]' (posthumous), trans. James Strachey in *The Standard Edition of the Complete Psychological Works of Sigmund Freud Volume I* (1886–99), London: The Hogarth Press.

Mehlman, Jeffrey (1996 [1975]) 'How to Read Freud on Jokes: The Critic as *Schadchen*', in *Writing and Psychoanalysis: A Reader*, ed. John Lechte, London: Arnold.

See ALIENATION; ECONOMY

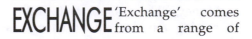 **EXCHANGE** 'Exchange' comes from a range of

Middle English, Latin and French sources. Exchange contains 'change' – to change something – while exchange implies changing something for something else. *Change* is also the French for 'exchange', as in the exchange of foreign currency. In English, 'change' also has a money connection, as in terms like 'loose change', or 'to change $100' for smaller denominations. Yet an English-speaking country can also talk about foreign exchange, when referring to the return on exports.

Immediately, then, exchange takes us to the economy* and to society and the notion of giving and receiving. In this context, reciprocity is an exchange which maintains equilibrium in the circulation of goods.

Since the beginning of the Industrial Revolution, money* has intensified the process of abstraction, or decontextualisation, mainly because it has become an abstract medium rather than a material substance. With arrival of the information* society in the twentieth century, all forms of materiality became problematic. Money is part of this process. With electronic forms of money (transfer of funds by changing numbers), and the access to funds through electronic means, exchange is also becoming more abstract.

Money is the general equivalent that accommodates differences (between products and services, objects and time) and thereby allows exchanges to take place. As Georg Simmel says: 'Exchange supposes an objective measurement of subjective valuations' (1990: 81). In other words, money is the quantitative measurement of subjective evaluations of the differences between things.

Money, then, is abstract and is becoming more so. But exchange is broader than money. It is just that

exchange value (price) is now the dominant form of exchange. It was not always so. Not only was money at one time a material substance (gold and silver), much sought after, but exchanges can constitute the very fabric of society itself. Karl Polanyi (1957) identified and defined three modes of exchange: reciprocal (gift calls for a counter-gift), redistributive (money or goods are paid to, and reallocated by, a third party), and market (exchange through money with reference to price). Polanyi argued that these three modes of exchange can be found singularly or in combination in economic organisations of societies around the world.

Despite Polanyi, the two modes of exchange that are now most discussed are reciprocal and market exchange. With regard to reciprocal exchange, the anthropologist, Claude Lévi-Strauss (1987) speaks of the exchange of goods, the exchange of women, and the exchange of signs. Lévi-Strauss also shows that for some societies as a whole, and for some Western societies in part, the form of the act of exchange is more important than what is exchanged. In southern France, patrons at a restaurant might exchange a glass of the same wine. 'What has happened?' the anthropologist asks. And he answers that, 'From an economic viewpoint, no one has gained and no one has lost. But the point is that there is much more in the exchange itself than in the things exchanged' (Lévi-Strauss 1969: 59).

It was another anthropologist, Marcel Mauss, who initiated an interest in exchange through his study of the gift (Mauss 1990). What Mauss was able to show was that some societies could be called societies of the gift, because a gift called for a counter-gift. Every effort would have to be made to meet obligations of reciprocity, even if this is not entirely transparent to the participants themselves. For in practice there are no formal rules attaching to gift exchange, only a sense of honour or (moral) shame if the gift is not reciprocated at some point in the future, immediate reciprocation being unacceptable. Exchange here forces those involved (which is ultimately all those in society) to experience both the dependency of being in debt, and the power of having another indebted to them, as it also ensures the circulation of goods and women in the kinship alliances necessary for the survival of society. For Mauss, the pinnacle of gift societies is seen in the orgy of giving that occurs in the potlatch in North America or the *kula* in the Pacific, and the *hau* in New Zealand. For Mauss, the gift is the very foundation of social life in many non-capitalist societies. Even in capitalist societies, Mauss noted, there were still remnants of older social forms: in the presents given at Christmas, birthdays and marriages. Or, if we focus on everyday life, there is still often a sense of obligation to repay a gift, or a service done without payment, especially if the parties involved are not part of the family.

In summary, we have the following characteristics of exchange in societies of the gift:

1 Even though a gift presupposes a counter-gift, it is also possible that this might not happen. The gift approaches a giving without receiving – at least at the level of the individual.
2 Nevertheless, if someone gives, someone else must receive. But at the same time, one gives *in order to receive* (hence the notion of the counter-gift). (This implies that gift exchange cannot easily be appreciated from the perspective of an individual.)
3 In gift societies focus is on consumption more than on production. Consumption without production results in loss. The destruction of goods in the potlatch is thus an instance of loss. In extreme cases, destruction includes the ritual death of human beings (e.g. in Aztec society). Capitalist society does not countenance such wanton destruction.
4 Gift societies are thus societies of disequilibrium and loss, which has to be compensated for in the interests of the survival of the society itself.
5 These are also societies of prestige and hierarchy. To be able to engage in expenditure without limit is often the mark of power.
6 These, then, are societies with very limited forms of money, and thus with limited forms of exchange. They are, formally speaking, relatively undifferentiated societies. Individuality is not very elaborated.
7 These are societies of 'context' (being tied to material place), not of decontextualisation (abstract, not being tied to place, only to time). To leave the locale is to leave the society altogether.
8 These are not societies of utility (where the usefulness of something, or its instrumental value, is the dominant criterion), but societies of mutual obligation, based on intimate, effective relations.

By contrast to gift societies the dominant form of exchange in capitalist societies is market exchange mediated by money. This of course brings with it a depersonalisation of human relations not seen in gift societies. It also brings alienation* through the dominance of what Marx called the exchange-value (the market or monetary value of a commodity) of things, over their use-value (the good as consumed to satisfy a need). On the other hand, the argument in this field for modernisation has been that what is lost in the intimacy of human relations is compensated for in modernity by greater formal freedoms and a more highly differentiated society, one that allows for more sophisticated expressions of individuality. The question that some are now asking, however, is whether this process of modernisation and, latterly, postmodernisation, and the depersonalisation of social relations which seem to be their correlate has not gone too far, so that there might now be a need to investigate new ways of inventing and experiencing deeper human intimacy.

Lévi-Strauss, Claude (1969 [1949]) *The Elementary Structures of Kinship*, trans. J.H. Bell and John von Sturmer, Boston: Beacon Press.
Lévi-Strauss, Claude (1987) *Introduction to the Work of Marcel Mauss*, trans. Felicity Baker, London: Routledge & Kegan Paul.
Mauss, Marcel (1990 [1923–24]) *The Gift: The Form and Reason for Exchange in Archaic Societies*, trans. W.D. Halls, London: Routledge.
Polanyi, Karl (1957 [1944]) *The Great Transformation*, Boston: Beacon Press.
Simmel, Georg (1990 [1900]) *The Philosophy of Money*, trans. Tom Bottomore and David Frisby, 2nd edn, London and New York: Routledge.

See DIFFERENCE–INDIVIDUALITY; GIFT; LABOUR-POWER

FAMILY

Family can be looked at in terms of differences in space and time: that is, what makes a family in one place (in one culture) is not the same as in another. This version of the meaning of family is becoming more important as polities become multicultural.

The dictionary is also illuminating: here we find that 'family' derives from the Latin, *familia* (household) and gives *pater familias* (head of the household). From the Anglicised version, we easily see the derivation of familiar (closeness), and the opposite: unfamiliar, or strange (from Old French: *estrange* and Modern French: *étrange*, whence, *étranger*: foreigner). The stranger then is, in the first instance, one who is not part of the familiar, who is unfamiliar, is non-family, or, 'who is not one of us'. A stranger is also someone who is not a member of the Houses of Commons. Connected to 'strange' is 'estrange' – whence, 'estranged': to be alienated from (cf. estranged wife of husband). These meanings open the way to the figurative meanings of family, which, as we shall see, have become important in politics in the twenty-first century.

Historically, family originates in the Greek word for household, *oikos*, which gives economy*, meaning, in the first instance, domestic economy. The *oikos* is the private domain in the 'public–private' opposition. The *oikos*, whose members are of the same kin group, ministers to the physical needs of its members. Life*, as physical survival and the satisfaction of basic needs, takes place in the *oikos*. This is so for the Greeks, and those, like the philosopher Hannah Arendt, who follow them, even if the idea of culture* makes the idea of bare life (*zoë*) problematic. For in cultural terms, even the satisfaction of basic needs is never just instrumental, but is culturally inflected. Thus the *way* basic needs are satisfied is of crucial interest and importance when considering the role and nature of the family in modern society.

No explanation of family would be complete without addressing the notion of marriage and kinship relations. In the Western style nation states, the extended family, with several generations living together, is in decline. Marriage is, however, still generally public and legal with the nuclear family – mother, father, children – being the dominant form of the legally constituted family structure, even if, at the same time, there are sole parent families, homosexual families, and people living alone. Blended families, and partners who have been previously married, are alternative forms of the legally constituted family.

While marriage is publicly constituted, it is privately lived. In effect, it is the quintessential form of private living in the West followed by *de facto* relationships and single people living alone. Even in a *de facto* relationship the law has a place because there is an interdiction against incest, although the notion of what constitutes incest is culturally inflected.

For anthropologists such as Claude Lévi-Strauss, the meaning of incest depends upon the way that a given society or culture defines permitted unions. In Ancient Egypt, as in Samoa, marriage between a brother and an older sister was permitted, while marriage between a brother and a younger sister was condemned as immoral. In Western culture, this form of marriage would not be permitted because of the close blood relations of the partners. Lévi-Strauss suggests that marriage is a form of exchange*, and that 'it is the exchange which counts and not the things exchanged' (1969: 139). Marriage and kinship structures are thus fundamentally symbolic, and not based in some biological or natural aversion to sexual relations with close kin. In fact, the law against incest, qua law, is a symbolic form that determines what constitutes incest. As such, marriage, and the family structure that this implies, is also a fundamentally symbolic form.

In modern family relations in the West, the driving force behind couples cohabiting and marrying is often thought to be love*. And indeed, in the history of social relations since the eighteenth century, love, as giving rein to and following the dictates of one's passion, has been a strikingly important, if often baffling phenomenon. Love emerges against the dictates of the aristocratic families, for whom marriage alliances are a key mechanism for the maintenance and accumulation of wealth and status. Hence the idea that one ought not to marry above or beneath one's station. Love breaks out of such a constricting code of privilege – at least in appearance. Love directs the lovers to form their own society – or rather, their own community – by following the dictates of desire and passion. Love brings outsiders together, as it brings together those of whom families disapprove. Love has, moreover, been about the coming together of strangers (as opposed to the usual situation in the aristocracy, where the partners not only know each other but are often related). It is from strangers that family emerges: that is, from the strange and the unfamiliar, the familiar is born. At least that is the myth behind the modern family. The question that arises is whether a relationship begun in love between partners who were – or at least who can in principle have been – strangers, can survive the familiarity that is the modern family.

The sociologist, Niklas Luhmann (1986) thus contrasts love with family (rather than defining family as that institution which gives rise to love which is different from the love upon which it was first established). And another sociologist, Anthony Giddens (1997), says that the freedom to enter into a relationship – and thus marriage and family – implies that the continuation or ending of the relationship is also in the hands of those who first started it. There is no longer the same social pressure (stigma of divorce, etc.) beyond the control of the partners, which might induce them to continue to 'make a go of it'. Instead, the relationship survives or is dissolved according to the will of the partners. The members of the relationship are alone responsible for their joint fate. This brings with it its own form of anxiety, according to Giddens.

The family – like school – has always had detractors. People can point to the authoritarian, father-dominated, family of the past as well to the cruel nature of family relations where discipline had become a fetish, particularly as far as females and children were concerned. The miserable, or at least difficult, childhood has been the source, and still is the source of literature that moves people – Dickens being but one example. And so, in the twenty-first century, departments of social welfare will often talk of dysfunctional families, where everything expected of a family in terms of care and emotional richness is absent, where children are abused, where domestic violence reigns, and parents have long ago ceased to be in charge of their lives. In short, family members have become estranged from one another. All secure familiarity has vanished. Life on the street and drug abuse is often the lot of the offspring of such dysfunctional unions. There is, then, the negative as well as the positive family in today's world.

In a more figurative vein, 'family' has been used to refer to the 'family of man', or, in nationalist terms, to the 'family of the nation'. An implication of the latter is the idea that a nation only includes those who are not foreign, or strange. No doubt family operates (despite its legal basis) at an affective, or emotional level. And this is being projected on to the large entity of the nation.

But if various forms of love are present in the family, hate is often there, too. This is why family members are not called upon to judge in each other's case, and why the law would be corrupt if it simply operated in the interest of a given family, or families. The Mafia in Italy does, of course, challenge this legal, objective basis of justice*, and, having given itself the status of 'The Family', aims to make things work in its own interest, rather than in the interest of justice.

Giddens, Anthony (1997 [1991]) *Modernity and Self-Identity: Self and Society in the Late Modern Age*, Cambridge: Polity Press.

Lévi-Strauss, Claude (1969 [1949]) *The Elementary Structures of Kinship*, trans. J.H. Bell and John von Sturmer, Boston: Beacon Press.

Luhmann, Niklas (1986) *Love as Passion: The Codification of Intimacy*, Stanford, CA: Stanford University Press.

FANTASY/PHANTASY, FANTASM

To say that a story is a 'pure fantasy', implies that it is a figment of the imagination, that it is not literally true. This meaning of fantasy – or phantasy, if we want to evoke the Greek root of the word – corresponds to the notion of illusion, unreality. Looked at as a 'phantom' of the imagination, a story, or an image, evokes the idea of delusion, or worrying and ghost-like presence, which is neither real nor entirely unreal. The ghost, or phantom, of Hamlet's father lacks a certain material form, but this does not mean that it does not have a presence in Shakespeare's play.

A further clue to the cluster of significance which surrounds fantasy comes from the Greek etymology, where *phantasia* literally means 'a making visible', the term deriving from *phainein*, to show. In classical Greek, phantasy could mean spectre or apparition, the faculty of sensuous perception or of imagination. The Old French meaning of *fantaisie* comes through in English in words like fancy and caprice. In music, a 'fantasia' is a piece composed without premeditation or concern for classical form. Similarly, a French perfume is a *fantaisie* when its fabrication breaks away from the 'classical' scent patterns.

The Latin origin of fantasy has emphasised its fanciful, daydream aspect, and has continued to highlight the working of the imagination and its products. We are dealing here with a relatively innocent, and even pleasurable, notion of fantasy/phantasy – a notion that is very much in harmony with the conscious engagement of the imagination, just as a child does when thinking of Santa Claus, or the Tooth Fairy.

Less innocent uses of fantasy have emerged in psychology, where the explicit expression of fantasy can assist in plumbing the depths of a subject's personality, without this being hindered by conscious and unconscious defence mechanisms. The patient is thus led to 'betray' the workings of the inner life, as one might betray a liking for a certain type of movie in light of a survey of one's cinema-going habits. Rorschach ink blots have also been used to the same end, with the information about what different people see in the blot used to determine the personality type to which they supposedly belong. Now, the distinction made between fantasy and objective reality begins to look a little weaker. This point is evocative of a general tendency to use the indirect knowledge gained from interviews and other sources, such as films and novels, to form a picture of the patterns of subjectivity which exist in a given social milieu. From here, one can begin to speak of a social imaginary. Within this, fantasy becomes the avenue through which otherwise inexpressible

sentiments are expressed – for example the complex feelings a society might have about relationships, or foreignness.

Within the field of literary criticism, Roland Barthes (1915–80) analysed the plays of Jean Racine (1639–99) using structuralist techniques and came up with aspects of figures of unconscious obsessions and fantasies, much to the consternation of more conservative literary critics (Barthes 1964). Barthes did a similar study of the historical writing of Jules Michelet (1798–1874), and found that blood, assuming a variety of meanings as it appeared in different contexts, was an abiding motif in Michelet's work. At one point Barthes proposes that Michelet's writing evokes someone traumatised by blood (Barthes 1987: 159). Other organising elements in Michelet include: female grace and virile justice organising all of Michelet's writing; the hero as he who 'deposits Justice with History'; alcohol and tobacco 'stop history' (because leading to a failure to act).

Fantasy really came on the scene since 1960 with the revival in interest of Freud's (1856–1939) theory of unconscious fantasy (Freud 1979a, 1979b). Freud places emphasis, not on the difference between fantasy and reality, but on the fundamental role psychic reality plays in human experience. What Freud is continually groping for is a way of explaining the importance of fantasy in relation to formative aspects of psychic life related to separation from the mother and sexual difference, the intervention of the father and the castration complex – not to mention the Oedipus complex. Sexual difference, as the prototype of every encounter with difference, and thus with what is inexpressible and fearful, needs a mode of expression. For Freud, fantasy is this mode. In effect, the subject of castration is searching for a way of compensating, in symbolic terms, for the lack of castration anxiety. Freud takes the notion of fantasy away from the French *fantaisie*, as the sweet reveries of the imagination, and finds in it indications of repressed material and unconscious desire. Fantasy is a serious thing when it comes to understanding the nature of psychic space. And it has epistemological implications. It is not that psychic space *is* everything, and that there is no objective reality – for this would be solipsism – but that the structure and nature of psychic space must be taken into account in any quest for truth.

Perhaps the most influential interpretation of fantasy is that of the French psychoanalyst, Jacques Lacan (1901–81). In order to distinguish fantasy from the working and products of the imagination, Lacan (1978) uses the French term, *fantasm*, for which he has the following notation: $\$\Box a$, which depicts the relation of the (barred $\$$) subject to the lost object of desire, *a* (also known as *objet petit a*). The separation of the subject from the mother, which comes with the experience of castration anxiety, inaugurates the attempt to fill the gap between self and other symbolically. The '*a*', in one of its avatars, stands for the mother as the lost object, the one with whom that subject-child wants to reunite. However, the child must come to accept his or her individuality and relative autonomy, *vis-à-vis* the mother. Of course an object, *as* essentially lost, can never be found (for separation from the mother is permanent). The object is lost, structually speaking, so that no symbolic form will ever be equivalent to it – no *fantasm* will ever fill this gap, for it is the fantasm, in Lacan's sense, which is the tangible

expression of the attempt to fill the gap, or to compensate for a lack in the symbolic order. This object is also called the lost object of desire (= desire in general): for it is symbolic of the lack which sets desire in motion.

The lost object and the myth of castration thus come to occupy, in psychic space, the position of primal fantasy or founding scene, a scene which is not consciously accessible to the subject, except indirectly, in a displaced form through fantasy productions. How much more important, then, must art productions be for the psychoanalyst, geared as he or she is to find evidence of unconscious desire in fantasy structures which the non-analyst might see as the most unpromising of places.

Barthes, Roland (1964) *On Racine*, trans. Richard Howard, New York: Hill & Wang.
Barthes, Roland (1987) *Michelet*, trans. Richard Howard, Oxford: Blackwell.
Freud, Sigmund (1979a [1908]) 'Hysterical Phantasies and Their Relation to Bisexuality', trans. D. Bryan, in *The Freud Pelican Library, Volume 10: On Psychopathology*, Harmondsworth: Pelican, 83–94.
Freud, Sigmund (1979b [1919] 'A Child is Being Beaten', in *The Freud Pelican Library, Volume 10: On Psychopathology*, trans. A. and J. Strachey, Harmondsworth: Pelican, 159–193.
Lacan, Jacques (1978) *Seminar, Book XI: Four Fundamental Concepts of Psychoanalysis*, trans. Alan Sheridan, New York: Norton.

See IDENTITY; IMAGINARY; IMAGINATION

FRACTAL

FRACTAL Etymologically, 'fractal' is formed from the Latin word, *fractus*, past participle of *frangere*, to break.

Subsequently, 'fractal' emerged in mathematics, and is adapted from the French, *fractal*, a term which came to prominence in B.B. Mandelbrot's book, originally published in French, as *Les Objets fractals* (1975), and published in English as *Fractals: Form, Chance and Dimension* (1977). The reality of fractal patterns is closely associated with what has become known as 'Chaos theory'; indeed, the fractal is the 'footprint of chaotic systems' (Shroyer 1993: 71). Although it is essentially a mathematical notion, 'fractal' now has wide currency outside mathematics, in politics, economics and art.

Strictly speaking, a fractal is a mathematically conceived curve such that any small part of it, once enlarged, has the same statistical character as the original. Mountain reliefs, island coastlines, the holes of Emmental cheese, the structure of vegetables such as cauliflowers, the craters of the moon, the distribution of stars close to us in the galaxy and a good deal more can be described by the use of generalised Brownian movement and the idea of the fractal dimension.

According to Mandelbrot (1977), classical geometry is unable to describe many important spatial patterns of nature because these are so irregular and fragmented. Traditional representational models just cannot do them justice. To remedy this absence of geometric representation in the classical Newtonian sense, Mandelbrot proposed a family of shapes called 'fractals – or fractal sets'. If classical geometry simplified patterns, reducing them to their most basic form but bereft of complicating detail, fractal theory attempts to indicate the unpredictable complexity that underlies all domains of the natural and human world. Put simply, the apparent chaos, or randomness, of the shape of a coastline or of the crystalline structure of a snowflake come, in fractal modelling, to take on a perceptible, if unpredictable, pattern, often of astonishing beauty. Fractal configurations make it possible to appreciate that order begins to emerge out of true randomness, but that this order is never absolute, while every apparent order is riddled with random or chaotic elements. Classical Euclidean geometry, based on analytical, a priori principles, is not adequate to grasping natural formations because 'clouds are not spheres', 'mountains are not cones', 'lightning does not travel in a straight line' (Gleick 1988: 94). Gleick, in his book on Chaos, goes on to say: 'The new [fractal] geometry mirrors a universe that is rough, not rounded, scabrous, not smooth. It is a geometry of the pitted, pocked, and broken up, the twisted, tangled, and intertwined' (Gleick 1988: 94). Nature – and no doubt the human world as well – is thus riven by an essential complexity, a notion that, once again, throws into doubt the Cartesian idea of an essential simplicity underlying apparent complexity. The great merit of fractal geometry, for the specialist and lay person alike, is in its capacity to render visible, without simplifying it, the very patterns of complexity*.

Another dimension of complexity made evident by fractal geometry is the fact that the small changes (the famous 'beat of a butterfly's wings') can have inordinate effects. Similarly, the smallest rounding of numbers in mathematical calculations can have large effects when it comes to the prediction of patterns: meteorological patterns, for example. The point, as some have failed to understand, is not that a tiny event (the motion of butterfly wings) can, in itself, have catastrophic effects, but that a large number of tiny events – events that are barely observable – can have vast cumulative effects.

Fractal geometry, with its emphasis on changes over time, is a mode of synthetic thinking, as opposed to analytical thinking, which is based on constancy. Analytical approaches to the understanding of social and natural phenomena imply that a complete knowledge of an existing state of affairs (= description of equilibrium) will, in principle, give rise to a perfect prediction of events. To be sure, human knowledge, being historically limited, will fail to come up with complete knowledge. However, if powerful tools are invented in the future the possibility of complete knowledge exists in principle under the old paradigm. Fractal modelling, by direct contrast, implies that there can be no complete knowledge in principle, not just in fact. For complexity (randomness) is at the very heart of order itself. The future – the weather, for instance – is thus only ever predictable within well-defined limits. In practice, this means nothing more nor less than that there is always something new on the horizon, and that time* is at the heart of all things.

What a fractal approach also shows is that patterns emerge, despite – or even because of – randomness. And instead of saying that, by definition (that is, analytically), disorder is unthinkable or unobservable or impossible to model, a certain *tendency* towards order is often perceptible, just as, from the opposite side, random elements will be present in even the most highly ordered phenomena.

Ultimately fractal geometry suggests that complexity, not simplicity, is the order of the day, and that attempts to smooth the rough edges of things and people is a travesty of nature as

it is. Humans are fractal; they are complex, not stereotypical and clone*-like. This can be seen in the range of human faces. Each one is the same: it is human, with eyes, ears, nose, cheeks, etc. A model of the typical human face can even be proffered. This, however, is to view the human face in a Cartesian, Euclidean manner: as a collection of simple elements that can be reproduced. But each face is also unmeasurably, and qualitatively different. There is a difference in the sameness which cannot be measured, or fully represented. This is the fractal effect. The more the fractal effect is given currency, the more consideration will have to be given to chance, difference and singularity in human affairs, as well as in the affairs of nature. The oversimplifications that have served humans for millennia may well continue to do so, but they can never again be wielded as a truth used to subdue undesirable (because complex without a model) parts of culture or of nature.

Gleick, James (1988) *Chaos: Making a New Science*, London: Cardinal Sphere Books.
Mandelbrot, Benoit (1977) *Fractals: Form, Chance and Dimension*, San Francisco: Freeman.
Shroyer, Jo Ann (1993) *Quarks, Critters, and Chaos: What Science Terms Really Mean*, New York: Prentice-Hall.

See ANALYTIC–SYNTHETIC; DIFFERENCE–INDIVIDUALITY; TIME

FREEDOM
When referring to human action, there is hardly a term more often used in the world's media than freedom. People live – or should live – in freedom, in modern democratic polities; freedom of

choice, freedom from hunger, freedom of conscience, freedom to be who we are, freedom of the individual, etc. – all these phrases are endlessly repeated until it seems that freedom risks becoming a cliché. Were this to happen, it would, for many, be a terrible thing because it would destroy the almost sacred nature of freedom in human life.

Historically, freedom, in its human form, especially in relation to politics and morality, has been understood to be a condition of self-determination, so that a person is able to act free from any coercion – in particular, free from the coercion often employed by Church or State. This is close to Sir Isaiah Berlin's famous notion of negative freedom, or 'freedom from' (Berlin 1969). The contrast here is with positive freedom, or 'freedom to', which implies that the agent is unhindered in achieving a given end. Closely aligned to Berlin's idea of freedom is the liberal view, often represented by John Stuart Mill's 1859 essay, 'On Liberty' (1991), which says that an individual should have the right to do what he or she wants to do, provided that these actions do not have undesirable effects on others. Mill thus distinguishes between 'self-regarding' actions – which only involve the individual agent – and 'other-regarding' actions, which impinge upon others. Whether or not it is possible to keep these two domains separate is one of the abiding issues of liberal philosophy.

From a moral point of view, it is often argued that an action done under duress, or out of a sense of self-preservation, is one that is not free. If, at gunpoint, or through starvation, a person acts in a particular way, the moral worth of the action will be reduced to the extent that it is decided that the agent was not free to act

otherwise. Even though great moral gestures have been made in just such extreme circumstances, who could judge another who failed to live up to such high moral standards? In other words, who would say that, in face of the extreme, an agent was *free* to act otherwise?

In his theory of pure reason, Kant (1724–1804) defines freedom as the 'unconditioned cause' (1970: 392). Practically speaking – i.e. in the sphere of morality – freedom is said to be a condition of the will (see Kant 1997). That is, no act of will can be said to be free if it is conditioned in any way. Freedom is therefore the product of a transcendental idea. Freedom can cause things to happen, but cannot itself be caused. Modern sociology has challenged such an idea with its emphasis on action as always being socially conditioned, or socially caused. Freedom, in the pure sense that Kant refers to, according to the sociological view, does not exist. Only freedom that is socially based can be realised, if it can be realised at all. Individual freedom is far more problematic. For this reason, a sociological approach to freedom tends to privilege political over moral freedom. Kant understood freedom in the context of a society that was still religious. And indeed, Kant says that the conditions of morality are God, freedom and immortality. Sociology, by contrast, heralds the secularisation of society. Despite the certainty by sociology, Kant is very clear: 'The denial of transcendental freedom must ... involve the elimination of all practical freedom' (1970: 465). This is because freedom cannot have a cause. It is completely autonomous – almost by definition.

Discussion of Kant's idea of freedom also raises the issue of the relation of freedom and necessity*, the great dialectical couple that figures in the work of German idealist philosophy, Marx's writings, and the writing of Hannah Arendt (1906–1975). Everything here turns around different kinds of action: action done for instrumental reasons (for human survival, for example), or from necessity, and action done for its own sake, or completely free acts. According to Arendt, modern society, in making welfare and the production and consumption of commodities its *raison d'être*; has given up on freedom is the sense of actions done for their own sake, actions entirely separate from need or necessity. Action – the free act – for Arendt is not useful in any obvious sense. Instead, it is an end in itself, creative, essentially public, and discloses 'who' we are by comparison with 'what' we are as humans (in our biological nature). According to Arendt, the Classical Greeks had such a notion of freedom: action done in the public sphere would reveal the identity and personality of the actor – both to the community and to the actor himself. 'In acting and speaking, men show who they are, reveal actively their unique personal identities' (Arendt 1958: 179).

Although in a different way to Kant, Arendt also places freedom beyond the easy reach of objective description. And so in attempting to say *who* someone is, 'our very vocabulary leads us astray into saying *what* he is' (Arendt 1958: 181). The sphere of the 'what' (enumeration of qualities) is the sphere that, ironically, hides the 'who', instead of revealing it. Sociology would thus hide the realm of freedom in its obsession with the 'what' of things. Sociology also hides action to the extent that it focuses on necessity – the social and material conditions that

form individuals – rather than on freedom, freedom here being the point at which individuals transcend necessity and engage in action.

Does this then mean that freedom is a mystical domain beyond the reach of ordinary mortals? Arendt, for one, has an intriguing answer to this question. It is that because every human life* between birth and death can be told as a story, everyone can, potentially, experience freedom, since the public narration of a life – the *telling* of a life story – is also action in the fullest sense as an end in itself. A life story is also revelatory of the *who* that we are; this form of revelation, exemplified perhaps by Jean-Jacques Rousseau's *Confessions* (1781–88), can therefore make a mark on the otherwise instrumentalised public stage (Arendt 1958: 184–185).

Arendt, Hannah (1958) *The Human Condition*, Chicago and London: University of Chicago Press.

Berlin, Sir Isaiah (1969) *Four Essays on Liberty*, Oxford: Oxford University Press.

Kant, Immanuel (1970 [1781]) *Critique of Pure Reason*, trans. Norman Kemp Smith, London and Basingstoke: Macmillan.

Kant, Immanuel (1997 [1788]) *Critique of Practical Reason*, trans. Mary Gregor, Cambridge: Cambridge University Press.

Mill, John Stuart (1991 [1859]) 'An Essay on Liberty', in *On Liberty, Utilitarianism, Considerations on Representative Government, The Subjection of Women*, Oxford: Oxford University Press.

FUZZY LOGIC

In fuzzy logical terms, we can say to someone that they had better come 'pretty soon', otherwise the dinner will be ruined. How long, precisely, is 'pretty soon'? How long is 'in a moment'? Digital logic – the logic of either/or; true or false – has an answer to such questions: 'pretty soon' means precisely 'x' amount of time; in a moment means precisely 'y' amount of time – neither more nor less. If, from a digital, true–false, logical point of view it is not possible to be specific about the length of time involved, the result is a diminution in knowledge. If, to bring space into the picture, we say that the house was 'terribly large', digital logic questions us and demands that we give precise measurements – 185 square metres, let us say. Digital logic wants exactness; fuzzy logic seems to give inexactness, and, say the digital advocates, is therefore of doubtful validity.

Interest in fuzzy logic has arisen against a background of the hegemony of digital processes of all kinds. Digital processes are analytical and 'left brain' in orientation, whereas fuzzy logic is more 'right brain' and synthetic in orientation (see analytic–synthetic).

While digital logic is bivalent, fuzzy logic is ambivalent. It evokes ambiguous borders – between a hill and mountain, for example. At what height exactly should we speak of a mountain rather than a hill? There is no exact answer to such a question, even if we know that an extremely tall land formation (20,000 metres high) is a mountain and a small one a hill (100 metres high). Of course, it is possible to digitalise the issue and say that a land mass rising above 10,000 metres is a mountain; below 10,000 metres is a hill. But the *reality* is that things are fluid. We drift into mountainness out of hillness; the actual border cannot be specified exactly. Digital logic always held out the hope that with more sophisticated precision instruments

exactness could be achieved, and that, in principle, inexactness could be eliminated. Something must be either true *or* false, one thing *or* the other; it cannot be neither, and it cannot be both at the same time. Such would be the stricture laid down by digital logic.

It has been suggested that bivalent logic is Western in character, that classical Greece inaugurated the law of non-contradiction, fundamental to the working of this logic: something, said Aristotle, must either be or not be; to claim that it both is *and* is not (p and not-p) is a contradiction. Clear thinking in everyday life, and rigour in science and philosophy, are said to result from avoiding contradiction. Avoiding contradiction becomes a veritable 'law of thought'.

Poetic works often break with this law so that something can simultaneously be and not be, thus breaking the above law. More generally, the realm of art often plays with contradiction by affirming on one level what it denies on another. Dostoevsky's 'polyphonic' novels, which enact a range of political and social positions, have been described as 'ambivalent': they are religious and non-religious, socialist and conservative, the voice of the devil and of God, of the living and of the dead. Carnival is also an ambivalent art form because it is the enactment of all social positions. And of course, carnival spills over into society at large: everyone gets swept up by carnival.

In painting ambivalence arises with René Magritte's *Ceci n'est pas une pipe* ('This is not a pipe')(1928), which is a painting of a pipe, and which, as a painting, is not a pipe, but a representation. Maybe all realist art forms are ambivalent in this sense. For a representation (of an Olympic athlete in a photograph) both is and is not what it is.

Fuzzy logic has given rise to the fuzzy set, a notion introduced by an electrical engineer, Lofti Zadeh in 1965. The idea behind the fuzzy set is that in any collection – all the tall men in Paris – the qualities that best describe the collection are, most often, approximate values like 'more or less', rather than that tallness is every man of exactly two metres. There may not be any man of two metres tall, or only one, with the others clustering around, being more or less than two metres. Fuzzy logic says that if the degree of tallness of all the men in Paris were to be described, all men are more or less tall. Or: every man is tall and not tall to some degree. In other words, 'tallness, like most properties in the world, is a matter of degree' (Kosko 1994: 147).

What we learn from fuzzy logic, then, is that it is wrong to be dogmatic – black or white – about the properties of the human and the natural worlds. Fuzzy sets and meaning in language go well together, for the meaning of an individual word is never exactly one thing. There are, as we say, shades of meaning. This is why it is possible to draw out more than one meaning from a text and why, despite attempts to prevent this, legal documents are also open to interpretation.

The aim of fuzzy logic, however, is not to valorise inexactness, but to recognise complexity. It is not a substitute for existing analytical methods, but supplements them, in order to foster a richer understanding of phenomena.

Kosko, Bart (1994) *Fuzzy Thinking*, London: Flamingo.

GENERAL WILL

GENERAL WILL In an age when populism is gaining ground, the concept of the General Will is being pushed ever further into the background. From its inception in Jean-Jacques Rousseau's putatively subversive tract, *The Social Contract* of 1762 (Rousseau 1973), the General Will has been looked on with suspicion by politically conservative and progressive forces alike. One side has seen the General Will as opening the door to disorder; this is because such a Will can be interpreted as uniting democracy with certain high standards of government, standards which would form the basis for a challenge to the existing order and its current rulers. In the name of the people, the General Will stakes a claim in the name of the true will of the people.

The other side – political progressives – have, for their part, seen the General Will as a problem because it makes a distinction between the will of the people as measured quantitatively in an election or opinion poll, and a qualitative notion of this Will, a distinction which, clearly, entails the imperative to judge, to evaluate. This might leave the way open for tyrants and anti-democratic forces to come to power based on the claim that they *really* speak in the name of the people. Such was the claim of 'living real'

communism in the USSR and Eastern Europe. No wonder such polities have embraced free-market democracy with such vigour.

Although it is difficult, it may still be necessary to keep the General Will in mind when 'the people' vote for violations of human rights in dealing with asylum seekers, or when a certain amount of corruption occurs when the police deal with drug dealers and addicts, in the interest of 'clearing the streets' of such people. The latter exemplifies the 'result' mentality which police around the world are beginning to exhibit in relation to both organised and unorganised crime. Indeed, we could do worse than define the General Will as the basis of law in its broadest sense, as opposed to police action in the broadest sense (= the rule of force, as in the notion of a police state).

While many imply or exclaim that, because the two are essentially different, a choice has to be made in the end between the law and the will of the people (the law supposedly being too far removed from the people), Rousseau, in *The Social Contract*, argued that the spirit of any law worthy of the name coincides with the will of the people. The difference between law and democracy is thus merely apparent. However, even Rousseau was forced to ask how a people that did not, most of the time, seem to know what it wanted could have authored the General Will. How would it be possible to avoid the General Will becoming authoritarian and paternalistic, a set of orders telling people to do what is in their own interest – if only they knew what the latter was. Or if only *someone* knew what the latter was. And indeed, Rousseau's inadequately argued point that people might have to be 'forced to be free', made with the aim of illustrating the nature of the General Will, has provided a field day for libertarians like Bertrand Russell, who saw in such a statement the origins of totalitarianism itself. Even more directly, and more perplexingly, though, how could the General Will possibly be enforced? But why precisely should it *need* to be enforced if it was the true will of the people?

There is, however, more than one way to approach the General Will, as there no doubt is in relation to Rousseau's work generally. And it is that, whether or not the details of the argumentation are sound, the General Will points to a dimension of political and social life that cannot simply be swept away. Apart from the fact that Rousseau, in equating the General Will with *their* will, gives to the people the qualities of foresight and wisdom – the people for him are not essentially an unruly mob – there are moments in the political and social life of every democratic polity when there is a need to invoke something like the General Will. What would these moments be? Already, we have pointed to the violations of human rights in the interests of social and political convenience. If a poll, taken at a given moment, were to show that a majority of people favoured having the police break the law in the interest of an easier life

(ridding the streets of drug dealers – or of political protesters), must the one who opposes the sentiment expressed in the poll have to accept that they are also opposing democracy? Even though John Stuart Mill pointed to the 'tyranny of the majority', is there any way round equating the will of the people with the quantitative measurement of it at any given moment in an opinion poll? It is only by invoking an argument based on qualitative criteria that one can claim both a democratic and a just approach to the problem. In other words, the General Will can be seen to *legitimise* (see legitimacy) a just and democratic approach to political action.

We sometimes hear the phrase 'popular democracy', when the people deal with paedophiles in their own way. A populist press which, if challenged about contempt of court or the like, can always shelter under the cloak of democracy, plays on – exploits – the contingent feelings of people (the question of the actual number is rarely addressed). More importantly, if governments break human rights conventions (maybe in times of war, but maybe not) in claiming that they are following the will of the people (meaning by this that the latest opinion poll says they should), what recourse do we have other than to invoke some form of the General Will argument? If individuals claim (or if others claim on their behalf) that they gave up their human rights freely and voluntarily in full knowledge of what they were doing, what recourse do we have other than invoking some form of the General Will argument? If women, living under a totalitarian regime, claim that they have given up their freedom* and individuality of their own free will, as some women living under the Taliban regime in

Afghanistan have claimed, what recourse other than to a version of the General Will argument exists which can simultaneously do justice to a democratic position and to freedom and human rights?

Let it not be thought that there are no problems with Rousseau's famous concept. Let us recognise, as many have, that the possibility for abuse exists, and that the full nature of the General Will remains inscrutable. However, Rousseau's term is not there to be rated according to the consistency and power of its argument; it is there because the issues to which it alludes are deep seated and enduring, and this is so more than ever because now – today – these issues tear at the heart of democratic political life.

Rousseau, Jean-Jacques (1973 [1762]) *The Social Contract* in *The Social Contract and Discourses*, trans. G.D.H. Cole, London, Melbourne and Toronto: J.M. Dent & Sons, Everyman's Library.

GIFT While the gift has been analysed as a form of exchange*, the nature of the true gift is to be without any obligation to reciprocate, without the need for exchange. A gift that elicits a counter-gift is not a gift in the strict sense. There can perhaps be the gift of life – but a Christmas gift? Is it really a gift when everyone spends money* to buy gifts for everyone else, and expects – or morally demands – that they receive gifts in their turn? Exchange there may be, but a gift…?

The difficulty of comprehending a gift as a gift may explain why the precise format of the counter-gift in certain non-Western societies (Samoa,

Alaska) is shrouded in mystery. If one is to reciprocate, this must be a reciprocation that is to some extent disguised. An appropriate amount of time must elapse; the good returned must be of a similar value but of a different nature; there must be no indication that the gift is a reciprocation, even though both parties might intuit that it is. On the other hand, the one to whom the gift is given is under an obligation to receive, otherwise gift giving as an institution would be impossible. A whole social structure can thus be based on the gift and its moral ties, just as money, in a different way, constitutes itself as an institution in Western society.

As the anthropologist of the gift, Marcel Mauss (1872–1950), put it: the gift entails a threefold structure: to give, to receive and to reciprocate (Mauss 1990). As an institution, the gift is never a simple exchange of goods, but involves honour and a specific use of time; it is something which touches every aspect of life, ensuring the circulation of women in marriage as well as the circulation of goods. The latter, it should be noted are not limited to materials, but include services of all kinds, sexual favours, festivals and dances. Even when material goods are involved, these are not the inanimate things they are deemed to be in capitalist societies, but have a 'soul', a spirituality.

In certain societies giving can reach such heights that destruction of goods is the result. In North American societies, as in New Guinea, prestige and honour are gained and maintained by the one who can expend the most. In extreme cases, destruction includes ritual death of human beings, as occurred in Aztec society. This is what characterises the society based on a general economy*. Relations of power, which underpin the gift in general, are made explicit here.

These are, then, societies of prestige and hierarchy, as they are societies of community* (= context). Here, forms of money are often very limited. Gift societies may be contrasted on this point with highly developed, and highly complex and differentiated money economies founded on decontextualisation and the dissolution of community as a closed system. Again, in contrast to capitalist, money societies these are not societies of utility, but often religious societies based in the achievement of ends.

A key point here is that Mauss suggests that the reciprocity of gift exchange still remains with us. Every gift elicits a counter-gift. Is this true? The gift is an institution, not just a contingent event, which means that, as an institution, the gift is distinct from the actions of specific individuals. Or rather: specific individuals are formed by the institution of the gift. Those who sense that a complex money society is also one of alienation have begun to wonder whether a revitalisation of the gift might not be the antidote needed. Indeed, in a world where rational choice theory posits self-interest and competition as the driving forces of human behaviour, practices of the gift seem well nigh altruistic by comparison. In an essay which examines ways in which the gift might come to prominence in capitalist societies, Godbout has asked what stops people giving. He responds by saying that giving can be a threat to identity. That is what makes people reject the gift, 'what makes them hold onto things instead of allowing them to circulate' (Godbout 2000: 40).

Put another way: gift giving is constitutive of community, and is driven by a tendency to homogenise rather than differentiate. Giving hospitality is, after all, a way of making the stranger the same as community, even if this is for a limited time. The tendency towards individualisation in modernity would thus make the institution of the gift a very secondary one under capitalism.

Godbout, Jacques T. (2000) 'Homo Donator versus Homo Oeconomicus' [Gift-giving Man versus Economic Man]', in Gifts and Interests, ed. A. Vandeveld, Leuven, Belgium: Peeters, 23–46.
Mauss, Marcel (1990 [1923–24]) The Gift: The Form and Reason for Exchange in Archaic Societies, trans. W.D. Halls, London: Routledge.

GLOBALISATION

When Marshall McLuhan coined the phrase, 'the global village' in 1962 to indicate how electronic communications were connecting all parts of the world, little did he know that this very process might bring about anything but a 'village' effect. Simply being connected does not entail the kind of community* connoted by 'village'. Everyone knows everyone else in the village, but no one person can know even a fraction of the possible internet or other connections brought by new information* technologies. The internet – to cite but one form of connection – is a labyrinth without a centre, not at all like a village with its square, and familiar fountain or some other public work. McLuhan's mistake was to speak in purely qualitative terms of a phenomenon that has a predominantly quantitative persona. Some would say that globalisation is essentially quantitative because it is reinforced by international money markets; it is therefore to be treated with caution. Anti-globalisation demonstrations in the US, Italy, Australia and elsewhere have taken place in an atmosphere of suspicion about the motives of global capital.

Communications networks are one important element of what is called 'globalisation'. While, within a limited sphere, communications (to stay with this dimension for a moment) may allow a greater degree of familiarity, for qualitative interaction to emerge on a worldwide basis, more sophisticated communicative facilities are by no means enough. In fact, overcoming distance – making connections – does not in itself entail overcoming cultural, or even political and economic barriers.

As a factor in the development of the information society, globalisation has, quantitatively, equalised the distribution of information, much as money* has equalised through price a knowledge of the value of goods and services, if not the accessibility of these. In other words, there is now, in principle, one market for commodities, by contrast to the profit (often corrupt) that could be made in the past by buying the same item in one market, and selling it in another. That is, if, through some means not generally available, one was able to find out that the price of gold was selling at a lower price in Tokyo than in the rest of the world, it would be possible to buy gold in Tokyo and sell it in London. A profit could be made because part of the market had imperfect information. The black market still retains an echo of this past. Now, in the era of globalisation, it is in principle almost impossible, at a broad international level, to find such anomalies.

This is not to deny that in other areas there is still differential access to information. This is illustrated by that fact that, in the 1930s, Australia depended on Britain's news service (the ABC depended on the BBC) for information about events in the rest of the world, and therefore Australia was slower to learn of European events than were Europeans (and vice versa – but, then again, why should Europeans need to know what was happening in Australia, except as concerns the tennis and the cricket?). Globalisation, in informational terms, means that differential access to information is overcome and that, in principle, any event can be known in any part of the world at the speed of light – which means, effectively, that the occurrence of an event and an audience's knowledge of it is instantaneous: 11 September, 2001, is a grim case in point.

Apart from extreme fundamentalist regimes, like that of the Taliban in Afghanistan, which decide to withdraw totally from the international communications network, even the poorest nations, through the satellite dish, can have access to international television services. The chief difference between access to such services in India as opposed to Europe or America is that access in India is by the village as a whole, whereas access in the latter is by individuals or households. Although poverty must still be recognised as an obstacle to equal access to information, the continuing downward trend of prices for key forms of communications technology such as the telephone and computer means that villages very often bear the cost, even if individual households cannot.

Globalisation evokes the speed at which it is possible to move between any two points on the globe. The three-month journey by sail from England to Australia in the late eighteenth century has now become a 24-hour flight by conventional jet, or 13 hours by Concorde. In addition to the time factor, many parts of the globe were outside transportation networks, so that opportunities for travel were severely limited. Even though the dream of transporting oneself to a new location merely by thinking oneself into it is an impossible one, the fact remains that the whole of the globe is now, in principle, accessible by all (lack of money of course constitutes an economic limitation, but this a contingent matter, and thus raises other issues).

Globalisation is also manifest in economic terms through the phenomenon of the multinational corporation. Now, no longer respecting national state boundaries, the multinational is able to buy in the cheapest market and sell in the dearest. The multinational thus seeks out cheap labour and fights to have local restrictions on its activities relaxed. Politics for the multinational is always a relatively local, and thus provincial, phenomenon. From a multinational point of view, politicians rarely grasp the big picture, which, for such organisations, is very big indeed, for it is global.

The multinational corporation is illustrative of the force for decontextualisation that characterises globalisation. Such globalisation implies that place, in relation to many activities in life, is no longer relevant in a material sense. What is done is increasingly independent of where it is done – whether in the fields of education, manufacturing, film-making (cf. Fox studios in Sydney), or forms of employment. Often, what began as a local tradition is replicated in other parts of the world (cf. French and Chinese cuisine, Hawaiian shirts, Rolls-Royce engines, Montessori pedagogical techniques, Chinese writing, and even religions). It has often been said that ethnic communities, establishing themselves away from their country of origin, sometimes appear more 'authentic' than their compatriots back home. The Chinese community in New York in the 1940s and 1950s is one example. Globalisation builds on these tendencies inaugurated by movements of migrants throughout the world. In so doing, local tradition suffers another blow – the first one (the growth of cities) having been delivered by modernity and the Industrial Revolution.

Although not always thought of in the same context, globalisation introduces an awareness of the finite global resources. The oceans, deserts and forests of the world are not closed systems, but are linked to the rest of the world, so that pollution in one area will have consequences in others. Global warming is an example of this.

If globalisation entails the possible replication and reproduction of everything from consumer goods to lifestyle, does this mean that a mass standardisation of life is taking place as never before, so that originality and uniqueness begin to disappear? As the French anthropologist Lévi-Strauss said in his UNESCO address of 1952 (1978: 361), we must 'never forget that no fraction of humanity should dispose of formulae which could be applied to all, and that a humanity merged into a single way of life is inconceivable because it would be an ossified humanity'. To sustain diversity, he says with great prescience, it is not enough to preserve the content of local traditions. What needs to be preserved is 'the fact of diversity'. In this regard, there has to be a readiness to accept the surprises that the evolution of human cultures holds in store; that is, all the people of the world need to appreciate the dynamism of difference and originality where, and whenever, it appears.

Lévi-Strauss, Claude (1978) 'Race and History', in *Structural Anthropology 2*, trans. Monique Layton, Harmondsworth and New York: Penguin Peregrine Books.

See COMMUNICATION; LOCAL

GOVERNMENTALITY

Governmentality is as much a research strategy as a conception of governing. Although governmentality (which might sound, to some, like a mental condition) is a term linked to the origin of the word, 'government' (originating in the Latin, *gubernare* and the Greek, *kubernan*, to steer), it is not government in the more conventional, if unfamiliar, sense. Government has always implied a clear distinction between the governor and the governed within a given territory in the context of politics, whereas governmentality theory has questioned the rigidity and narrowness, if not the very foundation, of this distinction and the political context which it supposedly evokes. Might there not be numerous contexts (the family) that also throw light on the relationship between the governor and the governed? Might not the governor and governed, in specific circumstances, be one and the same? This is the implication of the term, as it developed in the work of the French philosopher, Michel Foucault (1926–84). For Foucault, governmentality seeks to explore power relations, particularly in the domain of what constitutes conduct (from the French *conduire*, to drive, and *se conduire*, to act – or to conduct oneself – properly, or

appropriately). From Foucault's work in the 1970s – and possibly from a single lecture – the term 'governmentality' came into being.

In this much-cited lecture given in 1978, Foucault (1979) indicated that the term 'governmentality' served to move the meaning of government away from the idea that the State worked to regulate that part of a citizen's behaviour which, if allowed to go unchecked, might pose a threat to the good order of society. Essentially, in this view government is understood as a negative force; it is only there to ensure the security and well-being of society. Beyond that, what people did was no legitimate concern of government.

For Foucault, this negative approach to government was too heavily indebted to the view of a power which forbids: which essentially says 'no'. It assumes that the State only tends to be involved when the actions of citizens become criminal, and that the task of government is to conduct relations with other states and to ensure that citizens do not act in a way that is detrimental to others. This, however, is to assume that a modern American, economic rationalist, view of government is the right one. Foucault, by contrast, sees government as guiding conduct in an active and positive sense throughout the whole fabric of society, not just in the formal, legal domain of the State. Government includes reflection on the question of the best way of governing in a given context – in health, work, education, family and community relations, or religious practices. Here, it is not just a matter of coercing people to behave in the right way, but of acting upon the actions of others so that their conduct is the result of the field of possibilities that government makes possible.

It should not be concluded from what has been said that governing constitutes a limit to freedom*, while individuals engage in autonomous, free activity; nor should it be thought that actual freedom and governing are opposites, so that in saying that governing permeates the whole of society, and in saying that no actions exist outside a mode of governing, it is implied that freedom is being eradicated. According to Foucault, once a different inflection is placed on governing as an art (as it was in sixteenth-century Europe), an inflection involving trial and error, rather than as a science (where everything would be under control and predictable), then we can appreciate the full meaning of 'governmentality'. Now, governmentality must be understood as a set of actions or practices enacted over free individuals, actions realised only to the extent that individuals are free.

'Governmentality', then, points to a domain which covers more than the legitimate forms of politics and government; it is imbricated in all the actions of people; for this is what the art of government entails. In itself, it is neither good nor bad, desirable nor undesirable. Rather, it is the very field of contestation itself, should there be contestation, as it is the very field of acquiescence should there be acquiescence – whether on a macro or micro scale. The appropriate term here is 'agonism', implying a certain equality of forces, and a reciprocity of 'taunts' of one opponent against the other. More generally, as Foucault puts it in his famous lecture: 'governmentality was born out of, on the one hand the archaic model of Christian pastoral, and on the other out of a diplomatico-military technique' (Foucault 1979: 21). The formation of its specific instruments 'is exactly contemporaneous with that of the art of government and which are known, in the old 17th and 18th century

sense of the term, as police' (ibid.). The term 'police' is the key here. It derives from the French, policer, which in the eighteenth century meant 'to govern' by 'civilising' modes of conduct and refining mores and morals through the establishment of institutions, and all this in relation to the development and supervision of culture.

Governmentality returns to this earlier meaning of police in order to emphasise that governing is more than the public face of government and penetrates the deepest recesses of a nation's being. In this sense, governmentality turns the gaze towards, if not the hidden face of government, at least towards that face which remains unnoticed because it is so much taken for granted. This 'taken-for-grantedness' is typical of liberal-democratic styles of polity, where minimal government is claimed to exist or to be an ideal to be achieved. Here, if government were simply equated with the public and conventional face of government, little – from a governmentality point of view – would be understood about the real working of power. In the United States, for example, where minimal government is a widespread aspiration, the moral sphere of life has come to assume an importance not seen in other forms of democratic state where resistance to government is less marked. Thus governmentality, as a research strategy in relation to the working of power, enables a more profound understanding of the operation of liberal-democratic states and their practices of governing.

Foucault, Michel (1979) 'On Governmentality' *Ideology and Conciousness* 6: 5–21.

See PANOPTICON; POWER

GRAMMATOLOGY

The term, 'grammatology' comes from 'grammar', originating in the Greek adjective, *grammatikós*, 'of letters', and *logos*, meaning 'discourse'. It is linked to the Greek, *grâmma*, meaning letter and 'something written on the page', as well as *gráphein*, 'to write' (source of the English word 'graphic').

Grammatology has been used as a synonym for the history of writing*, as found in the work of Gelb (1952). Here, writing is seen to evolve towards Western phoneticism and as being a representation of speech. In the work of the French philosopher, Jacques Derrida (b. 1930), however, writing has fully assumed its status as grammatology, where the elementary unit of the *grammē* is neither fully oral nor literary, but is both oral and literary at the same time. As we see, the gramme's logic is double, ambivalent.

Rather than investigate phonetic writing as, among other things, a transcription of speech, an *aide-mémoire*, and a means to communicate over distances, we can gain insight into grammatology by looking at speech (the voice) itself. For if we can explain how speech has some of the qualities of writing, we will have moved closer to understanding the nature of grammatology as it is found in Derrida's work.

If writing is a means for communicating at a distance, speech is often viewed as absolute intimacy, an intimacy exemplified in the internal monologue where, in speaking to myself, no problem of interpretation exists because the gap between sender and receiver does not exist. I, as both addresser and addressee of the same message am, in short, absolutely present to myself.

Like the computer technology that has succeeded, without superseding, it, writing has often been thought of as an alienating medium by comparison with the intimacy of speech. As we say, to talk face to face is much more personal than communicating by letter. Here, speech is supposed to be informal and intimate, while writing is more formal and distant. Derrida, in his well-known book, *Of Grammatology* (1976), has drawn attention to the way that Jean-Jacques Rousseau (1712–78) argued strongly in favour of speech, because he saw it as the medium of the heart, and therefore as the medium of love and feeling in general. It was for Rousseau barely a medium. Speech, or better: the voice, was thought to be so close to the inner person that it could give direct access to the heart, and thus to the true self. Pity, which implies an immediate identification with the feelings of another, is thus of the order of the voice. Through pity we begin to occupy the very place of the other.

Rousseau, then, is the most famous early advocate of the intimacy of the voice, a view that is still more or less a commonplace today. Added to this view, we hardly need add, is the notion that writing merely *re*-presents the voice and that, as such, it is secondary to it. Writing by comparison to the voice is thus alienating.

Derrida, for his part, questions both the idea that speech and the voice can embody an absolute intimacy giving rise to absolute self-presence, and the idea of writing as secondary to speech. Instead, he claims that the gap between speech and meaning (the message) cannot be eliminated. And so when looking at Rousseau's belief that the inarticulate human cry is immediate communication* instantly evoking pity, we see that Rousseau is forced to concede that even here there is at least a modicum of articulation, which is a key characteristic of writing. The cry, then, is never a pure cry. It is the *expression* of emotion. Moreover, the cry is the measure of the distance, albeit tiny, between a self and its other. And let us not forget gesture: it is neither vocal nor entirely articulate and is potentially elemental (like the cry); yet it is visual and thus distancing, like writing. In this way, the absolute intimacy of the voice, as an embodiment of self-presence, begins to fall away. This, at least, is the argument of the grammatologist.

When he encounters an argument similar to Rousseau's in the work of the philosopher, Edmund Husserl (1859–1938), Derrida again contends that there must be a minimal difference between the sign* and meaning when something (e.g. a feeling) is communicated, even if this communication is entirely internal. To claim, as Husserl does, that communication takes place, even though the sender and receiver of the message are identical – even though the communication is composed of purely idiomatic (i.e. personal) signs – is to stretch the meaning of communication beyond plausibility. For there to be communication there must be a difference between sender and receiver. Moreover, the grammatologist contends, for a sign in a communication to be a sign, it must be formalisable, and thus repeatable. It cannot be entirely idiomatic. Writing, need we add, is such a vehicle of formalisation. A signature is emblematic of writing in this sense. For although it marks the individuality of the person whose signature it is, a signature must be repeatable and recognisable as the *same* signature in every new instance. A signature has an ideal, formal aspect, however personal it might seem.

Without this aspect a signature could not be forged.

Therefore, at the origin (the origin of the self, for example), there is an original difference (= writing), rather than an original plenitude. This is grammatology's key point and the source of its significance.

Grammatology also exploits a structuralist approach in the sciences with its emphasis on language as a system of differences. Unlike Saussure, though, Derrida sees writing as a more instructive indicator than speech or language in general. If language is essentially a system of differences, each element evokes other elements, and not just itself. This evocation of other elements, Derrida has called 'trace'. Since difference entails articulation (sign as a vehicle of expression), the meaning of linguistic elements is formal. (It is not the 't' itself in the word 'tree' which has meaning, but the relation it has with the other letters, even to the point of it not being identifiable as a 't'.) Trace, then, is articulation. But this is also observable in the pun form of language. James Joyce's *Finnegans Wake* would be an instance of writing as such for this reason. The pun is thus the work of the trace, which can be perceived in the double meaning of words and sounds, but also might not be so perceived. For consciousness has a predilection for identity*. The point is that there are always other meanings, other senses available, which are distant from the first but which are echoed in it. The echo-trace breaks the identity of original meaning. Derrida summarises the key points as follows:

Nothing, neither among the elements nor within the system, is anywhere ever simply present or absent. There are only, everywhere, differences and traces of traces. The gram, then, is the most general concept of semiology – which thus becomes grammatology. (Derrida 1981: 26)

Another sense of grammatology related to difference and articulation, is decontextualisation. To recall: writing as grammatology is difference and articulation, so that writing as distancing is also present in speech: there is always a difference between sign and meaning. A written text, or a recorded voice, as reproduction, can transcend the context in which they were produced. Indeed, a written text is not at all dependent for its meaning on the continued existence of its author (= equivalent to an original context). Writing as difference certainly requires a context, but this does not have to be fixed. Indeed, a new context can bring out new meanings (traces) in the text concerned – as, for instance, in a citation, where a text, taken from one context and inserted into another and thus recontextualised, says something more or something other that what it 'originally' said. Decontextualisation raises the question of whether there is anything essential in writing which would anchor it in some way. Or whether, on the contrary, writing is a kind of algebra, or pure code*, which is abstract in principle, and thus open to a continual process of decontextualisation/recontextualisation, so that no text is ever connected for more than a moment to any given context.

The main artistic genre of grammatology is collage, where images assume a double status: one, in terms of the set of relationships constituted by a current composition; the other, in terms of the allusion to the former context from which an image, or images, was taken. This gives images the rebus quality Freud described in 1900 in *The Interpretation of Dreams*. The rebus principle was also exploited by surrealism, although with more emphasis being given to the current composition. In collage no image* can be interpreted univocally. Images are always equivocal.

Overall, grammatology itself has an equivocal status. On the one hand, its task is to reveal the univocity bequeathed by the Western metaphysical tradition, while on the other hand, its implicit claim is to be able to work against metaphysics while still working within it. Perhaps even more fundamentally, though, grammatology participates in the further erosion of the sacred in postmodernity. For the sacred meaning is inevitably univocal, and its being is singular rather than double. In fact, it is the becoming singular of plurality. In this light, grammatology becomes yet another secular force in the land. Maybe this is for the good. Then again, if the sacred is the sustenance needed by the human imaginary*, the loss brought by complete secularisation may be greater than was at first thought. Here, grammatology should be allowed its place (a return to the harshness of the former religious world is not tenable), while at the same time being put in *its* place, a strategy grammatology has also endeavoured to carry out in relation to other (overweening?) intellectual and artistic movements.

Derrida, Jacques (1976 [1967]) *Of Grammatology*, trans. Gayatri Spivak, Baltimore and London: Johns Hopkins University Press.
Derrida, Jacques (1981 [1972]) *Positions*, trans. Alan Bass, Chicago: University of Chicago Press.
Gelb, I.J. (1952) *A Study of Writing: The Foundations of Grammatology*, Chicago: University of Chicago Press.

See DIFFÉRANCE; DIFFERENCE–INDIVIDUALITY; ; SACRED– PROFANE

H

HABITUS

HABITUS 'Habitus' derives from sixteenth century Latin, where it meant 'a way of being'. In a medical context, it referred to the appearance of the body as an indication of its general state of health.

Used by Leibniz in the seventeenth century, and later in the twentieth century in the field of art history, the term has received renewed attention in the work of the French sociologist, Pierre Bourdieu (e.g. 1977b, 1990). Habitus does *not* mean habit. For while habit is a conscious repetition of actions, habitus is a structural notion related to the way individuals and classes inhabit the world. To inhabit the world is always to be already in it prior to the possibility of consciousness of it. As rational choice theorists, symbolic interactionists and ethnomethodologists focus on contingent and conscious interactions, they are unable to account for the principle that structures such actions. In short, habitus, as a product of history, produces the 'collective practices, and hence history, in accordance with schemes engendered by that history' (Bourdieu 1977b: 82). Habitus is almost like a kind of 'practice-generating grammar' – a grammar that includes a psychological disposition. Through habitus one internalises the legitimacy of one's inclusion (the bourgeois) or exclusion (the working class) from privilege. Acquiring a habitus is perhaps like acquiring a first language: one has no choice in the matter.

The reason for pointing to habitus as grammar is to emphasise that class position does not determine how actors will act in any narrow sense. With a given habitus there is a wide range of possibilities, just as grammar enables a wide range of possibilities in a natural language. Indeed, a habitus allows for a certain degree of spontaneity, initiative and improvisation. Just as the content, or even style of a single speech act cannot be predicted on the basis of the structural rules of a language, and yet is made possible by them, so habitus makes social actions and interactions possible without making them entirely predictable.

Habitus is connected, then, to Bourdieu's view (or empirical discovery) that modern, capitalist societies are societies of inequality. In short, class conflict (the dominant against the dominated class) means that certain people receive a disproportionate share of cultural, economic and symbolic capital. Privilege thus exists, and privilege generates privilege. It is only in myths and folk-tale (the American West) that all 'possibles are equally possible for any possible subject' (1990: 64). 'The relation of what is possible is a relation to power' (ibid.).

Here, privilege should be grasped as being manifest not only at the level of economic capital (level of wealth), but also at the levels of the symbolic (e.g. education, language acquisition, aesthetic appreciation), and the body (what Bourdieu calls 'the cues of specific body *hexis*').

If a habitus largely exists beyond the consciousness of individual actors (for it is what goes without saying), access to it can be gained only by collecting a wide range of statistical and other data relating to social life. Studies of parents' occupations and educational attainment demonstrate that privilege is passed on; the children of doctors and other highly placed professionals also tend to get into medical, and other high, professional university faculties. Studies of taste tend to suggest that privilege and the dominant paradigms of taste are connected. Those with an appreciation of the canon in the arts, and who represent 'good taste', have similarly privileged parents and other relatives. Studies of academic institutions suggest that, in the humanities and social sciences, a particular facility with language relates again to economic and social privilege. In effect, Bourdieu's claim is that once the objective data have been gathered across the board, it is possible to construct a map of social privilege.

In sum, Bourdieu takes the statistical correlation between occupation and education and researches the additional aspects of home and the social environment, aspects which illustrate a correlation between the amount of cultural and symbolic capital and life-chances. Such capital appears in lifestyles. A habitus is connected to a lifestyle to the extent that it enables this lifestyle to be reproduced (which means: enables the same inequalities to be reproduced).

Habitus, then, consists of the transposable dispositions (transferable to a range of contexts), perceptions and appreciation an individual acquires through being a member of a given class, as this is articulated in a given set of material circumstances. Through habitus class conflict is played out. Class conflict is the coming into contact of different forms of class habitus. Habitus therefore implies that class conflict is deep seated. It is not always obvious and superficial. It is not directly related to an ideology*: this is why, ideologically, bourgeois intellectuals can be Marxists, and why working-class, or lower middle-class, people can be (ideologically) conservative. For Anthony Wedgwood-Benn (aristocrat) to become Tony Benn (socialist), a name change is not enough. Habitus transcends the name.

But despite Tony Benn, is it at all possible for someone to change their habitus? For Bourdieu, it is extremely difficult if not impossible to unlearn a habitus. Moreover, learning, he claims with his colleague, Jean-Claude Passeron, is 'an irreversible process' (Bourdieu 1977a: 43–44). This is why habitus might be true, but it is also a somewhat pessimistic view of society. Bourdieu's response is to say that habitus is linked to a knowledge of necessity*, and that such knowledge is the way to the only freedom* human beings have.

Bourdieu, Pierre (with Jean-Claude Passeron) (1977a [1970]) *Reproduction in Education, Society and Culture*, trans. Richard Nice, London: Sage.
Bourdieu, Pierre (1977b [1972]) *An Outline of a Theory of Practice*, trans. Richard Nice, London, New York and Cambridge: Cambridge University Press.
Bourdieu, Pierre (1990 [1980]) *The Logic of Practice*, trans. Richard Nice, Cambridge: Polity Press.

See ALIENATION; FREEDOM; LABOUR-POWER

HISTORY

Etymologically the word 'history' derives from the Latin word *historia*, meaning narrative of past events, account, tale, story. Another root is the Greek, *istoria*, a learning or knowing by inquiry, an account of one's inquiries, narrative, history, from the Greek *istor*, meaning a knowing, learned, wise man, or judge. The implication is that the emphasis is as much on the act of telling/narrating itself, as on what is told. The middle voice dimension of history implies that the narrator is not separate from history, but is in history – in the story.

Still in the Greek idiom, we have, as Herzfeld (1987: 42–43) has pointed out, the term *istories* – the people's histories, the plurality of stories – as opposed to official history (*i historia*), which smooths over the differences of individual 'stories'. So the stories the people tell to themselves become a way of opposing homogenising, official history.

For a long time – since Voltaire and Hume in the eighteenth century – history in the European West has been about relating the facts in a neutral voice. Or at least were a historian to engage in potentially subjective commentary and interpretation, the change of voice should be clear to the reader. With Carlyle (1795–1881) in England, Michelet (1798–1874) in France, and Ranke (1795–1886) in Germany in the nineteenth century, history writing came of age, and it was felt that a nation's, and by extension an individual's, cultural identity was located in the very interstices of historical discourse. Nations were historical, culture* and society were historical,

politics was historical. To know the progress brought by the Industrial Revolution, was to know the origin of things – things which grew in irreversible time, as the paradigm of thermodynamics* would have it. The life and death of nations, and indeed, of civilisations, could be documented and recorded, so that knowledge could be held in perpetuity for future generations.

Not only was history the key to understanding how the world worked, but the past offered lessons for those in the present. By studying the past, one could avoid making the same mistakes – or so it was thought. Part of the force of this status of history is the idea that, unlike myth or fiction, history is based on true facts. In short, true history emerges in descriptions of things as they are, not as they ought to be, or as humans imagined them to be. History writing proper, in short, participates in the secular scientific revolution that was witnessed by the nineteenth century. To know the present was to know the past.

The fever of history as an explanation for the present gave rise to historicism, the idea that events could be explained with reference to a given historical era, that the significance of facts was relative to historical change. Marx sometimes appeared to subscribe to such a framework in statements like: 'men make their own history, but not in circumstances of their own choosing'. Again, Marx emphasises an historicist orientation when he says that, after being a force of development, forces of production turn into social fetters and so come into conflict with the prevailing relations of production, or existing property relations, 'then occurs a period of social revolution' – i.e. historical change. Marx's stress on historical change as the essence of social life is the key aspect of his materialist conception of history. For Marx, social and political – not to mention economic – life is historical through and through. For him, only a truly conservative view of the world would deny this.

The return to origins – to the past – also led to the realisation, questioned today, that the past determined the present and the future. Marx seems to confirm the implicit determinism here when he says that one set of forces of production and property relations give rise to the next. Or: the new society comes into being in the womb of the old. Again, this is evocative of the thermodynamic paradigm, which holds that a perfect description of a given moment, or set of conditions, in history would provide a knowledge of future conditions. Time*, here, is effectively time as the accumulation of static moments, each one of which could, in principle, be isolated and studied in its own right. History thus attempts to capture a past present, not the past as essentially in time and therefore as different from the present. To travel in H.G. Wells's time machine is to return to a past present moment, a moment as it actually was, a moment recaptured and lived a second time. Here is historical writing wanting to become totally transparent, so that it is unnoticed and able to transport the reader back to the past moment in all its fullness.

Of course, even liberal historians, who do not often pay more than lip service to ideology*, have conceded that there is always a perspective informing historical writing. Marx was correct on that, they admit. The historian always has to choose which set of documents, which set of facts, or which events, will be the focus of study. Selection is inevitable.

But, in addition to this, critics such as Hayden White (1973) in America and Roland Barthes (1986) in France studied historical writing as though it were not transparent, but instead offered a great example of different styles – or rhetorics – of presentation. All descriptive writing tends to be organised metonymically, emphasising contiguity (one fact connects to another). Other historians, such as Michelet, used particular metaphors around which their text is organised. Barthes lists, for example, the different ways blood figures in the Michelet's text (Barthes 1987: 119–129). There is, *inter alia*, 'blood-as-corpse', 'blue blood', 'white blood', 'crazed blood and sealed blood', 'conjugal blood', 'flower of blood', etc.

In the climate of the twenty-first century, the critique of origins has been powerful and has affected the status of history – if not in published work, at least in the fibre of society. Intellectually, this tendency was given a fillip by the structuralist emphasis on the synchronic (static moment) aspect of a system of differences, rather than on a return to the past – the diachronic – in order to explain the present. The past has come to be seen as an interesting read, but eternally quaint and not of much relevance to life as it is lived, in the present.

Finally, we should not neglect the work of historians such as Michel Foucault (1974) and Fernand Braudel (1972, 1973, 1980), who, far from subscribing to either an historicist or a determinist view of history, have revamped the notion of historical time. In Foucault's case this has meant taking a deeper, archaeological approach to history, where events cease to be filtered through human consciousness and become implied by historical materials themselves:

manuals, buildings, older philosophical treatises, textbooks. Here, it is not just a matter of what the documents say, but also of what the documents *are*. Moreover, it is not just a matter of the debates that went on in history over topics such as language, but also one of the conditions of possibility of these debates. These conditions – and this is the second key characteristic of Foucault's histories – could be the result of historical discontinuities. In other words, instead of a smooth and logical transition from one era, or invention, to the next, based on continuity, there is frequently a mutative event that seems to be unrelated to what went before. Thus, in the eighteenth century the botanical grid seemed to be the dominant epistemological paradigm; but by the mid-nineteenth century, the very different, biological paradigm had taken its place. What such an approach lacks in explanation it gains in not being determinist. Foucault, in short, moves away from the strict necessity implied by the thermodynamic paradigm.

Fernand Braudel works with four levels of time in his historical writing. The first looks at the time of the environment, or geographical time, which implies slow, almost imperceptible change over millennia; the second level is the time of social and cultural history – the time of groups, empires and civilisations. Change here is more rapid than with geographical time, but it is not as rapid as change in the time of immediate events (*histoire événementielle*). This is the time of the individual human actor in history. A fourth level is the time of the moment, situation or conjuncture, a time that is yet to congeal into an event proper*. The four

levels of time intersect. Each has a rhythm that is specific to it. To focus uniquely on the third or fourth levels, as historians were prone to do in the nineteenth century, is thus superficial, and gives only a small part of the story.

Quite possibly, then, it is through an archaeological and multilayered approach to time that historical writing might be destined to endure in the twenty-first century.

Barthes, Roland (1986 [1967]) 'The Discourse of History', in *The Rustle of Language*, trans. Richard Howard, Berkeley and Los Angeles: University of California Press.
Barthes, Roland (1987 [1954]) *Michelet*, trans. Richard Howard, Oxford: Blackwell.
Braudel, Fernand (1972 [1949]) *The Mediterranean and the Mediterranean World in the Age of Philip II*, Volume I, trans. Siân Reynolds, Glasgow: William Collins.
Braudel, Fernand (1973 [1966]) *The Mediterranean and the Mediterranean World in the Age of Philip II*, Volume II, trans. Siân Reynolds, Glasgow: William Collins.
Braudel, Fernand (1980 [1969]) *On History*, trans. Sarah Matthews, Chicago: University of Chicago Press.
Foucault, Michel (1974 [1966]) *The Order of Things: An Archaeology of the Human Sciences*, Social Science Paperback, trans. from the French, London: Tavistock.
Herzfeld, Michael (1987) *Anthropology Through the Looking Glass: Critical Ethnography in the Margins of Europe*, Cambridge: Cambridge University Press.
White, Hayden (1973) *Metahistory: The Historical Imagination of Nineteenth-Century Europe*, Baltimore: Johns Hopkins University Press.

See THERMODYNAMICS

ICON Icon comes from the Greek, *eikōn*, meaning image*. The significance of the term pertains to the link between the image and the object – whether in the Eastern, Byzantine religious context, where the icon often depicts the Madonna and Christ child, or in the work of the semiologist, Charles Sanders Peirce (1839–1914), where an icon, also called a 'likeness', is defined as an image or representation that has the same features as the object depicted (Peirce 1991: 30, 181). An icon, therefore, never exists in isolation, but has an essentially dual structure; it also has non-conventional features – features that cannot easily be codified because they belong to the depicted thing itself. This is the realism of the icon.

The latter point has been challenged by semiologists like Umberto Eco (1976: 190–216), who argue that, analytically speaking, a representation, or an image, cannot literally be said to have the same features as the object. There is in reality always a difference between word and thing, image and imaged, the represented and the representation. And indeed, as Plato pointed out, if the image was identical with the imaged, there would be no image; for we would be dealing with the thing itself (Plato 1980: 466–467, 432b–e).

In the Eastern Church, an icon is a devotional painting – often an image of Christ, or another holy figure. As devotional, an icon brings the image to the viewer in a special way. An icon of Christ brings Christ into presence. Although the iconoclastic debate of the eighth century AD, is complex, one of its aspects involves the question of whether an icon can succeed in this function or not. If not, the love of icons becomes another thing entirely: the worship of an idol (*eidolon*). No doubt the material aspects of any religion open the way for the outsider to raise the question of whether icons (connections with the sacred) are in fact idols (material objects effectively loved for their own sake). The missionary was always able to see the other's religious observance involving a reverence for certain material objects as idolatry, while considering Christian objects truly sacred (as such, icons become a link to God). The iconoclastic debate seems to mirror this instability, an instability which is perhaps present in contemporary debates about realism, where claims that symbolic forms that connect us to the material world are said to be naïve because, after all, words are only words, an image is only an image – and a conventionalised, and thus coded, one at that.

In other respects, icon refers to the semi-realist images on the computer screen, or can refer to something, or someone, that stands out in society. Hence the saying: 'he is a real icon of the sporting world'.

Eco, Umberto (1976) *A Theory of Semiotics*, Bloomington: Indiana University Press.
Peirce, Charles Sanders (1991) *Peirce on Signs*, ed. James Hooper, Chapel Hill and London: University of North Carolina Press.
Plato (1980) *Cratylus*, trans. Benjamin Jowett, in *The Collected Dialogues of Plato*, ed. Edith Hamilton and Huntington Cairns, Princeton, NJ: Princeton University Press.

See CODE; INDEX; SIGN: SIGNIFIER/ SIGNIFIED

IDENTIFICATION

Like identity*, identification comes from the Latin, *idem*, meaning the same. Identification can mean 'to identify', when the identity of a person is being established. Someone may have the official task of confirming the identity of a dead body*. Or, in the well-known procedure on police drama films, a victim might be asked to participate in an identification parade. In other respects, the state provides its citizens with means of identification: passports, drivers' licences, identity cards, and the like.

The most important theory of identification doubtless comes from Freud (1967: 37–42), whose understanding can also be applied to the crowd identifying with a leader, or the individual with the group. For Freud, the subject establishes his or her identity through identification – first with parents, then with significant others, then with all kinds of figures which (usually) attract the subject. To 'identify with' is to make the other (person or thing) the same as oneself, at least at a psychic level, and at least for a period of time. To make the same as oneself means to render familiar, to obliterate difference. Mystical states offer an extreme form of this, but everyday life also calls upon people to engage their powers of identification. To identify with a character in a film or on the stage or on television is to reduce, in the mind of the subject so affected, the difference between self and other.

Identification calls upon the powers of the imaginary. For to identify with someone is both to be and not to be that person. Or, in short, it is to be that person in the mode of identification. For a child between the ages of six and eighteen months, the identification with the mirror image is an important development in the formation of the self. The mirror is not the same as the one who looks into the glass; yet as an index, the image could only have been caused by the one who looks and becomes a reflection. This mirror image is the self in the only mode in which it is possible for a subject to see him or herself. Without the process of identification, we would have no possible way of seeing ourselves as others see us. It may be said that the visual dimension is a mere surface, but this surface is, nevertheless, the only avenue available. The process is seen as less superficial to the extent that the recognition of self through identification also initiates processes of reflexivity: 'Am I, or am I not like that?' 'Do others see me as this image or not?'

If identification makes the other the same, at least at some level, is it ever possible to do justice to the other? Film theorists have often said that the success of certain popular movies is due to the way the audience is able to identify with the characters and situations. Against this, it is necessary to recall that Freud also saw an element of differing embedded in the process of identification. For an individual self is, in the end, made up of identifications, and is not an identity produced by a single identification. Because difference is involved, with people changing over time, sometimes quite radically, the effects can be quite disturbing, to the extent that the subject feels invaded by feelings of a loss of self. Identification thus becomes a two-edged sword. On the one hand, it is very much a temporal rather than a spatial process; the individual evolves, or changes over time due to the heterogeneous nature of his or her identifications. On the other hand, identification in childhood opens the way for the self as such to emerge. Without a capacity for identification, there would be no self, and consequently no self-love. And there would be no love* either; for love is also a product of identification, of the self becoming other. If the self cannot do justice to the other, can the self do justice to itself? For the self, for the reflexive mind, is also an object; this is why it is possible to talk about self-love. The subject must identify with itself – despite the changes – in order to be a person. Identification shows us that the process is complex, that it involves difference as well as identity.

Were the self reducible to an identity, it would also be a closed interiority; identification, as a process, opens up the self to the outside world; it renders the self at least partially, and essentially, social. Language is crucial in this situation, for as a mother tongue, it is as close as it is possible to get to the 'real self'. Yet language is also essentially social and cultural. It is other. It comes as much from the outside as from within. Identification enables language to be transparent, when this is necessary. Instead of seeing the words, one is able to see meanings, things and images. All symbolic forms have this transparency, a transparency made possible through identification.

The depressive is a person for whom identification has failed. For the depressive – and, even more, the melancholic – person no longer 'believes' in words. Words have become entirely empty. The world for the depressive is characterised by an emptiness that symbolic forms cannot overcome. Identification no longer infuses these symbolic forms with life.

Film criticism and analysis – especially of a feminist persuasion – has often seen identification in cinema as an identification with stereotypes and ideological views of political and social life. Put simply: this kind of criticism implies that people see what they want to see – for example women in subordinate positions in society and the home, who never speak too much and are always passive sexual partners. Now, the idea has to be entertained that identification, as a process, also exposes audiences to what they do not want to see. Shock in a film, while not immediately called for, is implicitly desired as the desire for something other than the 'same old thing'. Identification opens the self to the new; this is undoubtedly its most profound aspect.

A potentially dangerous dimension of identification comes from the possibility that the individual gives up the power to decide and is swayed by the leader, as evidenced in Fascism. Such power to persuade can lead to scapegoating (cf. Jews under Nazism) and other forms of injustice. As a result, this form of identification has to be kept under control.

Freud, Sigmund (1967 [1921]) *Group Psychology and the Analysis of the Ego*, trans. James Strachey, revised edition, London: The Hogarth Press.

See COMMUNITY; DIFFERENCE–INDIVIDUALITY; IDENTITY

IDENTITY

Martin Heidegger begins a discussion of identity and difference by stating that the principle of identity (in philosophy) currently takes the form: A = A (Heidegger 1969). Otherwise expressed: identity means that A is the same as itself, thus evoking the Latin origin, *idem*, meaning 'the same'. In fact, in terms of the law of identity, A = A is a tautology.

Before Heidegger (1889–1976), Leibniz (1646–1716), then Hegel (1770–1831), had called identity the self-identical, essence. By extension, identity is the essential element.

Logically, identity enters into the picture in relation to the law of contradiction. In Hegel's view, contradiction 'is the root of all movement and life' (Hegel 1966: 67). In other words, contradiction is a reality in the world – not just an abstract principle.

However, over the years since the Marxist renaissance of the 1960s, Hegel has fallen into desuetude and a more subdued logic has taken over. In part, then, the law of identity says that something cannot both be and not-be (the case). For a long time, reason was thought to be exclusively tied to ensuring the prevalence of identity, and hence the maintenance of the law of non-contradiction. In contemporary culture*, however, difference has come to challenge identity in philosophy, politics, culture and psychology, difference being precisely that which is not identical to itself. (See difference – individuality).

At stake here is that fact that the rigid adherence to the notion of identity can entail a failure to see the real complexity of thought and the world. The world includes things that cannot be included within identity. Even when speaking about difference, however, are we always forced, in order to get some idea of it, to refer also to identity? Are identity and difference inextricable, or is this to give an identity to difference? Sometimes this is easy to do. If, for example, we think of two people, they are the same (identical) to the extent that they are human beings, but different to the extent that they are individuals. To say that two people are individuals is to say that one can be distinguished from the other. One person is tall, the other short; one has blue eyes, the other has hazel; one has a round face, the other, a square face, etc. Blue eyes are an identity (blue = blue); hazel eyes are an identity (hazel = hazel). Difference here is the difference between two identities. Because: b = b, b ≠ h. What, though, is the quality which distinguishes blue from hazel? Perhaps some would say that the colour grey is the difference between blue and hazel, but immediately, an identity (g = g) has been given as difference, and this is a contradiction, since it implies that difference is an identity.

True difference, then, cannot be named, since naming is to make something identical with itself, and difference is not this.

In psychology, it was thought, until Freud's work at the end of the nineteenth century, that to be an individual was to be an individual identical self. René Descartes (1596–1650), in proposing the *cogito* (I think therefore I am), established, so it seemed, the self as identical with itself, in so far as the only thing that could not be doubted was the 'I' who thinks. The theory of the unconscious changes all this, for it opens up a division in the subject, as the analysts might say, which turns the self into a conscious *and* an unconscious subject. The subject, in short, becomes simultaneously self (consciousness: I *am* me) and other (I *am not* me), or, as the nineteenth-century French poet, Rimbaud, put it: 'I is an other'. The unconscious also points to unconscious desire, to the unconscious fantasm and to sexual difference (see Fantasy/Phantasy, Fantasm). If we think about it, the very reality of time entails that the self is an entity struggling for identity, but time makes this impossible in any absolute sense. The difference between childhood and adulthood is simply a broader confirmation of this. If, then, self-certainty can be achieved only in a given instant, we must die a thousand deaths every day. For the instant is ephemeral. The actual moment of self-consciousness is thus ephemeral too.

Issues about the nature of the relation of self-consciousness to the unconscious have divided the psychoanalytic community. There are those in the United States who privilege the place of (self) consciousness and the ego as identical with itself, and those in continental Europe, influenced by Lacan, who argue that the subject is not identical with itself because of the effect of the unconscious. Much debate has gone on over the years about whether either approach is scientific. But this is another story.

Culturally speaking, there is the phenomenon of 'multiculturalism': a plurality of cultures sharing the same geographic space, or place. If it is a question of a multicultural nation, the principle of identity seems to have been violated, and difference has entered the scene. A tension arises when an individual or group feels that the plurality of multiculturalism means a loss of collective, group identity. In extreme cases, this sense of loss can spill over into violence against those seen as other to the true identity. In this way, multiculturalism can have serious political implications. Identity seems to offer unity and thus the security of sameness, while multiculturalism offers diversity and perhaps disunity. Others see cultural plurality as the way to a more complex, and therefore richer, form of unity.

We have been speaking about the substantive qualities of identity; however, there is also formal, civil identity, and this has come to be an important source of debate in a world where there are greater movements of people than at any other time in human history. Civil identity links an individual to a state, confers rights (citizenship and the right to live in a particular country, the right to vote, freedom of speech and association, free trial) and demands obligations (payment of taxes, obeying the law). Civil identity is the identity on a passport or identity card, the identity needed in order to travel, the identity which makes a person the member of civil society. It is the public face of the self.

During the period between the two world wars there were many stateless people, who had no home country, no place in which they could live legally. The condition of illegal immigrants and asylum seekers in the twenty-first century echoes this, in the sense that the only way the stateless can come under the protection of the legal system is to break the law. As a criminal, the illegal immigrant or asylum seeker at least has rights which citizens have under the law (e.g. the right to legal representation) – they have at least some sort of formal equality and recognition. Not to have a civil identity is to be in dire straits: it means total anonymity and being the victim of arbitrary police action. Indeed, the police state is essentially the rule by force, not by law. And the citizen is the one who has rights under the law.

Although civil identity might not be substantive (i.e. refer to the true moral being), it is the basis of liberty in modern democratic polities. To lose civil identity, as the Jews did under the Nazis, is to lose part of what it means to be human.

Hegel, G.W.F. (1966 [1812–16]) *The Science of Logic. Volume 2*, trans. W.H. Johnston and L.G. Struthers, London: George Allen & Unwin.
Heidegger, Martin (1969) *Identity and Difference*, trans. Joan Stambaugh, New York: Harper & Row.

IDEOLOGY

'Ideology', in its suffix, '-logy', evokes *logos* (see logos-mythos) and literally means the study of ideas. This is indeed the meaning it had in 1796, the work of the eighteenth-century thinker, Destutt de Tracy.

Marx and Engels in 1845 described ideology as a *camera obscura*, or a distorting lens, through which classes view the world according to their class interest. More broadly, Marx argued that the 'ideas of the ruling class are, in every age, the ruling ideas'. In other words, the dominant material power is, *ipso facto*, the dominant intellectual power. By 'ruling ideas', Marx presumably does not mean scientific ideas like thermodynamics*, even though this was becoming a dominant idea in science, and therefore in society, during the mid-nineteenth century. He must rather mean political, religious and cultural ideas – ideas about the nature of society, about work, about property, about history, about art, about God, about power, etc. At this socio-cultural level, the ideas of the bourgeoisie – the dominant material power – become so naturalised and taken for granted that the real partisan element becomes invisible. The discipline of political economy – as it was then – speaks the language of bourgeois interest (centrality of the market), and yet appears generally to be the voice of reason and objectivity. Thus, the market system, the dominance of the owners of property over those selling labour-power*, seems entirely natural – not just to the owners, but to the workers as well. Ideology is working in the most effective and fundamental way when it is not perceived to be ideology.

For Marx, then, ideology is only secondarily a doctrinal system (religious, political, moral). As doctrine (as an '-ism'), ideology is perfectly visible, but this is not ideology in the deepest sense; it is not ideology as the sustainer of ruling power.

Two features of ideology as made famous by Marx have rendered it limiting as an analytical tool today. The first is that it leads to a focus exclusively on consciousness. Ideology is about what people think, rather than about what they feel, or what they do – although this has changed, as we shall see; ideology has now also become what people do. The limiting thing about consciousness is that it presupposes a potential lucidity about what is really going on. Even Marx recognised this limit. Merely explaining the truth about the world to the working class is not going to lead to revolution; for the working class also have a material investment in the way things are.

The second point about ideology is that it presupposes that one can distil from it, in a coherent way, the ideas of which it is composed. The phrase, 'ruling ideas' presupposes, for instance, that bourgeois rule can be encapsulated in certain key ideas: 'market', 'money', 'interest', 'property', etc. There is a risk of oversimplification in this approach.

With the decline in the popularity of ideology as an explanatory tool, which took place after the structuralist revolution in the 1960s, some attempts at recuperation were made. These consisted in the idea that ideology was in fact embedded in the practices – often everyday practices – people engaged in. Ideology indeed became the network of practices which constituted a person as a social subject. This makes ideology more than a set of beliefs, and more than a person is necessarily able to articulate at the level of consciousness. The work of Althusser (1971), and latterly, Žižek (1994), best represents this approach.

Another criticism of ideology is that it depends on the distinction between science and truth on one side, and ideology and error on the other. In fact, the separation of the scientific from the ideological is extremely difficult to sustain – especially in the humanities and social sciences, and especially in fields like psychiatry, psychology and social behaviour. Once ideology in Marx's sense is used, it becomes a two-edged sword: were it as profound

as Marx suggests, it would seem impossible for anyone – Marx included – to escape its tentacles. So we are left wondering how we can speak scientifically *about* ideology from within ideology. There seems to be no escape from this dilemma.

A possible response comes from the French sociologist, Pierre Bourdieu (1990). He accepts that ideology is at the level of misrecognition (*méconnaissance*), and that experience and thought cannot reveal the ideology because ideology, qua misrecognition, is a sphere not open to experience and reflexivity. As a result, it is necessary to set out all the objective markers of social activity, beginning with correlations between occupation, education level, type of education, place of living, parents' occupations, artistic preferences, language competence, etc. From the information gleaned from all these forms of data, a person can be given a place in a map of social space, a map which will not correspond to the anticipated image of self that experience (ideology) might give. The map of social space is society's other, unknown face, a face that can be given only by means of objective indices.

Two main difficulties seem to arise from Bourdieu's approach: the first is that naïvety (about the truth of social life) is presupposed as an unassailable given: objective indices cut through the naïveties reinforced by ideology. Objective social science can, by definition, never show a coincidence between thinking and reality. This is thus a theoretical limit to Bourdieu's approach. Secondly, the objective indices must be interpreted – something which seems to bring us full circle: what is to prevent ideology, or the naïve attitude, distorting the interpretation of the significance of objective indices?

Althusser, Louis (1971 [1969]) 'Ideology and Ideological State Apparatuses', in *Lenin and Philosophy and Other Essays*, trans. Ben Brewster, London: New Left Books.

Bourdieu, Pierre (1990) *The Logic of Practice*, trans. Richard Nice, Cambridge: Polity Press.

Marx, Karl and Engels, Friedrich (1967 [1845]) *The German Ideology*, in *Writings of the Young Marx on Philosophy and Society*, trans. and ed. Loyd D. Easton and Kurt H. Guddat, New York: Anchor Books.

Žižek, Slavoj (ed.) (1994) *Mapping Ideology*, London and New York: Verso.

See LOGOS–MYTHOS; POWER

IMAGE Since the Iconoclastic debate in the eighth century, the image has had the rights of the city in Western culture. It has become commonplace to assume that the image as such is the one that appears in the media, the arts, medical science, computing, and other areas where images are reproduced. It is also commonly held that the image can have a subjective dimension as the mental image produced and reproduced in the imagination*. Indeed, image and imagination are often confused.

The truth is that what many people understand by the term 'image' could be better captured by the term, 'simulacrum*'. When it is said that in a mediatised society we are flooded with images – meaning that images take on a life of their own and, through tele-visual means of all kinds, completely surround us – confusion is implied between an image of reality and the reality of an image. An image that has itself become a reality, or seems to have become autonomous, I designate here as a simulacrum, and will consider

it at length in another entry. I note, however, that it is the simulacrum which is inseparable from its reproduction, a view that is often misleadingly associated with the image.

It is arguable that modern and postmodern understandings of the image go back to Plato. In this regard, most scholars agree that Plato did not condemn the image outright, but distinguished between a good and a bad image, as is captured in his distinction between *eikôn* (a good representation of the model or *eidos*) and *eidôlon* (a bad representation, semblance or simulacrum, also called an idol). According to the scholar of Ancient Greek thought, Jean-Pierre Vernant: 'The image falls within the category of the Same; by its similitude it is the same as its model' (1979: 110). If the image resembled its model exactly, there would be no image. This means of course that the image in Plato has the analogue character of being 'both... and' – both image and model. Plato condemns the bad form of the image, whereby the image appears as an image, and as such becomes a mode of pure appearance, rather being a mode of the model's appearance, or the appearance of what is imaged.

In this light, it is notable how closely much of the discussion (such as it is) of the image at the end of the millennium is couched in Plato's terms, with the difference that the equivalent of the *eidôlon* (simulacrum) has assumed pride of place in many quarters, for example in (semiotic) analyses of film and television. To read the image as a sign – which is consistent with the form of the simulacrum, not the image – that is, to treat it semiotically, presupposes that a clear distinction can be made between the image/sign and what it signifies. As a sign, the image can be analysed, reflected upon and thus made the object of a meta-language or discourse. This, however, is to lose touch with a much older understanding of the term, image which, as an *imago*, is entirely transparent and capable of effects that are barely analysable. With this understanding, the difference between the image and the imaged is erased.

In earlier phases of human history and prehistory, especially in relation to funerary rites and mourning, the image (as effigy, for example) had the same power as the imaged. An image would not just represent a dead person; it would *be* the reincarnation of that person. In Australian Aboriginal culture, to show, and even more, to insult or degrade, the image of a dead person is literally to insult or degrade that person; for, to repeat, there is no difference between image and imaged.

The image is associated, too, with icon*, and thus with iconoclasm. At the broadest level, two different interpretations of iconoclasm exist: one says that the war against images waged in the seventh and eighth centuries AD were about the belief that images were no longer sacred, that they were no longer seen as the incarnation of the imaged (God or Christ, for example). To worship the image thus came to mean to worship a simulacrum – an image which referred only to itself. Pagans were deemed to worship images because it could not be accepted that the spirit of the god could really be present in the image.

A second interpretation of the image in the iconoclastic period has recently been put forward by the French philosopher, Marie-José Mondzain (1996). It allows us to question the notion of the image as essentially visual. For at the time of iconoclasm, the icon was visual, while the image was not. Today, on the other hand, the image has become entirely visual and, in this sense, is too close to us for the image as such to appear. According to Mondzain, the image can only be fully appreciated if it is considered in terms of the Byzantine, Christian heritage underpinning a religious disposition, expressed in a theology. The following notions are particularly pertinent for understanding this theology: the idea, informed by Aristotle, of 'economy*' as a distribution of relations (relationship, for example, between the Father and the Son), 'consubstantiality', as understood in the Trinity, 'incarnation', in relation to a specific form of the image and what is imaged, 'mimesis*', as the becoming 'flesh' of the image (without flesh always being equated with materiality), and 'similitude', which is to be distinguished from resemblance, begin to deepen our understanding of iconoclasm and its opposite, iconophilia.

The simulacrum has none of the qualities of being the thing itself, as in the notion of mimesis as the becoming flesh of the image, from which, it could be suggested, all forms of realism derive their force, once realism is recognised as a quintessential form of the imaginary*.

If what passes for the image today should be more readily defined in terms of its reproduction (whether digital or analogical, painted or filmic, auditory or visual, virtual or material), which is to say in terms of its technology, this is because the imaginary relation to the image is weakening, and it is no longer a question of living as though the image provides something marvellous, as the surrealists said, or threatening, as Christianity has said, beyond itself. In short, the image is no longer transparent, but has, as simulacrum, become opaque and thus the possible object of the semiologist's method rather than the vehicle of the poet's truth.

Mondzain, M.-J. (1996) *Image, icône, économie: Les sources byzantines de l'imaginaire contemporain*, Paris, Seuil.
Vernant, Jean-Pierre. (1979) 'Naissance d'images' (The Birth of Images), in *Religions, histoires, raisons*, Paris: Maspero.

See: ANALOGUE; INDEX

IMAGINARY

The Imaginary, here as a noun with the first letter capitalised, is not to be confused with imagination, and has gained its importance in the context of Jacques Lacan's (1901–81) psychoanalytic theory, where it is contrasted with the symbolic and the real. Lacan's theory of the Imaginary was first outlined in his article, 'The Mirror Stage as Formative of the I' (Lacan 1977: 1–7).

The chimpanzee initially surpasses the child in learning to deal with the outside world, thus indicating the infant's extreme vulnerability. Certainly, the human infant's motor capacity is very limited in the first year of life. Consequently, the recognition of a whole image*, and mimicry in front of the mirror, or in relation to an other, brings a sense of triumph and jubilation. Identification with the mirror image leads to a transformation: the image is an *imago* and thus has formative effects on the subject. It brings about physical and psychological changes. Given the physical prematurity, where motor coordination is limited and evoked in the phantasy of the fragmented body, the mirror image offers an anticipation of wholeness.

This idea allows Lacan to go further and to say that language and the symbolic have formative effects. Without language and the symbolic, there would be no subject. Within this symbolic matrix, the Imaginary allows an identification to take place which is in turn the precondition for the formation for the symbolic 'I'. As with the mirror image, use of the first person pronoun entails that the subject is able, by way of the Imaginary, to 'be' its image or to assume the pronoun as its own, and yet not go to the extent of equating symbolic forms with reality. In other words, the mirror stage is a coming to terms with the simultaneous reality and unreality of language. This is expressed by Lacan when he says that the mirror stage is the place of misrecognition (*méconnaissance*): the infant treats the image as real – as it must do – when the image is only an image. Similarly, the use of a natural language treats words as real – or at least as access to the thing, or to meaning – when they are only words. The mirror stage, then, is equivalent to the child's entry into language.

The mirror stage also reveals that, in order to become self-conscious, an instrument (even an alienating one) is necessary; it is impossible to go through the process without an image as a kind of prosthesis. This can open the way to aggressivity; for images of aggression are necessary in order that real aggression can be acted out.

In light of misrecognition, the mirror stage brings with it an approximation to surrealist practice. The relationship of the subject to the image itself 'mirrors' the delirious subject's relation to the surrealist image. Lacan even gives an explanation that confirms the delirium: for the infant, the unified *imago* becomes identical to the one who views it. Correlative to the caption in René Magritte's painting of a pipe, the analyst takes up a position that, effectively, says: 'This is not a self'. The young child, inured to the Imaginary, effectively says, by contrast: 'That *is* me'. The sense, therefore, of the commonsense reading of Magritte's pipe painting (*La Trahison des images*, 1928) (The Treason of Images) is the prototype of the mirror stage itself, as Lacan theorises it.

In terms of the mirror stage, the difference between text and image in Magritte can be translated into the difference between primary narcissism and its libidinal investment in the image, and the alienating power of a text which, as purely symbolic, opens the way to 'mediatization through the desire of the other' (Lacan 1977: 5). Faced with the symbolic, the ego can experience an uneasiness and an anxiety that only the delirium of paranoia can alleviate. We note, then, that 'stage' and 'mirror' are not to be taken in a strictly empirical and contingent sense, but instead in the sense of an ontological structure of human experience, even if the effects of the image as *imago* is formative of the 'I' (that is, of the subject itself). For the *imago* shows that symbols can have real effects, despite their supposedly ideal nature.

The mirror stage is less a stage and more the effect of the relation of specularity, a relation that will come to include the identification with an other. The mirror is less a mirror than the instance of reflection and specularity as such. We have, then, a specularity and its effects which are not limited to the period of infancy and childhood, but which go to the heart of what is essential in the Imaginary and the symbolic. That is, it goes to the heart of what the human is in its destiny. The mirror stage, in short, is not something that one grows out of, but is a truly *formative* experience – even though Lacan's references to empirical

research in paediatrics and ethology might lead one to think that the mirror stage can be studied by an adult all the more effectively because he or she has 'been through all that'. Were we *not* dealing with a structure, the mirror stage, as an empirical and contingent moment, might easily vary depending on the actual individual involved. Similarly, were it a question of the empirical qualities of an empirically given mirror, the formation of the 'I' would in reality become tied to developments in technology – perhaps to the point where it could be said that the better the mirror, the more definite and effective would be the specular relation between subject and ego. The mirror is not, therefore, simply a prosthesis. It points to a universal and ideal relation that is constitutive of the Imaginary. This is ironical to the extent that in his early seminars Lacan situates the Imaginary purely and simply in experience, while the symbolic alone is the source of a priori principles (cf. Lacan 1978: 50).

Even with an *imago*, however, there has to be fixation or fascination. This is supplied by primary narcissism, which is also inaugurated by a libidinal charge. Without the leap over the hypothetical gap between inner and outer worlds (the inner and outer worlds being the prototype of the subsequent self–other dyad) made possible by fascination, there would be no mirror stage.

Despite these attempts at precision, it is illuminating to apply to the mirror the same division that is manifest in Magritte's painting of the pipe. As *imago*, the pipe is an already given set. That is, the recognition of 'pipeness' already exists in the Imaginary prior to the experience of any given pipe. The condition of possibility of this is the structuring force of the mirror stage.

'Pipeness', in other words, enables one to see a pipe as a pipe. It enables one to accept the image of the thing as the thing imaged. The pipe, then, is not just a unique image coming from the imagination, but is the realisation of an a priori entity – much as, for Plato, the image is a likeness of the *eidos* (model).

If the ego is an illusory product of consciousness, the subject is the real product of the symbolic. The symbolic is the truth of the illusory status of the ego. It is, for instance, the mirror itself as the bearer of the image as simulacrum* (the image as different from the entity in the mirror; the image *as* image and not the image as the entity imaged). The symbolic is the necessary foundation for the Imaginary as the mirror is the foundation of the image. A mirror is less the physical apparatus of an opaque and reflective surface and more an effect that can occur in diverse contexts. Even more: the mirror effect occurs when an ego identifies with its objects – be these words or another ego. The Imaginary is necessary in order to turn symbols into living entities. The image becomes the imaged in this scenario. But, as we have seen, the symbolic (as machine and as symbolic system) is the necessary foundation of the Imaginary – its raw material, as it were. The symbolic is what gives the Imaginary a sense of 'reality'.

Lacan, Jacques (1977 [1966]) *Ecrits: A Selection*, trans. Alan Sheridan, London: Tavistock.

Lacan, Jacques (1978) *Le Séminaire, Livre II: Le moi dans la théorie de Freud et dans la technique de la psychanalyse*, Paris: Seuil.

See FANTASY/PHANTASY; FANTASM

IMAGINATION

At one level, imagination is a psychic capacity which enables the subject to invent what does not exist in reality. More than this: imagination has been seen as the creative faculty *par excellence*. Without imagination, there would be no art or invention. In this vein, the Marxist formula famously claims that 'what distinguishes the worst architect from the best of bees is this, that the architect raises his structure in imagination before he erects it in reality' (Marx 1954: 174). Here, the imagination is the conscious use of creativity, and this faculty is very much tied to consciousness itself. This entails that the products of the imagination have a definite logic, whereas, at a superficial level – that is, at a conscious level – dream formations do not.

By comparison with the psychoanalytic notion of the imaginary*, the imagination does not entail misrecognition (*méconnaissance*). This implies that while the imaginary sees a reality in what are ultimately symbolic or fictional entities, the imagination produces works which it *knows* to be fiction. The latter point is, however, a commonsense view, and is rendered problematic when it is recalled that analysts and others have combed ostensibly fictional works in order to better understand aspects of personality, as structured by an abiding fantasy/phantasy*, or – as in the 'roman-à-clef – have treated fictional works as disguised works of fact. The greater the quantity of works of imagination, the more likely it is that an underlying style, or even truth, may be revealed. Or again, works of poetic imagination might disclose 'what conceals itself'. This is indeed Heidegger's view of poetry (Heidegger 1975: 223).

The singularity of the imaginary product is a key to grasping individuality as a profound and rich psychic space. What I imagine – qua imaginary product – is different from anything anyone else imagines. Although I am conscious of what I imagine, that it is unique, often escapes me. My own private language, or set of images, is often familiar to me but astonishing to others. The uniqueness of imaginary products is distinct from their aesthetic or artistic value.

By linking imagination to the singularity of individuality, we have also made it the enemy of community*, whereas those who equate imagination with identification* also see imagination as the key to the individual's integration into community (as in 'imaginary communities').

Edmund Husserl (1859–1938) has often been cited as accomplishing a 'liberation from the fact' in the search for 'eidetic', or essential, certainty. In *Ideas* (1982), the imagination becomes a quintessential resource in eidetic thinking; for no one more than Husserl was concerned to link the truth value of eidetic insights to the truth value of fiction or phantasy. Like the fictional object, eidetic objects are not 'real'. Or 'one can say in strict truth, that *"feigning" [Fiktion] makes up the vital element of phenomenology as of every other eidetic science*, that feigning is the source from which the cognition of "eternal truths" is fed' (Husserl 1982: 160, para. 70. Husserl's emphasis). Later, Husserl reiterates that

> As sciences of pure essence, geometry and phenomenology do not recognize any findings about real existence. Connected with just that is the fact that clear feignings not only offer them foundations as good as, but to a great extent better than, the data of actual perception and experience. (Husserl 1982: 183–184, para. 79)

How is this possible? How is it possible for fiction (feigning) – the imagination – to be on a par with the essential – with eidetic certainty? Fictional entities, together with products of the imagination in general, thus serve as the basis of a philosophical doctrine. The Husserlian essential realm is incomprehensible until the full force of the imagination as the foundation of eidetic certainty is appreciated.

Husserl repeats on a number of occasions that the question does not hinge on whether or not fictional entities have a real existence, but on what it means to engage in an inquiry into the eidetic sphere (the essential, as opposed to contingent, level). With regard to the latter, the search for essences is also the search for pure idealities. Enough commentaries on Husserl exist to warn us not to presuppose immediately that phenomenology is simply an idealism; rather it addresses key issues in relation to the working of the imagination and the imaginary. Indeed, an ideality is always an imaginary ideality. Science develops from its capacity to create ideal objects. There is thus a crucial connection between imagaination and science, for all the claim that science is objective.

Formerly, philosophy had to be purged of imagination; now, deconstruction* destabilises the imaginary in philosophy – or even philosophy as imaginary. This is not just any destabilisation, but would constitute the destabilisation of philosophy *tout court*. I must explain and justify this claim. A great deal depends on the Husserlian union of fiction and ideality.

If fiction (feigning) leads directly to the eidetic quest, this is because fiction, like ideality in general, is a perfection and as such is pure. Whether, in a given case, one can distinguish fiction from non-fiction is a contingent matter that has no significant bearing on the ideal essence of fiction as a product of the imagination. In a number of places, Husserl explains that an imagined entity (often an object) has the ideal perfection that an existing entity could never have. Thus a red triangle, as imagined, is perfectly triangular, is perfectly red, and exists nowhere; it has no determination, no spatial or temporal coordinates which would give it the qualities (but also the imperfections) of an existing object.

The ideality of language, and specifically of meaning, pertains to an ideal interiority. In talking with myself Husserl says, every barrier to transparency and thus to perfect expression is overcome, resulting in perfect communication. So perfect is the communication that, according to Husserl, the act of communication itself ceases to be essential. I always already know – in imagination – what I would communicate to myself. Actually to communicate becomes a sheer redundancy. Therefore, soliloquy is an absence of 'noise', of obstacles, and of all confusion. This is because the 'I' which engages in this internal monologue is homogeneous and identical with itself – or rather, it is present to itself. This imaginary monologue, in which one participates, and which is a perfect monologue, must not be confused with a monologue in the imagination, one that might be used, for example, in a piece of fiction. With regard to the latter, it is quite possible to take a position outside the monologue, and thus to represent the speech. For the latter is a medium.

Today, the question has arisen, for a society so dominated by the media, as to whether a rich internal life, centred around imagination, is still possible. It is a matter of knowing whether a fantasy world is still possible when so many manufactured fantasies – so many stereotypes – are so readily available.

Heidegger, Martin (1975) *Poetry, Language, Thought*, trans. Albert Hofstadter, New York: Harper & Row.

Husserl, Edmund (1982 [1913]) *Ideas Pertaining to a Pure Phenomenology and to a Phenomenological Philosophy. First Book: General Introduction to Pure Phenomenology*, trans. F. Kersten, Dordrecht, Boston and London: Kluwer Academic Publishers.

Marx, Karl (1954 [1867]) *Capital Volume I: A Critical Analysis of Capitalist Production*, trans. Samuel Moore and Edward Aveling, Moscow: Progress Publishers.

See IMAGE

IMMANENT/IMMANENCE-TRANSCENDENT/TRANSCENDENCE

'Immanence' and 'immanent' come from the late Latin *immanentem*, present participle of *immanere*, meaning to dwell, to remain. An immanent principle (in Kant) is a principle limited to the realm of experience, as opposed to a principle of transcendence. Philosophy – or at least certain forms of philosophy – has been thought to be transcendent in relation to the level of everyday life. Theology is thought to deal with entities and ideas which transcend the mundane world, and are thus transcendent in their turn.

Immanence – the fact or condition of being immanent – means indwelling, inherent. Immanence philosophy is based on a theory that evolved in Germany at the end of the nineteenth century, and which claimed that reality exists only through being immanent (already present) in conscious minds.

Modern phenomenology and humanistic existentialism move in the paths of immanence philosophy, for they examine what is embedded in human experience. It has been suggested in relation to Husserl's (1859–1938) Phenomenology that if we suppose that the absence of spatial contours could be a sufficient condition for immanence, then it seems that we should have to consider mathematical entities and axioms as immanent objects.

We see, then, that the literal meaning of 'immanent' is 'embeddedness', or 'indwelling'. This is to be contrasted with 'transcendent', meaning above and beyond any possible experience in the phenomenal world.

In *What Is Called Thinking*? Heidegger (1889–1976) says that 'thought and poesy are in themselves the originary, the essential, and therefore also the final speech that language speaks through the mouth of man' (Heidegger 1968: 126). When language speaks through man as thought and poesy (poetry), it speaks immanently. Often, because of its status as immanent, the speaking of language goes unnoticed, for attention is focused on the thought or the poesy – not on language as such. In the end, language speaking cannot be a special form of speaking; it cannot be a speaking that is different from language as it is used every day, although poetry begins to move in that direction.

In a similar way, an immanent God would become manifest through the things of the world, whereas a transcendent God would be distinct and separate from the world.

Social organisation can also be immanent or transcendent. In its immanent form, such things as marriage relations, government, education and the economy are organised through ritual and taboo, initiation ceremonies and festivals, the exchange of gifts and sacred artistic practices, rather than

through formal bureaucratic agencies, which exemplify a transcendent form of social organisation. The absence, in certain non-Western societies, of explicit forms of religious institutions, such as a church, often led Europeans to think that such societies had no religion.

In a philosophical vein, Jean-Paul Sartre argues against what he calls the 'illusion of immanence' (*illusion d'immanence*) (Sartre 1986: 17), where what is thought to have a reality (an image in the head) in fact has none. There may be an image* of reality (of the thing, object, individual, etc.), but there is no reality of the image in the mind of the subject distinct from objective reality. The illusion relates to the sense that there is a reality embedded in the image as image. However, in Sartre's view, the image is not a different version of the object: there is no unreal image on one side and a real object on the other. Nor should a true image be confused with a perception. In a *perception* of the Parthenon one will be able to distinguish the number of columns, and will probably be interested in doing so. In an *image* of the Parthenon, on the other hand, the number of columns is quite irrelevant; for in this case the 'columnness' of columns is the important thing. There is no reality embedded in the image.

For Sartre, too, a photograph has two aspects, as far as the photographic image is concerned. One aspect is the photograph as a physical object; the other is the photograph as an image. With a painting there is a similar situation regarding the distinction between the physical object of a perception and an image – as in any physical form of representation whatsoever. The perception of the physical object that has been assigned the task of representation is thus quite different from the imaging consciousness.

Kant raises the question of transcendence when he speaks about the transcendental ego, and, more generally, of the 'noumenal' world. This is the domain of ideas and categories that can then be applied to the phenomenal world. The noumenal world, because it is a realm of transcendence, cannot be analysed, since it provides the very tools that would be needed to do such an analysis. It is in this sense that the realm of transcendence has assumed such importance in religious doctrines and systems – but only as a domain that is named, not one that is known.

For psychoanalysis, the limit of transcendence is in reality a limit of consciousness. The unconscious*, as slips of the tongue, repetitions, forgetting of names, and a variety of symptoms, constitutes another domain which has its own kind of coherence. Indeed, the unconscious is immanent in the products of psychic life.

Heidegger, Martin (1968 [1954]) *What Is Called Thinking?*, trans. J. Glenn Gray, New York: Harper & Row.
Sartre, Jean-Paul (1986 [1940]) *L'Imaginaire: psychologie phénoménologique de l'imagination*, Paris: Gallimard.

See EXCHANGE; GIFT

INDEX 'Index', understood in the sense invented by C.S. Peirce (1839–1914), is a sign which is attached to what it signifies (as with a weathervane and the wind) (Peirce 1991: 251). Other examples would be: shadows, footprints (as an index of shoe size), warm air as an index of summer, fighter planes as an index of war and smoke as an index of fire. An index also corresponds to the rhetorical figure of synecdoche, where the part stands for the whole. A sail is an index of a ship and a wing the index of a plane.

Denis Hollier has identified the index as a key element of surrealism. Here, we can recall in particular Giorgio de Chirico's haunting paintings where shadows feature so prominently (see Hollier 1994). Thus, shadows, mirror images and, in writing, autobiographical elements figure prominently in surrealist art. By using indexical signs, surrealism aims to go beyond the notion of imagination* as a closed and unreal world quite separate from reality. Index provides a way of grasping the image* as the primary vehicle of the imagination. It also represents the split between a virtual and an actual object. The face in the mirror is virtual as an index of the actual face which is looking at the glass. But, in addition, the first person pronoun (in the novel or story) becomes the index of the author of the text.

In German expressionist cinema, indexical signs also serve as a key feature of the often stark, black and white contrasts, which highlight shadows and bring a sinister tone to the scenario. The shadow must be a shadow of something, or someone. That is the nature of the indexical sign.

Hollier, Denis (1994) 'Surrealist Precipitates', *October*, 69 (Summer): 111–132.
Peirce, Charles Sanders (1991) *Peirce on Signs*, ed. James Hooper, Chapel Hill and London: University of North Carolina Press.

See ICON; IMAGE SIGN; SIGNIFIER/SIGNIFIED

INFORMATION The theory of information

comes into its own with the development of cybernetics*. In this context, it has to be understood that information is a physical, not a theoretical or cultural entity. Taking a communication* approach, Umberto Eco offers an example of an information system, which he calls 'the elementary structure of communication' (Eco 1976: 32). Consider, then, an engineer who needs to know when a reservoir, closed by a watergate and ensconced between two mountains, reaches a certain height. He needs to know whether there is water in the basin, whether it is above or below a certain danger level and the rate at which the water is rising. So he invents a buoy that will activate a transmitter which will then emit 'an electric signal which travels through a *channel* (an electric wire) and is picked up downstream by a *receiver*; this device converts the signal into a given string of elements…that constitute a *message* for *destination* apparatus. The destination, at this point, can release a mechanical response in order to correct the situation at the source (for instance opening the watergate so that the water can be slowly evacuated)' (Eco 1976: 33).

From a linguistic and semiotic point of view, communication can be represented as follows:

message
(code)

sender   **receiver**
(telephone) $\Rightarrow$ (telephone)
channel
(telephone wire/cable)

To get the message through, the line needs to be free of 'noise' (sounds not revelant to the particular message); the measure of this is the response of the person on the other end of the line as interpreted by the sender. That is, we are dealing with meaning.

With Eco's information example, on the other hand, the code* has to ensure that a given signal will be translated into a given response. A potential obstacle to this is excessive noise in a channel. Therefore the code has to be sufficiently complex to ensure that noise does not interfere with information. In short, information here is mechanically produced and very much part of a stimulus–response system that is not hampered by ambiguity or complexity of interpretation. This is a digital, on–off, system, that breaks down under the pressure if there are too many variables. Turning an electric light on and off is based on a similar system.

But surely, some might argue, there is an element of interpretation involved when the engineer perceives the flashing light signal in the 'destination apparatus'. The flashing light could even be a 'WARNING' sign, in response to which the engineer needs to pull the lever to open the watergate to release water from the reservoir. However, the procedures involved here could also be programmed, to enable the valve to be opened automatically when the water reaches a certain level. There is no essential need for interpretation here. What we are dealing with are what Eco calls 's-codes'. These are 'systems or "structures" that can also subsist independently of any sort of significant or communicative purpose' (Eco 1976: 38). And, we can add, s-codes can subsist independently of any context.

Katherine Hayles makes the further point in the discussion of Shannon and Weaver's mathematical theory of information to the effect that, 'in information theoretic terms, no message is ever sent' (Hayles 1999: 18). For the information theorist, it is the signal that is sent, and this is important because it is quantifiable and thus objectifiable. The aim of information theory is to have a concept of information that can be applied across all contexts. Meaning is context specific; information is not. Moreover, while Eco's 'watergate model' of communication shows that, to be enacted, information needs a code and a channel, the information element as such is distinct from its physical enactment.

Hayles also reminds us that while the mathematical theory of information supposedly reduces uncertainty (through being able to calculate the probability of x occurring), there is a sense in which uncertainty is at the heart of information. The more unlikely the occurrence of an event*, the greater the information if it does occur. An event that has a high probability of occurring does not provide much information; the reverse is the case for an unlikely event. In informational theory terms, this means that when things are going according to plan, there is a paucity of meaning.

Many systems in computing are poor in information as meaning, since a given set of procedures produces a predictable response – even to the point where a computer can shut down automatically after an 'illegal operation' quite independently of the system user. Indeed, a key aspect of many computer systems is that they are increasingly informational rather than communicative (decontextualising rather than context specific). The significance of a communicative response is that it engages the initiative of the 'destination' – i.e. it is not predictable, as many information systems are.

The phrase, 'the information society', often implies the dominance of the media. In this regard, Bernard Stiegler (1996: 124) has pointed out that information only exists in the strict sense when it is differentially possessed. What everyone knows is not information. This implies that information does have potential political implications, or even that information is essentially political, in that 'those in the know' are at an extreme advantage in the market and elsewhere.

From another, less technical angle, a distinction can be made – and indeed needs to be made – between knowledge* and information. Information, especially as gathered by the media, is contingent, for the moment, and then forgotten, whereas knowledge is connected to a cultural heritage, and is accumulated in the body of knowledge – as in history or mathematics. Knowledge is cumulative (one element builds on the next), while information is dispersed and fragmentary. For some, the fear is that information, as the expression of an eternal present, is taking over from knowledge as the dominant form of knowing in post-industrial societies.

Eco, Umberto (1976) *A Theory of Semiotics*, Bloomington: Indiana University Press.
Hayles, N. Katherine (1999) *How We Became Posthuman: Virtual Bodies in Cybernetics, Literature and Informatics*, Chicago: University of Chicago Press.
Stiegler, Bernard (1996) *La technique et le temps 2: La désorientation*, Paris: Galilée.

SEE CYBERNETICS

INTERPRETATION

Interpretation used to mean 'translation', but is now clearly distinguished from it. With interpretation, there is a question concerning meaning; with translation, there is a question concerning the equivalence of expression. Interpretation has such a wide application that it is impossible to set out all its contexts. Certainly, interpretation concerns the search for true meaning in fields such as theology, where the task is to establish the meaning of the word of God in the Bible; in the Jewish tradition, there is the matter of the word for God: the tetragrammaton, JHWH. In the field of law, it is a matter of deciding on the true intention, or the spirit, behind the law; in the field of literature, it has been a matter of interpreting the meaning of the text; in the field of philosophy, it has been a matter of establishing the possible meanings of a thinker's work.

'Interpretation of Nature' is a phrase used by Francis Bacon (1561–1626) to denote the discovery of natural laws by means of induction.

In a parliamentary context, there is what is called 'attribution' in relation to the interpretation of legislation. Here, an interpretation clause, a clause in an Act of Parliament, defines the meaning of certain terms for the purposes of the Act.

Since the Second World War, two different, but fundamental, approaches to interpretation can be discerned. The first approach, which we could call hermeneutic, treats meaning as a domain beyond expression – beyond the words on the page, as it were, even beyond language itself. Meaning here is something other than the material manifestation of the means of expression. So we have the author's real intention, or the actual personality of the author as the true source of meaning, or we have the meaning of the text related to the true meaning of words. The material expression – the signs – of the author is the place where possible distortions take place. This approach assumes that, ultimately, someone is in control of meaning; or meaning is living in the text, but needs to be liberated from the everyday sense of words.

The second approach to meaning is best represented by structuralism. This approach says that whatever putative meaning may lie behind the text, or system of signs, it is the sign system with which interpretation is confronted. Even if it were possible to speak directly with the author – even with God – or even if the true meaning is not deemed to be in the signs, we would still be confronted with signs. All communication depends on signs that must be interpreted. Some, like Husserl, believe that an internal monologue escapes the sign system, and that, therefore, to speak with oneself is to experience signs as being absolutely transparent. However, it is doubtful if this is possible; it is also doubtful that anyone can be perfectly aware of all the connotations of a single word, or series of words. But maybe we can bypass words and signs – maybe we can bypass language – so that interpretation ceases to be necessary. Were this to be so, it is difficult to know how one could speak of communication, or of any form of mediation. How could one even know that anything at all has taken place?

The internal monologue is thus of doubtful validity when it comes to interpretation. What is more likely is that an intention beyond signs and other symbolic forms only leads to more signs, with the risk of an infinite regress. For all its faults, structuralism at least has the rigour to show that going beyond language is a very difficult thing, and that, consequently, interpretation is humanity's lot.

Interpretation is the lot in particular for those who use language as the characteristic which distinguishes the human from the animal world. This implies that the human world is a world of mediations, that language makes people human more than humans make language. That is, language is more than an instrument of communication, and also speaks in its own right. In fact, as Heidegger shows (Heidegger 1982: 57–108), the being of language and the being of Being as such are inextricably linked. Humans speak, then, but it is because language has made them human. And interpretation is intimately tied up with language as the making of the human, since distilling the richness (historical, poetic, emotional) of language is beyond the power of any single individual.

Even beside the richness of language, the infinity of contexts in which words and signs are instantiated entails that meaning is, ultimately, open-ended, and that interpretation is the order of the day. It is always a *question* of meanings, never one of a self-evident univocal meaning.

For Freud, in his great work, *The Interpretation of Dreams* (1976), the issue in dream interpretation centres on the dream's logic of disguise. At first encounter, dreams seem utterly devoid of meaning. No interpretation of the dream images seems possible. This, however, is a ruse. The dream attempts to elicit an interpretation of the images within a total picture, which makes little sense. It is only when the individual elements of the dream are looked at separately and the lines of association thus thrown up, followed, that progress can be made in determining what Freud calls the dream thoughts. The latter are to be contrasted with the manifest content of the dream, a content which is geared to mislead the interpreter. Ultimately, Freud discovered that dreams were infinitely complex, and that even after discovering the dream navel – the source of richest meanings – every interpretation had to remain to some extent provisional.

Freud's approach to interpretation has been influential to the extent that it has reinforced the principle of not taking things at face value. However, it has sometimes led people to assume that the manifest signs of things are always misleading. Perhaps the most successful disguise of all, we should not forget, is the one based on placing the truth in the most obvious place – as happens with the letter in Edgar Allan Poe's story, 'The Purloined Letter' (1982). The letter was missed because it was in such an obvious place – first on the King's desk, and then in the Minister's letter rack.

Interpretation has also been used in a political sense to suggest that each individual, or group, interprets reality in terms of interest, or location on social space. The phrase, 'situated knowledge', made famous by Donna Haraway (1990), can be understood in this sense. But before Haraway, the most famous exponent of interpretation as a point of view is Nietzsche, who says that there are no facts, only interpretations. (Nietzsche 1968: 267). Or, to invoke a current cliché, there are only 'ways of seeing'. Here, we encounter a potentially relativist approach to knowledge. The claim to objectivity through method runs into the counter-claim that, in 'fact', there are only interpretations. Clearly, a paradox arises here; for the implication is that any dogmatic claim in one direction or the other (whether this be for method or interpretation) is doomed from the start. A more likely scenario is that the world is composed of facts *and* interpretations.

Freud, Sigmund (1976 [1900]) *The Freud Pelican Library Volume 4: The Interpretation of Dreams*, trans. James Strachey, London: Penguin.

Haraway, Donna (1990) 'Situated Knowledges: The Science Question in Feminism and the Privilege of Partial Perspective', in *Simians, Cyborgs, and Women: The Reinvention of Nature* New York: Routledge, 183–202.

Heidegger, Martin (1982 [1959]) 'The Nature of Language', in *On the Way to Language*, trans. Peter D. Hertz, New York: Harper & Row, 57–108.

Nietzsche, Friedrich (1968 [1901]) *Will to Power*, trans. Walter Kaufmann and R.J. Hollingsworth, New York: Vintage.

Poe, Edgar Allan (1982) 'The Purloined Letter', in *The Complete Tales and Poems of Edgar Allan Poe*, London: Penguin.

See IMAGE; KNOWLEDGE; SIGN; SIGNIFIER/SIGNIFIED

JUSTICE

The term 'justice' comes from the Old French and Latin word, *justitia*. It is habitually linked to the law and equality before the law, an equality symbolised by the sword and the scales in balance being carried by a blindfolded maiden. The law, through the courts, weighs the facts (and only the facts) and delivers its verdict. The formality and objectivity of the law is inextricably linked to the idea of justice. There is, of course, the issue of whether the legal system is in fact just, or whether privilege is embedded in it – for the wealthy, or the most highly educated, for example. However, the ideal is that to be objective is to be just. It was not always thought to be so.

In the sociologist, Max Weber's (1864–1920) writing on law and bureaucracy, we find references to 'Kadi', or 'popular justice' found in Muslim countries, which preceded objective, or rational justice. In Kadi, the aim is not to arrive at a reasoned judgment, but to address substantive grievances. For this reason, it can be seen as arbitrary, more to do with the actual interests and conflicts involved than with the facts as established through jurisprudence (Weber 1967: 216–217, 219, 221). The dispenser of Kadi justice might feel strong sympathy, or indeed antipathy, towards a claimant, and give his decision accordingly. In other words, the feelings between the parties enter the picture, often giving the decisions an apparently arbitrary character. The fact that the Kadi judge acts in one way on one occasion does not oblige him to act in the same way on a future occasion. For the claimants have changed, the situation has changed and, in any case, the judge might also have a migraine! Even though the parties may have been satisfied by the outcome, Kadi justice does not lend itself to systematisation. The type of decision made often depends on who is in the chair. Personalities count.

The limits of Kadi and all forms of popular justice are seen when strong emotions result in the wrong person being punished for a crime. We assume then that the Kadi judge sits on Thursdays. A group of people in the village swear that the intellectually disabled boy, Albert, has killed all the village pigs. Feeling against Albert has been mounting for some time, and the judge does not like Albert either. The people want Albert to be put away so that he won't bother them any more. In fact, the evidence suggests that Albert could not have been the culprit because he was ill and in bed at the time of the alleged crime. But the people want action. The judge wants to keep in with the people, and to keep things simple. So he banishes Albert from the village. Everyone is happy – except Albert.

From a modern, jurisprudential point of view, Albert's case represents the height of injustice. First, because Albert may not have been able to understand the meaning of the charges brought against him, and, second, because he was not guilty of the crime – yet he was punished. *Billy Budd* by Herman Melville is a similar kind of story: Billy Budd becomes a scapegoat for the wrong done by others. He is both not guilty and innocent, in the deepest sense of these terms.

From this we can see that justice raises extremely important issues for a society to face up to. The call for justice runs deep in the human soul, even if the meaning varies according to the position of the speaker.

The rationalisation of the law, enabling consistent legal decisions to be made – decisions that are not subject to the personal whim of the individual occupying the office of judge, as could happen with Kadi – parallels the rise of the bureaucratic state. And the precise limit, with regard to justice, of the bureaucratic state is that its 'without regard for persons' ethic cannot take account of the substantive inequalities existing in society at large, the most notable being that the wealthy can gain access to the law (to legal advice and representation, and to the courts) more easily than the poor. The question then is: is it just that a rich person can do better than a poor person when it comes to access to the law? Marx and many left-wing thinkers have argued that equality and justice cannot come from the law until substantive economic and social inequalities have been eliminated.

Reference to Marx recalls the fact that justice as a concept is also seen by many thinkers to be broader than jurisprudence would suggest. Weber, too, agrees that the rational legal system cannot in itself decide what is just; rather, it constitutes the means through which justice is dispensed. The law, therefore, is much more about means, than being an end in itself. Thinkers from Plato (1963) to Rawls (1971) have recognised that there is also the question of a substantive meaning of justice.

In Classical Greece, we find Plato viewing justice as *the* critical political issue. 'What is justice?' Plato asks in *The Republic* (1963: 331c). His answer is that justice is virtue and wisdom, and that the virtue of someone or something is the essential quality of that person or thing. This, however, leads Plato to his famous claim that each person is 'naturally fitted for one task' (1963: 370b), and to his infamous division of political society into the philosopher kings (gold is in their souls – they are the most precious), the guardians (silver – the helpers), farmers and craftsmen (brass and iron). The virtue of each member of each group is in his soul, and justice is for each to live according to the character God has bequeathed. For justice to be maintained, a guardian cannot rule, and the philosopher ruler cannot be a soldier. Injustice therefore derives from people doing tasks for which they are not fitted. A well-governed state is a just state, where each does what he is destined to do.

Modern democracies are founded on exactly the opposite principle of justice to the one Plato outlined. Justice, in the modern context, entails that each has the right to participate in government and in governing, that governing cannot be the preserve of an elite. In addition, the whole idea of an essential quality of the soul is unacceptable to a modern polity. The idea and practice of education has taken the place of innate qualities.

The great thesis on justice in the twentieth century is that put forward by John Rawls. Justice for Rawls means equality in all things, so the existing unequal distribution of economic wealth is an obstacle. Being a liberal, and not wanting go down the socialist road, Rawls is interested in distributive justice, working out how the least advantaged in society can gain the greatest benefit from government legislation and other actions. Overall, though, Rawls proposes that justice is fairness: it would not therefore be fair (i.e. just) for someone to receive more than they deserved. Thus, although justice is essentially about equality, the fact that things are not in a state of equality means that fairness has to be the principle adopted.

More than something that can be realised in a material sense, justice is a 'sense of justice', which inspires people to action to oppose injustice. Maybe today that is it: it is more important to fight against injustice than to realise justice on this earth.

Plato (1963) *The Republic*, trans. Paul Shorey, in *The Collected Dialogues of Plato*, ed. Edith Hamilton and Huntington Cairns, Princeton, NJ: Princeton University Press.

Rawls, John (1971) *A Theory of Justice*, Cambridge, MA: Harvard University Press; Oxford: Oxford University Press.

Weber, Max (1967) *From Max Weber: Essays in Sociology*, trans. and ed. H.H. Gerth and C. Wright Mills, London: Routledge & Kegan Paul.

See LEGITIMACY

KLANGFARBENMELODIE

(TONE-COLOUR MELODY) In one sense, *Klangfarbenmelodie* is a technical, musical term describing tone-colour (*Klangfarbe*), or the melody of tones and timbres, in the work of the composers of the Second Viennese School: Arnold Schoenberg (1874–1951), Anton Webern (1883–1945) and Alban Berg (1885–1935). While Schoenberg claimed to have invented it, Webern's music in particular developed this dimension of musical sound. In effect, *Klangfarben* compositions are based on 'progressions of tone-colours equalling harmonic progressions in terms of inner logic' (Schoenberg 1975: 485). Schoenberg continues: 'These I called melodies, because like melodies, they would need to be given form, and to the same extent – but according to laws of their own, in keeping with their nature' (ibid.). Such compositions exemplify the use of the so-called atonal, 12 tone scale, where all the half-tones of the octave, or diatonic scale, are given equal value, in contrast to the eight steps familiar to modern Western music. The formalisation of the octave as the dominant scale in musical notation and composition in the West was only achieved in the eighteenth century in Europe. In this regard, Bach's *Well-Tempered Clavier* (1722) was a turning point in musical notation.

The octave was to have an enormous impact in constituting a particular kind of Western subject, much as perspective had done in the visual field during the Renaissance.

Schoenberg, Webern and Berg thus broke with the established musical language and became the avant-garde correlate of Mallarmé and Joyce in literature, Picasso in painting and Futurism in art and architecture. *Klangfarbenmelodie* reveals the familiarising, and even homogenising, function of 'well-tempered' music – the music that sounds 'musical'. The audience's outrage at Schoenberg's semi-, or multi-tonal pieces, such as *Piano Suite*, Op. 25 (composed in 1923), derives from the fact that, to the accustomed musical ear, the composer was tampering with the very essence of musical language.

From a sociological perspective, *Klangfarbenmelodie* can be used for metaphorical purposes. It may enable another way to think society as difference and multiplicity. Those who want to follow Heidegger and the notion of Being* would no doubt say that the thinking of multiplicity is equivalent to its very constitution.

In any event, we can envisage a community* founded on, and united by, multiplicity (a precedent set by the early Christian community of differences united through love). We might then find that a new system of community is ultimately prefigured in so-called atonal music, in a kind of *Klangfarbenmelodie* where each note is almost equivalent to its own 'keyness'.

A new, complex harmony, based on *Klangfarbenmelodie* is thus established. As a perceptible harmony, such a musical form has a transcendent aspect. It brings about new relationships between entities as well as new configurations of identity*. This is the coincidence of apparently diverse elements whose mode of regularity comes to constitute a revised and complex identity, a revised mode of belonging together.

A conventional state apparatus today does not necessarily have ears to hear such a proposal. It is unable to disengage itself from the instrumentalist logic that blocks its ears to (the structure of) music in order to appreciate the other forms of identity and community that are possible. Music, as body, music as difference – because of its fluidity, because of its non-representational aspect – renders identity all the more complex.

Klangfarbenmelodie could be seen as the opposite of 'well-temperedness', as Bach constructed it. In effect, Bach's principles of tuning provide an analogy with an 'in-tune' self, one that is pleasant to the ear, that has no atonal (in the sense of being off key) qualities. What is of interest is how this analogy might be developed so as to extend music as an analogy in order to gain insights into the structure of social relations. Rather than talking about 'well-temperedness', we can talk about 'keyishness'. While music can be seen as representing the self, it is also possible to talk about the relative autonomy of music. Music renders representation problematic. It would not simply be a medium or a means – even if we

agree that it can evoke certain moods, atmospheres, images, memories, etc. This evocation is not a repetition of the thing, although it can be metonymy – something associated, or contiguous, with what is evoked. Music is not an analytical thing. It is not equal to the sum of its parts, nor is it reducible to a simple essence. On the contrary, music is an end in itself, even if the process of its reproduction with digital technology can lead to an intolerable degree of repetition.

Music, as *Klangfarbenmelodie*, is also locked into the semiotic* as a way of rendering emotion more complex. For the semiotic, in one of its definitions, is the musicality of language. Musicality is as far from representing the subject as one can get. Musicality – the rhythm and song of language – *is* the subject, in a sense.

The notion of tonality and 'keyishness' implied by Bach's *Well-Tempered Clavier* is now open to development. Indeed, '[k]eys are entirely harmonic structures. They do not pre-exist. They are constructed by the composer' (Erickson 1955: 82). The key, or tonic is sometimes referred to, metaphorically, as 'the relation to home'. Thus, Erickson writes: 'This feeling of "keyishness" is one in which we are at all times aware in one way or another of "where we are in relation to home". We place ourselves harmonically, we orient ourselves in the music, by relating our position to the tonic. A key gives unity to all the musical events which happen in it' (ibid.). To construct the very diatonic scale of 'well-temperedness' of course requires two half-steps. In other words, 'well-temperedness' has a certain 'impurity' so that it can sound pure. 'Well-temperedness' also gives the illusion of remaining in key, whereas when we go beyond the capacity of the ear, remaining in a given key becomes quite academic. Even to play a single note is to introduce harmonics, notes or sounds which diverge from any given note. Music is now being made in light of these notions.

Suffice it to say, even if too abruptly, that the notion of musical configuration has a suppleness and a flexibility that every representation of a community or political totality lacks. Now, community could be thought of less as a moral person, a fixed group or a personality, and more as a form of organisation as subtle in its explicit form as is the organisation of timbre – of sound-colour – in *Klangfarbenmelodie*. The point, finally – which has implications for a new understanding of difference and community – is that *Klangfarbenmelodie* is not chaos; it is, on the contrary, a *form* of communication* and of order.

Erickson, Robert (1955) *The Structure of Music: A Listener's Guide*, Westport, CT: Greenwood Press.
Schoenberg, Anold (1975) *Style and Idea: Selected Writings of Arnold Schoenberg*, trans. Leo Black and ed. Leonard Stein, London: Faber & Faber.

See ANALYTIC–SYNTHETIC; SUBJECT

KNOWLEDGE

'Knowledge' has several important meanings: first, it can refer to a corpus of material that may have been accumulated over centuries, as in the fields of history or astronomy. Second, it can be 'know-how': a technical grasp of how to do things; this can range from knowing how to open a bottle of wine, to the know-how necessary to produce a supersonic jet aircraft.

Third, knowledge can mean being familiar, or acquainted, with someone or something – as in knowing a particular person, having a knowledge of a town or region, having local knowledge, having knowledge of the way things are done, of another language, of an event, or events.

Although there is, at the beginning of the twenty-first century, growing discussion about the relationship between knowledge and information (or between the media, as communication, and knowledge) a key debate in relation to knowledge is in the field which examines the relationship of the knower and the known – the field of epistemology*.

In other respects, knowledge is also associated with education and training. To be educated has, in a European context, implied being cultivated: having a general knowledge of areas like the arts and sciences in order to be able to appreciate the significance of developments in the world. A cultivated person is not always trained professionally in the fields in which he or she is interested, but has a good general knowledge of these. Through this, the cultivated person can be part of a community* of people of similar background. The salon in Paris in the eighteenth century, and the Bloomsbury group in the twentieth, are examples of groups valorising the cultivated person.

The opposite of this kind of personally or professionally acquired knowledge is ignorance. It goes without saying that the upper middle class predominates in the community of the cultivated person. Further, the cultivated person is disappearing in light of the instrumentalisation of knowledge, where knowledge is a means to an end – vocational, scientific, economic or political. By contrast, the cultivated person values knowledge for its own sake over and above its usefulness.

If the cultivated person's days appear to be numbered, another development in knowledge is also emerging. This is the proliferation of reference books of all types (dictionaries, technical monographs, self-help books, medical books, books on cuisine, compendia of discipline areas such as philosophy, science, history and art, secondary texts on thinkers, critical readers and the like). It is as though such works have as their mission the democratisation of the means to become cultivated through making general knowledge readily available to a wide audience.

A final aspect of knowledge might be called 'customary knowledge'. This is the informal knowledge passed down from generation to generation, characteristic of tradition: knowledge about parenting and childbirth, about mythology and stories of the people about ritual and taboo, artistic practices, death, burial and mourning, kinship relations and the ancestors, heroes and enemies, the powers of plants to heal and to cause pain, the land and its features, ways of hunting and cultivating animals and plants. This is knowledge as a gift*: its origin is as important as its capacity to constitute a community. It is no doubt a form of knowledge that is now extremely difficult to sustain, if the thinking of modern sociologists is correct and life on the planet is becoming increasingly secularised and professionalised.

L

LABOUR-POWER

Labour-power is a technical term that is used by Marx in his theory of the commodity (Marx 1954), but appears much earlier in his discussions of wage labour and capital of the late 1840s (Marx 1951: 74–97). In an economy in which there is a highly developed money* system and division of labour – in a highly mediated society, in effect – labour-power, like the goods it produces as commodities, is also a commodity; it has a market price, is bought and/or laid off, depending on the economic cycle. Does labour-power produce anything? Certainly. Labour-power produces, says Marx, surplus value for the capitalist. Or more precisely: labour-power is the equivalent of surplus value or profit, since the worker is only allowed to retain enough in payment to enable survival at a subsistence level. For the capitalist can sell, on the open market, the products of labour for a higher price than cost of production (= workers' subsistence level of survival). Without labour-power, there would be no surplus value – no profit – an indication that there is an essentially unequal exchange taking place. Indeed, Marx's view is that if the price of labour only covers the cost of the reproduction of the agent of that labour, there is exploitation. And even the cost of reproduction of labour does not relate to any particular labourer whose basic needs are satisfied, but rather to the anonymous labour pool. Thus, labour-power points to a system of exploitation that is structural in nature. This is what unequal exchange means here.

Since it is a market entity, labour-power is not the same as work. Where the worker produces the things necessary for survival, or in craft-based cottage industries we see a low level of a division of labour. In a craft-based economy, more value is attached by those involved to what is produced than to the brute fact of production. It is the latter which characterises commodity production in the capitalist system. The content of the goods or service becomes irrelevant because it is the exchange-value alone which counts, not the use-value. Everything, including labour, thus aspires to the condition of money, and form takes precedence over content – at least from the point of view of the individual labourer or capitalist. Through exchange-value, the worker acquires money, not goods, in order to subsist.

The idea of class struggle is mapped by Marx on to the notion of exploitation. Workers, or the proletariat, are the agents of labour-power; the capitalists, or the bourgeoisie, are the agents of capital and the accumulators of profit at the expense of the workers. Consequently, out of an abstract system Marx extracts a human core, a core of suffering on the one hand, and of greed on the other. Another way of looking at this is to say that labour-power is caught up in the logic of instrumental rationality, where things are not produced as ends in themselves but only as means to an end – the end of profit. Such a society is, in the Marxist schema, also one of alienation*. For individual workers – who, as a collective entity, actually do produce the goods for the market – fail to recognise themselves in the product of their labour.

One thing that is striking about Marx's theory here is that it takes industrial society as the quintessential society of labour-power. The age of steam, with workers in factories and down mines, is the age of commodity production for Marx. What happens to class struggle and to labour-power when the nature of work changes, due to the introduction of the new of information* technologies, and when different work practices no longer resemble the division of labour of the past? That is to say: what happens when the issue of alienation is actually addressed through new management techniques? The answer seems to be that the marked difference between the conditions of classes is radically reduced. And the capitalist mode of production seems to be ever more in the ascendancy – in particular, because its openness to reform has been vastly underestimated.

Postmodern theory (Baudrillard (b. 1929), Lyotard (1924–99)) has suggested that the very abstract nature of the commodity system that Marx highlighted has not diminished, but has intensified, to the point where labour and the products of labour have become pure signs. In other words, because production for need, or for an essential purpose, is a thing of the past, it is a question of what things signify – of what labour-power signifies – perhaps in relation to leisure. Lifestyles, or how people live, have taken precedence over life* as the satisfaction of needs, as necessity – as zoë (bare life). Labour-power, through the commodity form itself, has been integrated into the symbolic order, where signs dominate over reality. A commodity – and the labour-power that is its correlate – serves no *essential* purpose. Marx recognised this. A commodity may not have a purpose but it can have a meaning. Advertising does nothing but exploit this fact. In effect, the commodity has left the economic domain and has entered the sphere of language and culture. It is no longer a matter of production of goods and services for consumption, but of reproducing the system itself. Reproduction (of the system) has taken over from production (of the worker).

In its homogenised form, labour-power appeared to Marx to offer an insight into the communist society of the future. Workers might not have been aware of it (because the proletariat was still a class 'in itself', not 'for itself') but mass labour opened the way to a new form of community* which would overcome the tension between individuality and solidarity, and thereby be the very antithesis of capitalist social relations. What Marx missed, and what Simmel saw (Simmel 1971), was that labour-power is the way to new forms of individuality, precisely because labour is not an end in itself, but a means to achieve a whole range of new possibilities, possibilities which communism could hardly envisage, so concerned was it, in idea and in reality, to transform collections or aggregates of individuals into a homogenised society founded in solidarity.

Marx, Karl (1951 [1849]) *Wage Labour and Capital*, in *Karl Marx and Frederick Engels Selected Works in Two Volumes: Volume I*, trans. from the German, Moscow: Foreign Languages Publishing House.

Marx, Karl (1954 [1867]) *Capital, Volume I*, trans. Samuel Moore and Edward Aveling, Moscow: Progress Publishers.

Simmel, Georg (1971) 'Group Expansion and the Development of Individuality', trans. Richard P. Albares, in *On Individuality and Social Forms: Selected Writings*, Chicago and London: University of Chicago Press.

See DIFFERENCE–INDIVIDUALITY

LEGITIMACY

'Legitimacy' derives from 'legitimate', which is adapted from medieval Latin *lēgitimātūs*, past participle of *lēgitimāre*, meaning, to declare to be lawful, to cause to be regarded as lawful offspring (Latin, *lēgitimus*: lawful).

Legitimacy expresses a status which has been conferred or ratified by some authority, that is, something has been legitimised. In English it has taken the place of the older, French *légitime*, meaning 'to be based in law'.

Generally, then, legitimacy refers to the legal basis of an institution or practice. More colloquially, it has come to refer to the well-foundedness, or otherwise, of a wide range of actions and practices, especially in business. Here, legitimate sometimes means fair and honest.

Max Weber (1864–1920) set out three types of legitimacy of authority, or domination, of which the legal form was only one. These are: (1) tradition, where authority is accepted on the basis of what has happened in the past – the authority of the 'eternal yesterday'; (2) charismatic authority, which gains legitimacy from the sheer force of an individual personality deemed to have the 'gift of grace'; and (3) legal-rational authority, where legitimacy is based on 'rationally created *rules*' (Weber 1967: 78–79. Weber's emphasis).

The issue concerning legitimacy which is of the greatest importance now concerns the basis of the political system, and whether those who claim the right to govern have a legitimate basis for making that claim.

In Australia, the issue of legitimacy has arisen in two quite different contexts. The first concerns the dispossessing of Aboriginal people of their land after British settlement in 1788. Since ruling authorities want to avoid giving the impression that 'might' has dominated over 'right', there is frequently a concerted effort to show that colonial dispossession, when looked at in terms of the prevailing laws and customs of the time of dispossession, was legitimate. The principle of *terra nullius* – empty land – was invoked as a way of legitimising the British settlement of Australia. *Terra nullius* specified that no agriculture, and therefore no substantive ownership of the land, existed in Australia prior to European settlement, and that it was therefore legitimate for a colonial power to occupy the land without compensating the indigenous Aboriginal people. In 1992, *terra nullius*, was overturned in the Australian High Court, with the result that the legitimacy of the original occupation has been brought into question.

Another aspect of the occupation has concerned the question of whether or not a state of war existed between the Aboriginal people and the British authorities. Certainly, no state of war was formally declared, and much has hinged on the nature of the conflict that occurred between Aborigines and white people. If it could be shown that the Aboriginal people fought as though defending their land, then a state of war may have existed between the original inhabitants and the English settlers. A state of war gives legitimacy to later claims for a treaty, and even for compensation, if the war was initiated by the victors. In other words, a defeated people has legitimate rights. That it is defeated does not change this situation.

The difficulty of speaking of legitimacy in this context is that many in the Australian population simply look at things pragmatically in terms of who now has the power – possession being nine-tenths of the law, as they say. Populist governments find the courts and the complex legal arguments an impediment to pushing ahead with legislation that ignores Aboriginal rights. Legitimacy is rarely an issue in the popular imagination. And yet a democratic political system would not exist without it. For it is through the notion of legitimacy – through being voted into power – that governments are able to maintain touch with the 'will of the people'. Intractable political conflicts, such as the one between the Australian government and Aboriginal people, rarely allow legitimacy to be the main focus in the political debate.

The second example of legitimacy being brought into question was that of the dismissal, on 11 November 1975, of the Whitlam Labour government by the Governor-General, Sir John Kerr.

The opposition leader, Malcolm Fraser was sworn in as leader of a caretaker government, and subsequently led his Liberal Party to a substantial victory at the polls. For many people, the performance of Labour in government was not to their liking (too much social welfare reform) and so they wanted Malcolm Fraser to come to power. However, what one wants, and what is legitimate, can be, and often are, two very different things. Did the Governor-General, acting as the Queen's representative in Australia (the Queen being head of government in Australia in name only), act legitimately in dismissing the Labour government? Or was he the mechanism through which anti-Labour forces in society were able to get their party into government – whether legitimately or not? In the popular media the impression is frequently given that if the people want it (that is, if the opinion polls are over 50 per cent in favour), then it should be.

The idea of legitimacy is complex enough to require it to be the subject of political education. Today, such education is diminishing and a much more populist voice is being heard. While, in a practical sense, the consequences might not be serious in day to day activities, they are more so in a crisis, such as happened in 1975, and with the overturning of the principle of *terra nullius*. It is crisis, or instantiating situations and actions, which brings the issue of legitimacy to light. This is what the history of political theory from Hobbes's *Leviathan* (1968) to our own day demonstrates. It might be wise not to take too lightly the assignment of this tradition to the dustbin of history.

Nevertheless, establishing the legitimacy of institutions and governments can be extremely difficult. A Marxist might claim that, under conditions of oppression, talk of legitimacy neither makes sense nor is relevant to the aspirations of the oppressed. As a result, revolution can never be legitimate. For it can never find a legal basis in the existing framework – by definition. There is, in effect, a *differend**. Once in power, a revolutionary government has to work to establish its legitimacy and win the free consent of the people, otherwise it will have to resort to ruling a police state, where might takes precedence over right. The critical question is: to what extent do existing political systems makes provision for *legitimate* reforms, if not for revolution? The answer to that question would be the basis for constructing a typology of legitimate forms of government.

Hobbes, Thomas (1968 [1651]) *Leviathan*, London: Penguin.
Weber, Max (1967) *From Max Weber: Essays in Sociology*, trans. and ed. H.H. Gerth and C. Wright Mills, London: Routledge & Kegan Paul.

See POWER

LIFE Both the most obvious and the most obscure of notions, 'life' – its meaning and significance – is once again on the agenda. Aristotle's distinction between *zoë* (bare life, the mere fact of being alive) and *bios* (life as an achievement of something) has been extremely influential. The Latin, *vita*, evokes something of Aristotle's *bios*, particularly in Dante's sense of *vita nuova* (new life) as a transformation and reworking of who one is.

In the nineteenth century, fuelled by Darwin's idea of evolution, arose the discipline of biology, which literally means the study of life, and practically means the study of the evolution of animal and human life – particularly human life.

In the late nineteenth and early twentieth centuries, the philosophical idea of the *élan vital*, most notably as developed by Henri Bergson (1983), sought to evoke a life force that was irreducible to physical energy produced by animal and human bodies. The *élan vital* is thus a transcendental notion referring to a force beyond the biological understanding of life. The philosopher and scientist Hermann von Helmholtz (1821–94) demonstrated, in disputing the existence of the *élan vital*, that the energy produced by the human body was equivalent to the amount of food and other substances ingested. There was no evidence of an additional force.

In other respects, life has become an issue in the society of the twenty-first century from three different angles.

The first is life as a moral/ethical question in relation to euthanasia, *in vitro* fertilisation, eugenics, contraception and abortion. Here, decisions have to be made about when physical life begins and ends, and about when it *should* be understood to begin and end. Some opponents of euthanasia say that only God, or nature, has the right to end life, thus begging the difficult question that arises in some complex cases about *when* life has ended. Has a person's life ended when that person is brain dead? Or is it necessary for the whole organism to be pronounced dead? On the other hand, is bare life (Artistotle's *zoë*) a dignified and desirable state for a human being? Bare life is not human; only life as *bios* is truly human. This, at least, was Aristotle's view.

Contraception and abortion evoke the opposite question: about the beginning of human life. Again, to oppose these in the name of life is to reduce human life to bare life. On the other hand, someone could oppose contraception and abortion on the grounds that only God or nature can allow life and death. No human has the wisdom or majesty of moral bearing to assume such responsibility and the human tendency towards corruption – or at least the fact of human frailty – means that there is always a risk that impure (self-interested) motives will drive such decisions. Opponents of such a view, point out that modern life, with its highly sophisticated medical practices and accompanying new technologies, means that decisions about life and death just cannot be avoided. Even more: not to make such decisions would be tantamount to moral cowardice.

In the case of the sinister use of eugenics, life is linked, as it was with the Nazis, to a pre-existing model of perfection. Only those who conform to certain ideal criteria are deemed to be entitled to physical life. All crippled and otherwise deformed people, together with those said to be racially inferior, and thus a risk to the physical well-being of the human species, are not allowed to live under a strict and politically motivated form of eugenics. Sinister eugenics abhors difference and non-conformity.

There is perhaps a benign form of eugenics. Here, the aim is to use techniques such as cloning to eliminate certain life-threatening diseases and conditions. Before being introduced into the brains of human patients with Parkinson's disease, brain cells from pigs might be genetically altered so that the human cells will not reject the new pig cells. The latter then function in place of the damaged human cells. Or genetic engineering might be used to prevent a hereditary condition, such as haemophilia, manifesting itself in a male infant.

Despite such innocent uses of eugenic techniques, the reality is that nature is not simply being allowed to take its course, with humans being forced to come to terms with whatever might occur. There is nothing here of Nietzsche's *amor fati* (love of fate). Humanity may have to judge between a good and a bad use of eugenics, even if judging is something that a liberal society shies away from.

The second general aspect of the question of life is found in cybernetics*, where the debate is, in the first place, about the relative importance of consciousness and intelligence in human life. Artificial intelligence (AI) proponents proceed according to the view that consciousness and intelligence are primary in human life, so that once replication of the consciousness-intelligence system becomes possible, the artificial reproduction of a human being will also become possible. In the attempts to succeed in their quest, AI proponents, by making consciousness conform to the model of a giant computer, have adopted an analytical approach. Artificial life (AL) proponents, by contrast, have adopted a synthetic approach by allowing simple systems to reproduce and develop into unpredictable complex systems (see analytic–synthetic). In both AI and AL, there is still a tendency to privilege virtual life forms over incarnated, or bodily, life.

Thirdly, in another quite distinct approach to life that has been progressing in the early part of the twenty-first century, life is rethought in relation to the Aristotelian notions of *zoë* and *bios*. Giorgio Agamben's work looks at this, particularly his book, *Homo Sacer* (1998). Well before Agamben, however, Hannah Arendt addressed the issues arising here in her work on work and action, most notably *The Human Condition* (1958). For Arendt, action, in the fullest sense, is freedom*. Freedom is the public achievement which reveals *who* someone is, as opposed to *what* he or she is (the qualities which can be enumerated).

Freedom, as action (word and deed), is also a form of life: life as *bios*. As *bios*, life discloses the 'who' in the public sphere, because it is only in relation to others (who are essentially public others) that who one is can be disclosed. This disclosure is not entirely available to the actor him- or herself, and it means that a person in public, instead of self-consciously revealing who they are, *betrays* who they are through a thousand unselfconscious and unchoreographed words and deeds, which are both profound and banal: words and deeds as signs which, in their material incarnation, have nothing to do with action as such.

Since action is revelatory and betrays the 'who', it needs a witness – the historian – to enable it to enter into the collective memory. The thought that is immanent in it requires the thinker as a spectator to explicate it. Or, to put it another way: every action contains a story which must be told, but which cannot be told by the actor, for 'nobody is the author or producer of his own life story' (Arendt 1958: 184). And again: 'What the storyteller narrates must necessarily be hidden from the actor himself...because to him the meaningfulness of his act is not in the story that follows' (ibid.: 192).

From the distinction between *zoë* and *bios*, the idea of a *way of life* emerges. Dominated by survival and by doing as a means to an end, *zoë* will never be the life of action. From a position of instrumental doing, the world of action will always seem trivial and pointless. For the action can never answer the question: what use is it? As such, action seems to be essentially locked out of an economic rationalist environment, where the instrumentalism of the market dominates. On the other hand, action, due to its entirely unchoreographed, if not unpremeditated, character, can never be ruled out of even the most instrumental of environments. It is just that the work of the historian thinker spectator is that much more demanding.

Agamben, Giorgio (1998 [1995]) *Homo Sacer: Sovereign Power and Bare Life*, trans. Daniel Heller-Roazen, Stanford, CA: Stanford University Press.
Arendt, Hannah (1958) *The Human Condition*, Chicago: University of Chicago Press.
Bergson, Henri (1983 [1941]) *Creative Evolution*, trans. Arthur Mitchell, Lanham, MD: University Presses of America.

See ANALYTIC–SYNTHETIC; COMPLEXITY IMMANENT/ IMMANENCE

LOCAL The local refers to place, as the global (see globalisation*) refers to the compression of time. The local also evokes identity as familiarity, as in the expressions, 'local hero', or 'our neighbourhood'. This implies that the local is very strongly linked to context. What the local team does, or the local school or those who live locally do, cannot be generalised to fit a broader frame. Once this happens, the local ceases to be local. The local, then, evokes the notion of idiomatic – if not eccentric – features.

The family who, isolated in the mountains, sleeps with sheep in the bedroom because it is cold in the winter is acting locally. The action is specific to the place. A local place is therefore unique. A person who has local knowledge is someone who has *particular* knowledge, that is, who has knowledge pertinent to a specific context. Local knowledge is contextual knowledge. It cannot be applied elsewhere without risk of irrelevance.

Local habits and customs are usually characteristic of small communities. What many people worry about – those outside local communities as well as those within – is the loss of the local through the call of the city to young people and others. The globalising tendency of society means that the local seems to be a barrier to individual development. And indeed, the negative side of the local is the parochial – being blinkered by an attachment to a single place.

Migrants, who seek to start a new life elsewhere, often come from very localised environments, where unique cultural traits can make it difficult to adjust to a different locale. The unique nature of the local environment means that the full force of the local can really only be appreciated when one goes elsewhere. Often, the local resident does not know him or herself as local, so experiences another place as a shock. This can lead not only to an awakening, but also to insights about the local that more cosmopolitan people obtain only with difficulty. The limit to cosmopolitan experience is its failure to know the local as local, whereas the local can always become cosmopolitan.

Perhaps no one has managed to evoke the local with as much force as John Berger. In his book, *A Seventh Man* (1975), Berger, with photographer, Jean Mohr, captures in images and words the contrast between village life and life in European metropolitan conglomerations. The higgledy-piggledy disposition of dwellings perched on a hillside in Turkey contrasts with the network of freeways in the metropolis. The way round the village is acquired through local knowledge; the way round the city is far more about reading maps, signs and notices. In other words, in the city, everything is much more formal and decontextual, whereas in the village it is a question of context and informal, local knowledge. The message of Berger's book is that local life is disappearing at a rapid rate. This leads to the loss of strong community* ties and the dominance of formal relationships based on individual choice. These are the same things that Simmel (1858–1918) anticipated in his writing on the city and money early in the twentieth century (Simmel 1971). The disappearance of the local is no doubt a key element of modernity. Mass communications only serve to complete the job.

The uprooting experienced by those who have lost their local home country may well be a feature of what it means to be in the world. Technology contributes to this uprooting, or at least to the intrusion of the outside into the intimacy of the local community, and may have a negative impact on at least one level, since it undermines the existing form of the community. But it also can have a very positive effect: it can be the basis of a new type of community which benefits from renewal and enrichment. After all, we probably do not want to preserve some of the community prejudices revealed, for example, by Nikos Kazantzakis in his novel *Zorba the Greek* (1946).

Berger, John and Mohr, Jean (1975) *A Seventh Man: The Story of Migrant Workers in Europe*, Harmondsworth: Penguin/Pelican Books.

Simmel, Georg (1971 [1903]) 'The Metropolis and Mental Life', trans. Edward Shils, in *On Individuality and Social Forms: Selected Writings*, Chicago and London: University of Chicago Press.

LOGOS–MYTHOS

The *logos–mythos* couple originates in Greek philosophy's distinction between the word which 'makes manifest' (discourse) and poetry. *Logos* is also at the origin of logic and science, as is seen in bio-logy, psycho-logy, anthropo-logy. It relates to knowing, and has come to mean reason, judgement, definition. From an anthropological point of view, it has often been assumed that European culture*, inspired by Greek thought, is the culture of truth* and science, while non-European thinking is grounded in poetry and myth – or poetic discourse called *mythos*.

It has been suggested (Todorov 1984) that the defeat of the Aztecs by a relatively small number of Spaniards was due to the latter's possession of the *logos* and phonetic writing, or the 'technology of symbolism'. The Spaniards thus used writing as a means, not as an end. They engaged in calculation and improvisation – adjusted to circumstances – and saw time as irreversible. The Aztecs, by contrast, had total commitment to the *mythos*, which entailed a concern with the forms, rituals and poetry of the word, not its instrumental aspect. In such a society, without phonetic writing, the poetic word becomes constitutive of both power and social memory. The ruler as *tlatoani* is the best orator – the most accomplished

rhetorician – 'he who possesses speech'. Ritual speech is *huehuetlatolli*, 'discourses learned by heart'. These are of a set form and rhythm. The Spaniards marvelled at the (poetic) eloquence of the peoples they had beaten in battle (Todorov 1984: 79–80).

Mythos, as the poetic word, and the word of prophecy, is not instrumental, as *logos* has become instrumental. Societies without writing* (oral societies) are therefore often societies where the poetic and the instrumental word come together, so that speech becomes an end in itself as much as an instrument of communication*. At one level this is obvious, since, in an oral society, the musicality of the word is an aid to memory so that the instrumental and the poetic become inextricably entwined.

When the instrumental version of *logos* comes to dominate *mythos* – as has surely happened with the ascendancy of modernity – the former becomes a transcription of the real, that is, of contingency. Irreversible time dominates the reversible order of *mythos*. To the extent that a society refuses contingency, it risks becoming a closed system unable to tolerate difference within itself, to the point where its very survival is at issue. This is a point of the debate, however. Societies of the *mythos* are often those which can look death in the face: loss and sacrifice are the order of the day. Death is always present. *Mythos*, as the poetic word, is also a ritual lament, an institutionalised mourning.

If it has appeared that oral cultures, like the Aztec, placed too much importance on the word for its own sake, so that such cultures were unable to adapt to changing circumstances, the question arises as to whether highly instrumental cultures have gone too far in the other direction so that, in everyday life at least, poetic richness is lacking and people have lost touch with something called the inner and sacred self, which is still present in Ancient Greek culture.

Todorov, Tzvetan (1984 [1982]) *The Conquest of America: The Question of the Other*, trans. Richard Howard, New York: Harper & Row.

LOVE

LOVE is a key sentiment in human societies, and none more so than Enlightenment European society. As against violence, where is love placed now?

The question today concerns the extent to which love is about the spontaneous feelings of the people involved in a relationship, as opposed to being 'choreographed' by stories, myths, legends and, latterly, by novels and the cinema.

The view of Romanticism in late eighteen-century Europe is of course that 'love at first sight' is typical of true love, and that this had, until the French Revolution, been suppressed in practice. Not that people had not talked about love before the Revolution: from Greek myth, through Plato on eros, to the Troubadours, Don Juan and Romeo and Juliet, love is on the agenda. Love, in these historical instances, is equivalent to the absence of the loved object, and can only become manifest in the absence of the beloved. It is a kind of dream that can never be realised.

In the Greek myth of Orpheus and Eurydice, Eurydice dies a second time because, upon returning from the Underworld (Hades), her lover, Orpheus, turns and looks back at her – which the gods had forbidden him to do on pain of death. Orpheus, the wonderful singer, is thus separated from his love for ever. Some versions of the myth say that the Thracian women, angry at Orpheus's refusal to have anything to do with women after the loss of Eurydice, tore him to pieces – but the head just kept on singing… However, if love is the expression of it, the singing itself becomes love. The outpouring of emotion needs to be organised and expressed.

If this is the case, the Romantic view needs revision; even Romanticism's self-understanding would need revision. Jean-Jacques Rousseau (1712–78), for instance, wrote a novel of love letters called *Julie* – over 700 pages of expressions of love. People cried at the tragedy love brings when Julie, the heroine, dies (Rousseau 1964). People identify with love stories: they put themselves in the place of the imaginary lovers. This is even the case for the actual lovers. They, too, are involved in a process of identification. Therefore: love is always a love story, and there is no love without identification. However, the form of the story changes according to time and place: that is, according to history and culture.

As well as being a story, love can be the love of country, of nature, of God, of the poor, etc. Such objects of love also provoke a love story. We should keep this in mind in light of the historical aspects of love.

In a modern example of a love story, Salman Rushdie's novel, *The Ground Beneath Her Feet* (1999), the characters play out a contemporary version of the Orpheus and Eurydice myth. Irony is the form love's discourse has to take in this sceptical age (cf. Eco 1984: 67–68), and so in an ironical summary of the plot, we find the following dialogue:

—Hey, Calzbigi, what's this ending you're giving me here? Such a downer, I should send folks home with their faces long like a wurst? *Hello*? Happy it up, ja!—Sure, Herr Gluck, don't get so agitato. No problem! Love, it is stronger than Hades. Love, it make the gods merciful. How's about they send her back anyway? 'Get outa here, kid, the guy's crazy for you! What's one little peek?' Then the lovers throw a party, and what a party! Dancing, wine, the whole nine yards. So you got your big finish, everybody goes out humming.—Works for me. Nice going, Raniero.—Sure thing, Willibald. Forget about it. (Rushdie 1999: 12)

The main protagonist in fact is a photographer. He captures things for ever.

In other respects, Ormus Cama (the hero) seeks Vina Apsara (the heroine) in other women, thus emphasising the idea of love as identification.

Baz Luhrmann's film, *Moulin Rouge* (2001), is also supposedly founded on the Orpheus myth, with the heroine dying in the final scene. Love is the sort of emotional experience which has produced expressions, and representations, because it involves the separation of the lovers. Separation introduces the social dimension of love, takes it out of an essentially domestic context.

Modernity* (from the eighteenth to the twentieth century) sees the realisation of this dream of love through the realisation of the free choice of a lover, or marriage partner.

In the past, people wrote letters, even to members of their own family. Now the tendency is to write letters, if at all, only to those from whom we are separated in some way. The expression of love today is, as a result, much more problematic. In recognition of this, we have various efforts – such as that by Barthes (1978) – to invent a style that might be appropriate for the expression of love today.

Informality – closely linked to greater familiarity – militates against a sense of separation and, therefore, against love.

To the extent that sexuality brings together intimacy and familiarity, it, too, militates against the expression of love. So, from the point of view of love, the decline in the older style of marriage may not necessarily be a positive thing.

Poetic forms that arise as a result of the anguished soul's solitude must also be on the decline if sociological reality tends towards a combination of familiarity in the relationship and a lack of interest in making contact with (hostile others) outside the relationship. T.S. Eliot's poem, *A Dedication to my Wife* (1980) both expresses the points made above concerning the increase in familiarity and the decline in love, and then goes against them by making public, in the most hallowed of art forms, the intimate feelings a husband might have for a wife. In the poem, the lover-wife is both cherished and defamiliarised. The point is that love is a form of mediation, in the sense that the expression and the reality of love are one and the same thing. Love is (in) art. Passion needs its obstacles (= separation) for it to turn into love. *The Ground Beneath Her Feet* is, effectively, about the obstacles to love, and is therefore about love. The obstacles are equivalent to the love (as) story.

Society in the modern sense brings with it the impersonality of the economic system. It also exhibits a trend towards differentiation and individuality. Difference thus becomes a key issue of modern experience, and the ego becomes central. (See difference–individuality). People seek to differentiate themselves from their environment. Name, social status, etc. are no longer enough for the constitution of self-identity.

At the same time, differentiation brings a capacity to adjust to difference. Hence society's increasing complexity.

Now the issue, as Luhmann (1998) says, centres on the way that individual uniqueness and difference become part of the social fabric; whereas, previously, it was thought that individual difference might be a threat to the social fabric. Love enters the picture here. Love and friendship become the languages of individuation.

For Luhmann, love – beginning in the eighteenth century – comes to embody the notion of an open system: the open system is one that survives and is enriched by the absorption of new elements from the environment. A closed system is cut off from its environment and risks imploding for want of the revitalisation that comes from the introduction of new elements. Luhmann is influenced by systems theory. Julia Kristeva also takes up this idea at the beginning of her book, *Tales of Love* (1987b).

LOVE AS THE COMMUNICATION OF INTIMACY

Language is the medium of expression of new semantic forms which enable intimacy to be communicated. Love is perhaps a feeling, but more than this, it is one to be communicated – or expressed. The complexity of love discourse these days becomes the basis of the renewal of the expressions of love. Both Rushdie and Barthes recognise this.

Barthes, for example, writes in free indirect style:

'I look for signs, but of what? What is the object of my reading? Is it: am I loved (am I loved no longer, am I still loved)? Is it my future that I am trying to read, deciphering in what is inscribed the announcement of what will happen to me, according to a method which combines paleography and manticism [divination]? Isn't it rather, all things considered, that I remain suspended on this question, whose answer I tirelessly seek in the other's face: *What am I worth?* (Barthes 1978: 214)

'Passion' becomes a synonym for complex communication (what Luhmann calls a code*).

Initially, in the seventeenth and eighteenth centuries, passionate love was a deviation from social convention and had to be controlled, if not eliminated in the interest of formal moves and wit (see the French film *Ridicule*, 1996). How things are done (or said) takes precedence over what is done. Clichés can be repeated.

Then there is, perhaps paradoxically, a codification of *amour-passion*. Women read novels, and there are novels which show young men how to succeed in society. Gradually, self-referentiality begins to dominate thinking and feelings. This entails taking account of how one's own speech will appear to the other: that is, it is reflexivity, a form of feedback control. Love is open to fail because of the complexity of the communication required. This occurs in the movement from a stratified (tradition of aristocracy) to a functional mode of differentiation (modern democracy). Idealisation gives way to temporalisation.

For Luhmann, society is forced to develop new, more subtle codes of love. But even a code of love presupposes that love is something originating in the separation of the lovers. And this, no doubt, is the big difference between a contemporary experience of love and love in the past. For, today, love, intimacy and familiarity go together. There is no need for an expression of love when love is instead acted out, or is supposed to be. In the past, there was a certain degree of separation (partly constituted by a more formal demeanour) even in intimacy, thus blocking complete familiarity; today, those whom one really loves are those with whom one has grown most familiar. People today would never submit to the strictures (mostly moral) that lovers in Rousseau's novel put themselves under.

SIMMEL AND THE GENERAL FIELD OF LOVE

Simmel (1858–1918) considers varieties of love from a social psychological point of view (e.g. philanthropy, Christian agape love, erotic love.). Love is a force in its own right and is an utterly subjective event which embraces its object in a strict and unmediated fashion (Simmel 1984: 165). 'Once love exists, elements of the most diverse description may become linked with it' (Simmel 1984: 157). Overall, however, Simmel is taken up with the question of how love might be identified or distinguished.

Love brings a sense of freedom of choice. Love is formative and transformative, for the lover loves with the whole of his or her being. This is similar to the views of Julia Kristeva, for whom love can be a revolt, where a restructuring of the ego occurs because the boundary between lovers becomes fluid (I am you and you are me).

For Simmel, there can be no legitimate basis for love because love is an inner experience (a pre-given disposition) that cannot simply be provoked by external means (even by a love object). Love aims, to be sure, to transcend the means–ends nexus. Simmel reminds us that since the beginning of modernity there has been a madness in love as it leaves all biological and utilitarian aspects behind. Love pits itself against life. It is a kind of eternal, tragic drive, without historical content. 'In love this life has transcended itself' (cf. Simmel 1984: 172).

But most importantly, Simmel says: 'Love belongs to the quantitatively indeterminable values which, in principle, are not to be "earned"' (1984: 190). Consequently, there is a conflict between love and market values. However, there is also the question of whether someone is worthy of the love of another. Reciprocity is still there, if in the background.

SURREALISM AND LOVE

André Breton, in *Mad Love* (1978), shows that love must be convulsive, a shock, an unpredictable experience. It is mad in this sense. Mad love is not love that is sought in itself, but is an experience to which one opens oneself. It is a question of being receptive to love, wherever the experience may be. So mad love can occur in the most unexpected, everyday situations: it is another version of the surrealist principle of the 'extraordinary behind the ordinary'.

Mad love is also linked to the surrealist idea of beauty. This is convulsive beauty: 'beauty "envisaged exclusively for passionate ends"', not contemplative ends (ibid.).

Love, for the surrealist, is not analytical; it is not definable as a condition, or a set of elements. One cannot, in surrealist terms, say 'I have an ideal image of Mr Right – or Ms Right'. For in surrealist terms, we don't know what love is until we have experienced it; even then, there will always be more, or less, intense versions of love. There will always be, as in all surrealist experiences, incongruities in convulsive and passionate love. In light of such situations, Breton says: 'one's pleasure is always partly accounted for by the lack of resemblance between the desired object and the discovery. Whether this discovery be artistic, scientific, philosophic or as mediocre a use as you please, it takes all the beauty that I see in it from what it is *not*. In it alone is it given us to recognise the marvellous precipitate of desire' (Breton 1978: 163).

Love appears within the surrealist interest in indexical signs. The world thus becomes a 'forest of indices' (Breton 1978: 164). It harbours meanings of all kinds, just as it shows an index* of the object causing the shadow (as in the paintings of Giorgio de Chirico).

JULIA KRISTEVA'S THEORY OF LOVE

The 'love story' is love as expression and symbol based on separation. This conforms to Kristeva's psychoanalytic approach. But it is not the only kind of love there is. There is also, in Christianity, love as identification and fusion. Kristeva's work alerts us to this (Kristeva 1987a: 23–49).

We see then that love in Christianity is a gift (something that is non-reciprocal, a disequilibrium). In this and other religious contexts, love becomes an identification and a fusing with the other. This is the 'semiotic*' aspect of love; it may be compared to the symbolic aspect, which presupposes separation.

Love inspired by religious fervour retains the element of fusion (= identification). A public example of fusion,

as opposed to separation, in love might be the outpouring of emotion after the death of Princess Diana in 1997 (she was so young too!). Although there can also be identification in symbolic love (love of the love story), it takes second place to the 'story', or expressive side of love. In the love story, the expression of love becomes almost equivalent to love itself.

In the semiotic version of love, the expression gives way to identification. This is particularly strong in certain non-Western cultures. These are often cultures of the mask (British Columbia, Alaska, New Guinea) where assuming the mask of the god turns one into the god. In short, there is fusion. In the same sense, we can also speak about the psychoanalytic notion of transferential love, where there is identification by the analysand with the analyst. Here at least one of the parties involved is anything but indifferent to the reality of the other.

Kristeva, like Luhmann, also speaks about love as an 'open system': when one person encounters another in love, that person will be affected by the encounter. This leads to a restabilisation of the psyche at a higher level. The experience can be one of renewal, or rebirth (Kristeva 1987b: 15).

As Kristeva says, love 'is a flight of metaphors – it is literature' (Kristeva 1987b: 1). Love is a series of rebirths, of separations. Kristeva, like Barthes, takes up the issue of how love can be expressed in today's sceptical world, where the old moral codes have disappeared. Love is seen as essentially imaginary*, and is at play in the psychoanalytic session. If imaginary capacities falter, so will the capacity to love.

But today, says Kristeva, we are also in crisis because love discourse has become so impoverished. We are 'drowning in a cascade of false images' (Kristeva 1987b: 375) This, however, can lead to a 'resurrection' – a kind of renewal of faith in the power of language.

Barthes, Roland (1978 [1977]) *A Lover's Discourse: Fragments*, trans. Richard Howard, New York: Hill & Wang.

Breton, André (1978 [1937]) *Mad Love* (excerpts) in *What is Surrealism? Selected Writings*, ed. F. Rosemont, New York: Monad, 160–168.

Eco, U. (1984) *Reflections on* The Name of the Rose, London: Secker & Warburg.

Eliot, T.S. (1980) *'A Dedication to my Wife'*, in *Collected Poems, 1909–1962*, London: Faber & Faber.

Kristeva, Julia (1987a [1985]) 'Credence-Credit' and 'Children and Adults', in *In the Beginning Was Love*, trans. Leon S. Roudiez, New York: Columbia. University Press.

Kristeva, Julia (1987b [1983]) *Tales of Love*, trans. Leon S. Roudiez, New York: Columbia University Press.

Luhmann, Niklas (1998 [1982]) *Love as Passion: The Codification of Intimacy*, trans. Jeremy Gaines and Doris L. Jones, Stanford, CA: Stanford University Press.

Rousseau, Jean-Jacques (1964 [1761]) *Julie, ou La nouvelle Héloïse*, in *Oeuvres complètes*, II, Paris: Gallimard, 'Bibliothèque de la Pléiade'.

Rushdie, Salman (1999) *The Ground Beneath Her Feet*, New York: Henry Holt.

Simmel, Georg (1984) *On Women, Sexuality and Love*, trans. Guy Oakes, New Haven: Yale.

See ANALYTIC–SYNTHETIC; DIFFER-ENCE–INDIVIDUALITY

M

MEMORY According to the philosopher Martin Heidegger (1889–1976) memory 'initially signifies man's inner disposition, and devotion' (Heidegger 1968: 148). This 'inner disposition' relates to having forgotten, or having recalled, Being*. Memory is a keeping, which is also a keeping from oblivion. In effect, humanity has forgotten its place in Being. But because this place is also in memory it can come forth into unconcealment.

No bigger domain in philosophy can be found than that of memory. History of course connects up with collective memory. But what does it mean to remember here? Since humans inhabit the past, it is not simply a matter of consciously recalling the facts about 'what happened'. It is also a matter of allowing the past to come forth in human actions and thought. Memory begins to border on memorialising, on myth.

On a more individual note, a distinction can be made – as in Marcel Proust's writing – between voluntary and involuntary memory. Voluntary memory is involved when an effort is made to recall something: the date of the first day at school, or the formula for relativity ($E = mc^2$). Involuntary memory foists itself upon us and can send us on a spiral of associations that could never have been anticipated. For Proust, the famous madelaine cake and the cobblestones in Venice have the effect of generating such associations. Voluntary memory is related to consciousness, while involuntary memory is related to the unconscious.

To remember has, of course, a quite mundane aspect. Since the human capacity for recall is finite, it is necessary to supplement memory by recording things, whether by writing*, images, or simple marks on a rock. There are also mnemonic devices (designed to aid recall). These can be adapted to suit individual memory styles. Some will prefer a digital approach, with a code serving as the means of recall, while others will prefer to use images. Plato believed, as many still do, that the use of prostheses to aid memory in fact leads to an atrophying of the faculty. In Plato's view, only by using the powers of memory to the full can people hope to have a very good memory (Plato 1963: sect. 275a).

In Jorge Luis Borges's story, 'Funes the Memorious', the young man from Uruguay, Ireneo Funes, could recall every detail of the past and could perceive every detail of the present moment (Borges 1970). His mind was teeming with information, from which he could not escape. Such a condition made sleep difficult; for Funes could not turn away from the world. Even when he did finally get some rest, he recalled his dreams so vividly that they became like another world parallel with the world of perception. Not being able to forget, being blessed – or cursed – with total recall meant that Funes knew the richness of experience like no other, but he could not think, if it is agreed that thinking requires one to be able to work in generalities and abstractions.

The idea of total recall has for a long time been a shibboleth of popular culture. To do well at school – in mathematics and history in particular – one needs a good memory. The clever and the intelligent are thought to be those blessed with good memory. The condition of Funes, and those like him, gives the lie to this popular idea.

To recall – to remember – it is necessary to be able to forget. Shell-shocked soldiers from the First World War suffered, said Freud (1856–1939), from being unable forget. Nietzsche (1844–1900) also made the point that humanity needs to learn how to forget in order to act in the present and the future. For while it is important to remember, it is also important not to be dragged under by the past, so that 'the tradition of all the dead generations', as Marx said, 'weighs like a nightmare on the brain of the living' (Marx 1963: 15).

Because humans have finite retentional capacity, databases and archives of every kind – both hard copy and electronic – exist to enable easy reference. New technologies make the work of retention ever more exhaustive, ever more efficient.

Bergson (1859–1941) looks at memory from a different angle. For him, memory is not simply a weaker form of perception, which enables the recall – or representation – of an event, or events (Bergson 1991). Rather, memory has its own character and laws connected with emotion and subjectivity.

Memory is essentially time*, while perception relates to space. Memory is thus fluid, while perception is punctual. To equate time with a moment, or with a series of moments, is to spatialise time – as often happens in photography, within its quest to capture the present moment – to freeze it for ever. Cinema, by contrast, in presenting the moving image*, actually gives us time *as* time, time as subjective, as memory.

Gregory Ulmer has drawn attention to the distinction between 'lived' and 'artificial' memory (Ulmer 1989: 133–134). The idea of lived memory has been extremely influential in the history of thought. With respect to the recall of an experience of an event, lived memory would be the direct and unmediated representation of the perception of the event. In lived memory it is as though the event is being experienced for a second time as if it were the first time. Funes, in 'Funes the Memorious', had a memory which could be equated directly with lived memory. In fact, so much was this the case that for him there was only one time: given that the past was recalled with exactly the same intensity as the present – given that Funes's ability entailed that there was no loss – Funes's memory was identical with his perception. To the outsider, at least, Funes lived an intolerable life because he did not *know* anything precisely because there was no loss involved. To know, is, in a sense, to (partially) forget.

Artificial memory implies not only that memory entails a certain loss, but also that knowledge, understanding and insight are more important in recall than raw information supplied by perception. Memory becomes the code(s) individuals use to recall. In pre-printing societies, the skill of recall was embedded in a learned technique called mnemonics. One such system, used by

Cicero, was to put material to be recalled in specific places on an imaginary walk. Such a walk might also include the places where one had lived as a child. This technique can be called a code* to the extent that there is no necessary resemblance between the mnemonic and what is to be recalled. Memory – or remembering – can, in this way, be thoroughly individualised, derived as it is from biographical and other materials originating in personal experience or historical events. Here memory becomes a form of invention, since a link between the material to be recalled and the mode of recall is created.

Bergson, Henri (1991 [1939]) *Matter and Memory*, trans. Nancy Margaret Paul and W. Scott Palmer, New York: Zone Books.

Borges, Jorge Luis (1970 [1953]) 'Funes the Memorious', trans. James E. Irby, in *Labyrinths*, Harmondsworth: Penguin.

Heidegger, Martin (1968 [1954]) *What Is Called Thinking?*, trans. J. Glenn Gray, New York: Harper & Row.

Marx, Karl (1963) *The Eighteenth Brumaire of Louis Bonaparte*, New York: International Publishers.

Plato (1963) *Phaedrus*, trans. R. Hackforth, in *The Collected Dialogues of Plato*, ed. Edith Hamilton and Huntington Cairns, Princeton, NJ: Princeton University Press.

Ulmer, Gregory (1989) *Teletheory: Grammatology in the Age of Video*, New York: Routledge.

See WRITING

METAPHOR

Metaphor comes from the Greek *metaphora*, meaning, 'to transfer, or transport across'. As a rhetorical figure, metaphor means taking a word, or group of words, from one context and meaning, and placing them in another, so that a similarity appears between two elements once treated as different.

In discussions of metaphor, a question has been raised as to the scope of the term. Sometimes metaphor functions as a rhetorical figure in its own right, having its own characteristics, while at other times, metaphor – or the metaphorical – has come to stand for the whole domain of figurative language. However, if metaphor is so used, it becomes a part standing for the whole, and is, *ipso facto*, another rhetorical figure: a synecdoche. This is paradoxical at least, if not contradictory.

In a famous discussion of metaphor, the linguist, Roman Jakobson (1896–1982), distinguished metaphor, as similarity, from metonomy, as contiguity (Jakobson 1995: 115–33). Here, metaphor occupies the vertical axis, and metonymy the horizontal axis of linguistic activity. Metaphor comes to have a creative spark through linking between things that are initially unrelated. The true metaphor is not a cliché ('his speech cut the ground from under me'), but a completely new image* ('In the talk, he was the Tory cow to the Marxist lion'). Catachresis is a metaphor which has become literalised, and is found in expressions like 'the leaves of the book', where 'leaves' is a substitute for pages.

In another formulation, the psychoanalyst, Jacques Lacan (1901–80), inspired by Jakobson, equates metaphor with Freud's notion of condensation in dream work, where a single image contains multiple associations (Lacan 1977) – or, as Lacan says, where there is 'word for word substitution'. The link between one word and another would here be surprising and unexpected.

Jacques Derrida (b. 1930) looks at the way that metaphor has ultimately been linked to a real origin: in other words, figurative language has been linked to a literal reality (Derrida 1982). Because there is something real, there can be something metaphorical with which it can be compared. On this reading, there is a specific epistemology attached to the notion of metaphor. Metaphor is connected to ways of knowing the world. For Derrida, the real object, or the true reality, can only be present through a quasi-metaphorical structure. The image of true knowledge as enlightenment is one such example. Plato's image of truth as equivalent to going into the sun is possibly the origin of the idea of light being so important in relation to truth and knowledge. To know is thus to shed light on something. If, by contrast, something is obscure, it is an obstacle to knowing. Clarity also accompanies true knowledge. God is light. Gradually, it becomes difficult to separate the figurative from the literal, as Paul de Man showed (de Man 1979).

However, if language as such is metaphorical through and through (word does not equal thing; signifier does not equal signified, as the etymology of words begins to show), how is it possible for language to fulfil its literal function? No doubt, it is here that the imaginary domain of each language user comes into play. In its literal mode language, working through the user's imaginary, is transparent: the word, 'rose' brings the rose to us as though it were real. 'As though it were real': such is the key to understanding language as transparent. When confronted with the obstacle of language – as in the work of certain poets or when encountering a foreign language – the word as such appears before us. Transparency is gone and metaphor becomes opaque. Only a renewed effort to stimulate imaginary capacities can turn language into some kind of transparency once again. This, thinkers like Julia Kristeva have suggested, is a crucial task for those living in a society of the spectacle*, where the image as image – the image becoming a simulacrum* – tends to blot out transparency (Kristeva 1995).

From another perspective, metaphor has been a problem for philosophy and science. To the extent that their vehicle of expression is language, and the aim is truth, or factual description, the need for complete transparency is paramount. However, natural language is riven with metaphorical and figurative elements: truth is an 'island', it has been said. Moreover, it is often necessary to resort to metaphor in order to explain what would be otherwise inexplicable. Thus physicists describe 'waves' circling around a nucleus. They also talk about 'orbits', as though the micro level was a reflection of the macro universe. Metaphor is endemic to language and communication. To eliminate it would lead to atrophy in meaning and in the linguistic process itself.

de Man, Paul (1979) *Allegories of Reading: Figural Language in Rousseau, Nietzsche, Rilke, and Proust*, New Haven and London: Yale University Press.

Derrida, Jacques (1982 [1972]) 'White Mythology: Metaphor in the Text of Philosophy', in *Margins of Philosophy*, trans. Alan Bass, Chicago: University of Chicago Press.

Jakobson, Roman (1995) *On Language*, ed. Linda R. Waugh and Monique Monville-Burston, Cambridge, Mass., and London: Harvard University Press.

Kristeva, Julia (1995 [1993]) 'The Soul and the Image', in *New Maladies of the Soul*, trans. Ross Guberman, New York: Columbia University Press.

Lacan, Jacques (1977 [1966]) 'The Agency of the Letter in the Unconscious, or Reason since Freud', in *Écrits: A Selection*, trans. Alan Sheridan, London: Tavistock.

See SIGN: SIGNIFIER/SIGNIFIED; WRITING

METAPHYSICS

Metaphysics, it almost goes without saying, is rooted in the history of philosophy. For Aristotle, who wrote a text of the same name, metaphysics is a first philosophy, or an ontology*. In Medieval Greek *ta metaphusica* referred to 'the works after physics' (meta- and physics), and not a realm beyond the physical world. The title applied, from at least first century AD to the 13 books of Aristotle dealing with questions of ontology (Aristotle 1941).

Although the title, 'Metaphysics', initially described the received arrangement of Aristotle's writings (the whole collection of treatises on matters of natural science), the subject matter of the Metaphysics is the foundations of thought, or 'first philosophy'. From an early period, then, metaphysics was used as a name for the branch of study treated by Aristotle in the books following those dealing with the physical world; hence it came to be misinterpreted as meaning 'the science of things transcending what is physical or natural'. This misinterpretation is even found, though rarely, in Greek writers.

Metaphysics looks at being, or at 'what is', in the deepest sense. It goes 'beyond the physical' and examines questions that cannot be answered through referring to matters of fact, since it is precisely the basis of facts that constitutes the project of metaphysics. Indeed, the ground of science as a whole, or of the scientific method, is the focus of an inquiry in metaphysics.

Historically, metaphysics has never had much of a run in the Anglo-American tradition of analytical and pragmatic philosophy, as it is considered to be too speculative and imprecise (see analytic–synthetic). For this tradition, metaphysics deals with questions (what is Being*? what is essence? what is thinking? what is a world?) which just cannot be answered; or rather, one would have to be God in order to answer them. Metaphysics, the analytical tradition suspects, seems to get too close to theology, and too far away from the secular humanism of modernity* for it to be of much value today. In the 1930s the logical positivist movement claimed that philosophy, as a genuine branch of knowledge, must be distinguished from metaphysics. In 1937, Rudolf Carnap (1891–1970), a leader of the Vienna Circle of logical positivists, said that the sentences of metaphysics are pseudo-sentences which on logical analysis are proved to be either empty phrases or phrases which violate the rules of syntax.

While it is true that metaphysics, as the asking of key questions of Being, has been largely relegated to the work of Martin Heidegger (1889–1976), it is also significant that in the age of late modernity and postmodernity* it is increasingly difficult to address the idea of Being and the foundations of thought. This is almost the defining characteristic of the secular age, for better or for worse – and some would say, for worse. For a loss of spirituality is also implied here.

Heidegger is a proponent of the use of concepts of metaphysics as a 'comprehensive questioning' in order to reveal the nature of Being (Heidegger

1995: 24). Unlike the philosophers of the Anglo-American analytical tradition, Heidegger links metaphysics with the search for truth*. In other words, truth here cannot be limited to an empirical or factual truth. However, 'metaphysics' goes through an evolution in Heidegger's thought. Prior to the 1930s, it poses all the key questions of ontology, while after this time it refers to thought that has come to a standstill, since this thought reaches for a set of stock answers in response to key questions, rather than engaging in the activity of thinking. After Heidegger, metaphysics as a set of received ideas is a key theme in the work of deconstruction*, which shows that a metaphysical approach to issues installs determinism at the heart of thought on topics such as writing*, metaphor*, origin, difference, identity*, hospitality, logos, technology and others. Here, metaphysics approximates an unquestioned assumption. And the unquestioned assumption *par excellence* is the importance of 'presence'. Presence implies that an entity is given in a full, complete and irrefutable way (because without contradiction). Such a notion of presence means that difference is ruled out, along with any other terms which imply that an entity is not identical with itself, self-identity being the mark of presence. On closer inspection, the notion of presence also rules out time*: for presence is a present, timeless moment. Time, in the deepest sense – time as difference – renders presence problematic. Debate has ensued about whether Heidegger interprets Being as presence, or whether, as the title of Heidegger's inaugural work, *Being and Time* (1996), suggests, Being is essentially in time and therefore not entirely 'present'.

Marx said that, up until the modern era (the nineteenth century), philosophy was essentially contemplative. It attempted to say how the world was in its essential nature, forgetting that the act of contemplation itself is also part of the world and is therefore involved with what it contemplates. For contemplation to work, the philosopher would indeed need to be outside the world in the realm of metaphysics, as this term is commonly understood. Marx therefore points up an inherently analytical bias in the history of philosophy – at least as he understands it. 'The point is to change the world' (as Marx's 'Eleventh Thesis on Feuerbach' put it: Marx 1967: 402) and thus reject metaphysics.

Perhaps Marx also went too far. For it is not necessarily a matter of rejecting contemplation as a whole, but of using it as a creative force, much as Heidegger attempts to do when he says that Being is an original saying, or speaking. Language, then, does not reflect or express Being; it is the 'house of Being' (Heidegger 1993: 217) and as such, a mode of disclosing Being. Language speaking is itself original. Contemplation – or thinking – would similarly claim to be original.

Aristotle (1941) *Metaphysica* (Metaphysics), in *The Basic Works of Aristotle*, New York: Random House.

Heidegger, Martin (1993 [1947]) 'Letter on Humanism', in *Basic Writings*, ed. David Farrell Krell, London: Routledge.

Heidegger, Martin (1995) *The Fundamental Concepts of Metaphysics: World, Finitude, Solitude*, trans. William McNeill and Nicholas Walker, Bloomington and Indianapolis: Indiana University Press.

Heidegger, Martin (1996 [1927]) *Being and Time. A Translation of* Sein und Zeit, trans. Joan Stambaugh, Albany: State University of New York Press.

Marx, Karl (1967 [1888]) 'Theses on Feuerbach', in *Writings of the Young Marx on Philosophy and Society*, trans. and ed. Loyd D. Easton and Kurt H. Guddat, New York: Anchor Books.

See ANALYTIC–SYNTHETIC; DECONSTRUCTION; DIFFERENCE–INDIVIDUALITY; *LOGOS-MYTHOS*; TECHNICS

MIMESIS

For Aristotle and Plato, *mimēsis*, meaning 'to show', is contrasted with diegesis*, to narrate a story (including the spatiotemporal coordinates of that story). In Aristotle, this distinction turns on the difference between describing events – or narrative – and acting out events – or drama. Mimesis, then, centres in the showing as drama.

Subsequently, mimesis has come to mean imitation as representation based on a likeness between the representer and the represented. In this sense, mimesis tends towards the features of an icon*. And indeed, in its original, Platonic sense icon is a good representation. It is mimesis. Mimesis which simply conforms to the object imitated readily becomes a technical procedure. Instead of showing (which entails doing), mimesis becomes what is plausible, or credible in light of an understanding of what the (original) object is deemed to be. This mode of mimesis is comforting and conservative, whereas mimesis as showing is often shocking.

Walter Benjamin (1892–1940) says that mimesis – attaining its highest form in the human being – is 'the capacity for producing similarities' (Benjamin 1986: 333). With these words, the interpreter of modernity* succinctly provides an insight into mimesis that has not yet been fully appreciated. For not only does he avoid trying to solve the impossible problem of specifying the relation of the imitation to the imitated (the problem of representation), but he also gives mimesis a synthetic and creative twist. Indeed, Benjamin's approach recalls the surrealist art of bringing (different) things into proximity with each other, so that one *finds* similarities. Sense is thus made of Picasso's 'I do not seek, I find'. And so the child who is a train (to cite one of Benjamin's examples), *creates* the similarity: he makes his 'choo-choo-o-o-o' equivalent to the whistle, his body equivalent to the engine. Here, it makes no sense to ask whether the child is *like* a train because the issue concerns the creation of similarity, not the technical capacity to produce a realistic copy of the imitated. The latter, realist, or correspondence conception of mimesis throws light on one form of it, but has also inhibited the attempt to understand metaphor as a whole.

But instead of a so-called synthetic mimesis being a real advance in our understanding, might it not mean that mimesis is implicated in the projection of images into things, so that mimetic insights become a purely psychological phenomenon? In this sense, Gombrich invokes the Rorschach test in his discussion of 'likeness' (Gombrich 1983: 89). He invokes the same theme in talking about the mask and the face. Gombrich argues that recognition of facial features in a diversity of pictures implies that the human face has a universal structure, to which human beings have a propensity to respond. In other words, the objective features of the face correspond to the psychological predisposition to discover these features in what can be extremely minimalist representations. The complex human face, reduced to its simplest and most basic elements, can then be recognised everywhere. Indeed, it can then be reproduced in a codified form.

But likeness is also enacted in mimetic currents, as we shall see below. As such, mimesis does not just occur analytically, where complexity* is reduced to simplicity – to basic elements – and these then copied. It also occurs in a synthetic, creative way. Thus in the example, cited by Gombrich, of Picasso's portrait of Françoise Gilot entitled, *Françoise Gilot, 'FemmeFleur'* (1946), the portrait does not reproduce the face and body of Gilot reduced to its essential elements, but reveals part of the subject, as if for the first time (Gombrich 1986: 123). Revealing, indeed, takes over from representation as the repetition of what we already know. Revealing, in short, takes over from recognition. In this sense, art becomes a mode of discovery. But is it still mimetic? The answer is that it is, because something is now brought into relation with something else. Something is being imitated, or evokes something – Gilot's name is in Picasso's title, after all – even if it is difficult in the beginning to determine what it is. Indeed, inventive mimesis is intimately tied to naming. The point, though, is that mimesis can be inventive, and thus synthetic, as well as analytical. Inventive mimesis has its roots in surrealism.

Reminiscent of the surrealist effort to forge similarities is Benjamin's desire to make a book consisting entirely of quotations. As with collage, the juxtaposition of the elements of such a book opens it to the effects of chance*, effects which could not be predicted. Chance makes such a book of quotations a synthetic, not an analytical entity. The whole is not simply equivalent to the sum of the parts; knowing what each of the parts is does not automatically reveal the nature of the whole. Mimesis, in Benjamin's sense, then, is the kind of thing that is not given in the parts of which it is composed. Indeed, Benjamin's *oeuvre* as a whole is not analytical: its unity does not automatically emerge from the sum of its parts.

Now we turn, in the work of Sartre, to mimesis as an evocation. To show that perception and image* should not be confused, Sartre claims, is as important as showing that an image is not a simulacrum*. Thus, to think the image of a painting is not to think it as a painted image. In a painting of his friend Pierre, says Sartre, Pierre is not thought as the image of the painting; the painting is not an image of Pierre. Sartre thus concludes: 'In the imaging attitude, this painting is nothing but a way for Pierre to appear to me as absent. Thus the painting *gives* Pierre, although he is not there' (Sartre 1986: 54. My translation). Through a similar logic an image as an imitation is not an analogon of what is imitated; the imitation, in other words, is not a separate entity. Thus, the imitation of Maurice Chevalier does not produce a separate image in the mind which may then be compared with the imitated singer (an analytical procedure) (Sartre 1986: 56). Rather, the imitation is made by signs given by the imitator (impersonator), and these signs evoke Maurice Chevalier himself. In short, the imitator *is* Maurice Chevalier. As such, imitation evokes the possessed of primitive dance rituals (Sartre 1986: 64).

According to René Girard (1987: 7), all learning is mimetic. If this be true, to what extent is inventiveness – or creativeness – learned? Or better: to what extent is learning as imitation the antithesis of creativeness? An answer is given by Kant (1824–70) in the *Critique of Judgement* when he says that the creative genius 'is an example, not for imitation (for then that would mean the loss of the element of genius, and just the very soul of the work), but to be followed by another genius – one whom it arouses to a sense of his own originality' (Kant 1973: 181 para. 49). To be sure, to imitate originality opens up a paradox: a sameness (originality) in difference (creativeness). Mimesis in relation to originality would thus be founded on an experience, not a model. Teaching here would be about attempting to elicit an experience of originality – allowing originality to appear – rather than about imposing procedures and techniques on a student as though these were ends in themselves.

Benjamin, Walter (1986) 'On the Mimetic Faculty', in *Reflections: Essays, Aphorisms, Autobiographical Writings*, trans. Edmund Jephcott, New York: Schocken Books.

Girard, René (1987 [1978]) *Things Hidden since the Foundation of the World*, trans. Stephen Bann and Michael Metteer, Stanford, CA: Stanford University Press.

Gombrich, E.H. (1983) *Art and Illusion: A Study in the Psychology of Pictorial Representation*, 5th edn, Oxford: Phaidon.

Gombrich, E.H. (1986) *The Image and the Eye: Further Studies in the Psychology of Pictorial Representation*, Oxford: Phaidon.

Kant, Immanuel (1973) *Critique of Judgement*, trans. J.C. Meredith, Oxford: Clarendon Press.

Sartre, Jean-Paul (1986 [1940]) *L'Imaginaire: psychologie phénoménologique de l'imagination*, Paris: Gallimard.

See ANALYTIC–SYNTHETIC; TECHNICS

MODERNITY

Modernity has been a key idea in the social sciences and humanities, particularly in sociology. Sometimes confused with modernism, or modernisation, modernity refers to the historical reality which unfolded, first in Europe, and then in America, between the Renaissance and the twentieth century (1492–1939). Modernity includes the Industrial Revolution in its purview, and has cultural, political and psychological aspects. Modernity is the identity a whole era has given itself, an era that may only now be coming to an end.

Some of the descriptive features of modernity include the rise of a complex money economy and the market system that goes with it: exchange-value comes to take precedence over use-value, to use Marx's terms. Politically, modernity signals the rise of democracy and the republics through which it becomes manifest (French and American). Culturally, there is the rise in education and the analytical rationality which accompanies a literate society. Literacy leads to a revolution in forms of communication (newspapers and, subsequently, electronic media) and to the rise of public opinion. There is a focus on, and development of, individuality, as the traditional kinship forms of community in the countryside give way to city living. Georg Simmel is one of the great observers of this process (Simmel 1971). A new kind of freedom* and community emerge based on formal rights and obligations, rather than on solidarity. Love*, especially in its romantic incarnation, leads the way with its emphasis on an individual's choice of partner, and not on alliances pre-arranged by families.

Accompanying the evolution of individuality is the development of modern forms of the subject as actor and psychological being possessed of an intimate private self to which, in principle, only the subject* itself has unfettered access. This gives rise to a difference between a public and private self, which is hardly known in pre-Renaissance times.

Modernity, then, involves freeing the individual from tradition – as Simmel would say – or it means wrenching him or her from the tranquillity of a communal life now gone for ever. In Marx's terms it could mean alienation*.

A certain rationality emerges with modernity: what Max Weber calls *Zweckrationalität*, means–ends, or formal rationality, which he contrasts with *Wertrationalität*, or substantive rationality (Weber 1964: 184–186). Formal rationality valorises the mastery of technical means over moral, political or religious ends. Such rationality – also known as instrumental rationality – says how ends can be achieved; it makes no judgement of the value of the end sought. As purely formal, it is the rationality of bureaucracy – the ethic of bureaucracy being, 'without regard for persons', or the following of rational procedures regardless of the individuals involved. Corruption in politics tends to occur through the violation of this ethic.

And so modernity stands for the development of a particular form of reason and rationality. In Kant, the employment of this reason is equivalent to humanity's emergent maturity and autonomy, as opposed to its childhood and heteronomy (Kant 1977: 54–60). That is, modernity gives rise to the recognition by humanity that it is responsible for the law (political and moral) and, by extension, for the state of the world. Modernity in Kant, and to some extent in Marx's early writing, is thus about the secularisation and humanisation of the world. Humanity has to take responsibility for its own destiny; it can no longer rely on the props of tradition, God, myth, etc. In its clearest form in Ludwig Feuerbach (1804–72. Left-wing disciple of Hegel), man is responsible (for creating) God, and not the reverse (Feuerbach 1957).

With the growing secularisation of society, science – at least in the European world – and its rational method comes to challenge Christian religious views of the world. Evolution succeeds creationism as the dominant paradigm. Education becomes increasingly secular; Church becomes separate from State; religious allegiance becomes private; the sacred retreats into the margins of social and cultural life. The idea of a 'natural order of things' which cannot be changed is discredited in light of contingency and the historical nature of the cultural order. The world of modernity is thus a world of decontextualisation and abstraction; context as tradition (the natural order of things) takes a back seat.

Decontextualisation also contributes to modernity and its relation to aesthetics. Works of art become autonomous and disconnected from any specific context. The gallery system emerges. So-called traditional art can acquire qualities that are far removed from the work's embeddedness in a tradition. Australian Aboriginal art is a case in point. Art becomes tied to the value the art object is deemed to have in itself independently of context. Following this principle, beauty* in Kant's aesthetics* is independent of context (Kant 1952).

A secular culture* is one that begins to give precedence to time over place. Indeed, modernity is an epoch of movement and change. The information* age is the outcome of modernity's valorisation of time over space. Or rather, modernity valorises the irreversible time of contingency over the reversible time of tradition.

It is in this vein that Marshall Berman reads Marx, emphasising Marx's recognition of the progressive nature of a bourgeois class which destroys tradition, even while it 'produces its own gravediggers': the proletariat. 'All that is solid melts into air...' (Berman 1983).

For the poet, Charles Baudelaire (1821–67), modernity is captured in Edgar Allan Poe's (1809–49) short story, 'The Man in the Crowd' (Poe 1982). Who is this man? Before answering this question, we can consider Walter Benjamin's commentary in 'Paris, Capital of the Nineteenth Century' (Benjamin 1986). Much of what is of interest to us can be summarised by four key terms: 'fashion', 'panoramas', 'novelty', and 'flâneur'.

FASHION

To speak about fashion is to speak about what houses fashionable goods: it is the arcades built in the 1820s which are crucial here. Built from iron and glass, allowing the light to penetrate and thus enabling the cultivation of plants *inside*, the Paris arcades are the origin of the modern department store and the boutique shop. Here, too, we have the emergence of 'panoramas', 'an expression of a new feeling about life' (Benjamin 1986: 150). Panoramas are painted scenes illuminated by a light at the back. There were 'tireless exertions of technical skill to make panoramas the scenes of a perfect imitation of nature'.

PANORAMAS

- Panoramas point to photography and, beyond that, to sound films and cinema. The panorama is also another way of bringing nature into the city.
- Above all, the arcades, and thence the World Exhibitions, are places where merchandise of every sort can be displayed. They are where mass-produced fashion is first introduced into society.
- Exhibitions in the 1850s, and the World Exhibition of 1867, become the place for displaying commodities. 'Fashion prescribes the ritual according to which the commodity fetish wishes to be worshipped' (Benjamin 1986: 153). Fashion is luxury before it is utility. Benjamin speaks here of the 'phantasmagoria of capitalist culture' (ibid.) because the goods are the objects of phantasy and desire before they are objects of immediate need (see Fantasy/Phantasy, Fantasm).

NOVELTY

In the great exhibitions, goods are displayed for purchase. Do these goods correspond to the needs of the people? The answer is 'no'. Goods are bought and sold for their own sake, for the sake of novelty and fashion. Need ceases to have any immediate impact here. These are commodities, which have exchange or market value before they have the value of something that is needed to sustain human life (the use-value of a good).

Paris becomes the place of changing fashion and novelty in the range of goods available. All Europe is moving in the direction signalled by Paris, but Paris is the capital of the nineteenth century. And Baudelaire makes the city of Paris, in all its glory and horror, the subject of lyric poetry. The poet of modernity makes urban experience the subject of his work. Baudelaire's task is to find the beauty in evil.

THE FLÂNEUR

For the first time people leave their residences in order to walk, or stroll, as a form of leisure. So many things to see, even if their price puts them out of reach. The arcades, panoramas, shops of all kinds, exhibitions, are sights to be seen. Photography is invented. Images of all kinds emerge. Advertising is born. But above all, there is so much to see, so many little alleyways and courtyards that one would not have dreamed existed. The Sunday stroll along the river-bank is part of the arrival of the stroller, who, in French, is called a *flâneur*.

Because Baudelaire gives full rein to the streets of Paris and to the *flâneur* in his poetry and other writings, he describes things which the public of the time, as represented by the judgement of the courts, would have preferred not to know. Before Joyce, Baudelaire also had his writing censored, or even banned. Its references to sexuality and, in particular, to prostitution were too much.

Baudelaire's life was short. But had it been even shorter he might well have achieved most of what he became famous for. Much of his major poetry had been written by the time he was in his mid-twenties; he had travelled; he had formed the relationship that would weigh on him for the remainder of his life; he had contracted the venereal disease that would eventually kill him. In short, Baudelaire's life was like a steam-engine that ran out of steam.

Pleasure and work as mediated by time constitute the fate of the human being, according to Baudelaire. Time, clearly, is the irreversible time of the event that we spoke of earlier. Baudelaire's life, therefore, tends to be the embodiment of the time he thought dominated life. Or again, Baudelaire exemplifies the idea that pleasure ends in death. Without the replacement of the energy (i.e. without work) that is lost in pleasure, complete burn-out results. This is a logic of thermodynamics* – the incarnation of the law of entropy*. It is a different logic to the one now coming into being with the emergence of digital* technology: a 'cool' technology. This is the logic of the information society. But that is another story.

The *flâneur*, then, embodies thermodynamic logic. As *flâneur*, however, the walker does not run down but always finds renewed energy in order to keep strolling. The *flâneur* does not have anywhere to go because strolling itself is what drives him on. The *flâneur* revels in contingency and the chance events of experience. For the *flâneur*, there is always a new experience around the corner. Product of the modern city and the rise of commodities, the *flâneur*'s trajectory is no doubt partly determined by the search for novelty and the consumer culture that this implies. But, from a slightly different angle, what consumes his energy is the sense of the 'transitory, the fugitive, the contingent'. The story of 'The Man of the Crowd' illustrates this. The man of the crowd is the *flâneur* who is followed throughout the night so that one might learn where he is going. But, of course, this man is going nowhere in particular; instead, it is the journey that interests him; chance events determine his trajectory.

CONSTANTIN GUYS, PAINTER OF MODERN LIFE

Why did Baudelaire write so appreciatively of Constantin Guys, a painter of modest reputation and talents? (Baudelaire 1972: 390–435) The answer is that Guys painted 'this transitory, fleeting element of life'. He painted contingency. Every era has its own characteristics: its professions, classes, gestures, manners, fashions. Guys captures these. He did not immerse himself in the ideality of antiquity, but in the reality of modernity. He paints the soldier, the dandy, animals, women. He captures things as they happen. He takes a journalist's approach to reality. He focuses on detail rather than on form, on the ephemeral, rather than on eternal truths. Guys paints modernity.

Baudelaire, Charles (1972) 'The Painter of Modern Life', in *Selected Writings on Art and Artists*, trans. P.E. Charvet, Harmondsworth: Penguin.
Benjamin, Walter (1986) 'Paris, Capital of the Nineteenth Century', in *Reflections: Essays, Aphorisms, Autobiographical Writings*, trans. Edmund Jephcott, New York: Schocken Books.
Berman, Marshall (1983) *All that is Solid Melts into Air*, London: Verso.
Feuerbach, Ludwig (1957 [1841]) *The Essence of Christianity*, trans. George Eliot, New York: Harper & Row, Harper Torchbooks.
Kant, Immanuel (1952 [1790]) *The Critique of Judgement*, trans. James Creed Meredith, Oxford: Oxford University Press.
Kant, Immanuel (1977 [1784]) 'An Answer to the Question: "What is Enlightenment?"', in *Kant's Political Writings*, trans. H.B. Nisbet, Cambridge: Cambridge University Press.
Poe, Edgar Allan (1982) 'The Man of the Crowd', in *The Complete Tales and Poems of Edgar Allan Poe*, Harmondsworth: Penguin.
Simmel, Georg (1971) 'The Metropolis and Mental Life', trans. Edward A. Shils, in *On Individuality and Social Forms: Selected Writings*, Chicago and London: University of Chicago Press.
Weber, Max (1964) *The Theory of Social and Economic Organisation*, trans. A.M. Henderson and Talcott Parsons, New York: The Free Press; London: Collier-Macmillan.

See ANALYTIC–SYNTHETIC

MONEY

The value of money initially included its material form. Hoarding and flight of money was thus a problem in Europe in the sixteenth and seventeenth centuries. Money is also 'scriptural' (book-keeping) and, latterly, electronic. In this light, it is clear that money, as money, is now becoming independent of it material form. The materiality, or money's incarnation – no doubt necessary – is a representation, or is symbolic; it is not the thing itself; it is not value as such, any more than a word in language is the thing it represents. This is not to deny that money has been understood in the opposite sense as a pure materiality that has also been fetishised. Gold is the leading example of this. The search for gold in the Americas following the 1492 voyage of Christopher Columbus is surely the clearest example in European history of money taken as a pure fetish.

A fully developed money economy*, and the accompanying market mechanism, only gradually came into being in Europe, in an uneven way after the Industrial Revolution of the eighteenth century. Silver was originally reserved for everyday transactions – hence the French word for money is *l'argent* (silver). The progressive articulation of a money economy affects the whole of society (nothing can be left untouched – not even those who want to remain untouched). This is because money unleashes exchange at a vastly increased rate compared to barter transactions, or compared to the velocity of exchange in the money economy in its early stages, when the abstract nature of money is yet to be appreciated. Once it is, people know that exchange sends things out of the control of individuals; transactions eventually begin to approach the speed of light as money assumes an electronic form. Virtuality joins abstraction.

Money is not the same as wealth. It is the measure of wealth. Money is also the necessary component of an efficient budgetary system and is the means of accounting. Money, then, is not capital, but is the oil that lubricates the wheels of capitalism. This, too, was not well understood in the early days of the modern economy, when the fetishistic view of money predominated. Only the miser accumulates the material form of money for its own sake. The miser joins the fetishist in failing to accept money as money – that is, as failing to accept it as a purely abstract medium. Eventually, this aspect of money will lead many to feel that it is an alien and almost inhuman force which causes a sense of loss of context and the loss of the feelings which go with it. Money for service is never appropriate in the family home for this reason.

Trade was a key stimulus to the growth of the money economy. Money as a means enables exchange* to take place throughout the world, and is the precondition of a world market and the rapid circulation of people, goods and services this entails. Money, in this sense, facilitates the transcendence of all local forms.

A 'coded money value' evolves for 'all objects and occupations'. The world becomes a complex system of mediations and deferred actions and gratifications. Life loses its immediacy. Money undermines the idea of a 'simple' life. It breaks the one-to-one correspondence between production and consumption, which some believe to be characteristic of hunter-gatherer societies.

In short, money becomes part of a new circulation of people and goods and becomes the basis of intercultural societies. With traditional forms of barter, it was necessary for those involved to be there on the spot, in the community. Money, by contrast, enables movement, circulation and decontextualisation: people are no longer materially bound to their communities. Simmel remarks, at the beginning of 'Money in Modern Culture', that: 'This uniformity [of community] was destroyed by modernity' (1991: 17). And: 'This interdependence of personality and material relationships, which is typical of the barter economy, is dissolved by the money economy' (1991: 18). The emergence of a single currency, the Euro, will increase the volume of international economic transactions even further.

As Simmel (1858–1918) was one of the first to show, money contributes to the production of the following traits: independence, autonomy of personality, individuality. By contrast, the weavers' guild was not simply a number of individuals speaking/acting with one voice; it was an indissoluble community, like a family*.

Simmel reinforces the notion of money as completely divorced from its materiality and place of origin. It is a means only; a form of mediation that allows exchanges to take place, prices to be recorded, and wealth to be measured. Through price, money marks quantity; it does not mark quality. Simmel links money to all the features of urban life that have become so familiar: big cities; impersonality of exchange relations; the basis of the general equivalent (exactness), which indicates the way wealth is distributed; money as a commodity, where currencies are bought and sold against the changes in exchange rates. The last of these is made possible by the dominance of relativity (one currency against another, rather than currencies being measured against an intrinsic substance, such as gold). Money thus encourages a consumer mentality (interest in price of things); it is objective in nature and stands against all subjective sentiments; it increases the level of abstraction of modern culture* (this implies decontextualisation).

Money, it is said, rules out sentiment as the determining basis of human relationships. This is why people speak of love* or money. But is it as straightforward as this?

In 'The Metropolis and Mental Life' (1971), Simmel takes up a point made in his writing on money: he looks at the psychological foundation of life in the city. Money, and a highly complex money economy, have a great impact on the form and reality of the modern city. Some characteristics listed by Simmel are as follows:

1 The city produces the blasé* attitude, which is a mechanism for filtering out a surfeit of stimuli. This also results in more formal interactions between people.
2 Life takes on an increasingly intellectualistic tone: 'All emotional relationships between persons rest on their individuality, whereas intellectual relationships deal with persons as numbers, that is, with elements which, in themselves, are indifferent' (Simmel 1971: 326).
3 The city implies a decontextualisation, as life in big cities is international and cosmopolitan; cities contain people from a diversity of origins.
4 Despite the city's diversity, money deals with what is common to all, i.e. with exchange, and therefore with the division of labour. Labour-power* becomes a reality and barter disappears.
5 Community, which depends on an emotional bond between its members, is thus under threat in the city.
6 Through money – e.g. budgeting – the modern mind becomes a calculating one. Science dreams of turning the world into an arithmetical problem. It wants to quantify life, rather than deal with quality.
7 As 'punctuality, calculability and exactness' are key features of the modern city, village life stands in marked contrast. In the village, time is substantive (based on seasons), rather than formal (based on clocks).
8 There is greater freedom for the individual – greater independence – in the city, but a greater risk of alienation*.
9 The city overtakes every personal element, and brings intense specialisation. This is what Simmel calls the dominance of objective culture. The personality is no longer nourished as a whole – that is, spiritually in accordance with moral values. The implication is that individuals become increasingly normalised by the depersonalisation of life. There is no room for

idiosyncratic beings – or at least the struggle to be unique is thwarted by objectivising forces and liberal orthodoxy.

10 The fetishisation of money tends to be minimal in the city. Of course, people want wealth, but this is very different from the emotional attachment a Spaniard might have had for gold in Mexico or Peru. The miser and the stockbroker are very different animals.

11 The lust for money is very different from the drive for wealth. One sees money as an end in itself; the other sees it as a means to end. One adopts an absolutist approach; the other an instrumentalist approach.

Be all this as it may, the dominant characteristic of money is its status and function as a general equivalent. Money makes it possible to compare different things through price. Through price, money wipes out difference. Through price, everything becomes relative: the price of one thing (a university degree) can be compared with the price of another (a house). Like language, to which it has been compared, money can be said to constitute a system of differences without positive terms. Relativity is key to the nature of money. This is perhaps why it has also been associated with the rise of nihilism*.

Simmel, Georg (1971) 'The Metropolis and Mental Life', trans. Edward A. Shils, in *On Individuality and Social Forms: Selected Writings*, Chicago and London: University of Chicago Press.
Simmel, Georg (1991) 'Money in Modern Culture', trans. Mark Ritter, *Theory, Culture and Society*, 8 (3): 17–31.

See DIFFERENCE-INDIVIDUALITY

MONTAGE

Although montage – from the French, *monter*, to mount – is a term used in relation to cinema, it has also come to have a wider application in the idea of juxtaposing elements originating in different contexts. By splicing images together in a particular way, a film director can put his or her stamp firmly on the final product, which is a continuous film. This film is a new interlacing, or interweaving, of relatively heterogeneous elements. A new whole is created; the whole is not given automatically through pointing the camera at reality and letting the film roll. Along with cuts and takes (including out-takes) in the making of a film, there is above all the editing cut based on a final montage of images. The Russian film director, Sergei Eisenstein (1898–1948), developed what came to be called an intellectual montage, where strikingly different images were juxtaposed in order to suggest a particular concept (see Eisenstein 1949). The goal is to convey thought as well as action.

This is a very physicalist view of the montage process, as simply related to the splicing together of different celluloid images. But the issue is about ideas in cinema, a notion that is sharpened by Eisenstein's desire to make a film of the first volume of Marx's *Capital*. Here, the task is to work out how abstract ideas can be translated into a medium like film. What kinds of image would suggest the idea of a commodity? Clearly, a traditional, realist approach is not going to work; only a highly inventive approach will have any hope of success. Although Eisenstein only made notes for the project, the very idea of it broadens an understanding of what montage can be. For it is the technique of montage as suggestive of ideas (rather than objects) that would be the vehicle for the presentation of Marx's text on the 'big screen'. Cinema becomes metaphorical through montage.

Eisenstein also planned to make a film, based on a similarly inventive use of montage, of James Joyce's *Ulysses*. The aim was to have images that suggested a multitude of associations, much as occurs in dreams. In short, the images could not simply be read literally; they would require interpretive work as significant as that of Freud's when he set to work to make sense of dreams. In short, images now begin to be grasped as functioning discursively, rather than as representations.

The question that Gregory Ulmer has raised is whether the Eisenstein method of montage can be used for pedagogical purposes (Ulmer 1985: 265–315). For, if a discourse can be presented through images, it might be a means of communicating complex ideas in a new way. The wager is that images are so embedded in popular culture that it is to these that students are most receptive in the age of cinema, television and the internet. Rather than teaching about popular media, the point is to use popular media to present ideas – even classical ideas. Could a film, then, be made of this book, *Key Contemporary Concepts*? Eistenstein's version of montage implies that it could. On this basis, montage becomes the translation of images into words.

Eisenstein, Sergei M. (1949) *Film Form*, ed. and trans. Jay Leyda, New York: Harcourt Brace.

Ulmer, Gregory (1985) *Applied Grammatology: Post(e)-Pedagogy from Jacques Derrida to Joseph Beuys*, Baltimore and London: Johns Hopkins University Press.

IMAGE; MYTHOS (see *LOGOS–MYTHOS*)

NECESSITY

'Necessity' can be defined as something needed – from the Latin *necessitas*: need – but its social import has been seen in relation to freedom*. The philosopher, Hegel (1770–1831), for example, saw necessity as a form of dependence – the contingent object in itself, as opposed to freedom, as the subject for itself. In his *Science of Logic* (1966: 173–186), Hegel equates necessity with actuality, which is not immediate existence, but includes what is possible.

Hegel would not be as significant in relation to this if it had not been for Marx, who thought of the dialectic of necessity and freedom as the real movement of history*. Progressively, humanity, led finally by the proletariat – the class in itself, which had yet to achieve autonomy – would become for itself (i.e., self-conscious and aware of its destiny). It would negate the existing, contingent conditions of necessity, and thereby assume its freedom. The proletariat, then, was destined to bring about the transformation of a society of necessity (capitalist society) into a society of freedom (communist society) by negating necessity. History, Marx said, is made by man, but not always consciously. The class in itself has to become for itself, and this means becoming self-conscious (Marx 1967: 263–264).

In some ways, this is a beautiful myth that no longer has much currency. However, people frequently talk about the rights of individuals to act in freedom and not be told – let alone forced – to do anything against their will. There is therefore a residual sense of freedom even in a capitalist society.

For Hannah Arendt, the philosopher, who was passionately devoted to the cause of freedom, necessity is connected to a means – ends rationality (Arendt 1958: 121, 129–135). This is the rationality of instrumental reason. Action, here, has to have a purpose, has to be of some use, whereas the action of freedom can only be done for its own sake. It is necessity from which freedom has to separate itself. Such a task is all the more difficult in a society where the satisfaction of utilitarian needs to takes precedence, in the public sphere, over freedom, which is action.

Necessity, then, involves the satisfaction of needs – even basic needs – after which, it is often said, freedom becomes possible. Were this to be the case, freedom would be in the grip of necessity, almost to the point where necessity would have a hold over freedom. And indeed, this is Arendt's view. Society is now in the grip of necessity based in need and material conditions that do not allow freedom to flourish.

This raises a number of difficult questions: the first is that there is doubt about a freedom that cannot separate itself from necessity; on the other hand, it is no doubt the worst kind of voluntarism to expect that action can simply throw off the shackles of necessity through an act of will. Perhaps necessity is seen at its strongest in relation to the necessity to labour. This is connected to the necessity to survive, and so to the satisfaction of needs (for food, clothing shelter). The issue is whether or not this aspect of necessity can ever be overcome, or at least put to one side. For Arendt, this is the necessity of the private, or domestic sphere, whereas freedom is only ever enacted in the public sphere.

Finally, necessity is linked to causality. The cause of an event necessarily precedes the event; the event necessarily succeeds the cause. Necessity in science can mean logically, or physically, necessary, in the sense that things are determined in some way. The effect of a cause is not free to be other than what it is. The effect of a cause is thus determined. To speak about necessity in this way entails an important role for knowledge*. Necessity, then, is what we know must be the case; and it makes us realise that much of science is about reducing indeterminacy (absence of a cause) to some form of determination, which in a certain sense is also a loss of freedom.

Arendt, Hannah (1958) *The Human Condition*, Chicago: University of Chicago Press.
Hegel, G.W.F. (1966 [1812–16]) *The Science of Logic. Volume 2*, trans. W.H. Johnston and L.G. Struthers, London: George Allen & Unwin.
Marx, Karl (1967 [1843]) 'Toward a Critique of Hegel's Philosophy of Law', in *Writings of the Young Marx on Philosophy and Society*, trans. and ed. Loyd D. Easton and Kurt H. Guddat, New York: Anchor Books.

See FRACTAL; POWER

NETWORK

'Network' is a modern term that evokes the idea of a series of intersecting lines, much like those of a fishing net. In its most intense form, a network resembles a labyrinth, and can, in this incarnation, evoke the idea of the structure of an encyclopedia. Like an encyclopedia, a network has no centre; it is non-hierarchical; it can be augmented without limit. A network totality is only ever provisional.

People speak of a network of friends or of business acquaintances to refer to the wide-ranging circle of potential contacts who might help in some way, if need be.

More pertinently, as far as the structure of society is concerned, network theory is employed to track the range of contacts a person or group might have in a given society. In relation to ethnic groups living in America or Australia, one might want to know what the pattern of contacts is amongst such people. It would be significant to know, for example, whether the network of contacts of a migrant population living in a given city resembles the pattern of a closed community, geographically speaking, or whether, by contrast, the network is geographically dispersed. Also of import here is whether or not the network resembles the spatial configuration of the countries of origin of migrants. Often, the network in the country of destination is spatially more dispersed than that of the country of origin; but a network is discernible, none the less.

No doubt the most significant form of network is the internet, a network of computer-based sites, or pages, which can be accessed through a computer by anyone in the world. Contact through the 'net' is becoming more popular than person to person contact. Or is it that contact through the net has supplemented, rather than supplanted, face to fact contact? At the present, it is impossible to tell.

In his assessment of the situation, Manuel Castells argues that information* technology networks (a network being 'a set of interconnected nodes') constitute the 'new morphology' of society (Castells 2000: 500). This implies that information technology, and the networks of computer-based communication (or non-computer nodes connected by the internet), has taken over the entire social structure, to the point where it has become the social structure. Now, the 'power of flows takes over from the flow of power' (ibid.).

A network is an open system. Firms are now organised in networks within capitalism as an open global system. Capital becomes part of the system of flows. But then it becomes difficult to decide whether restructured global capitalism is the result of the rise of the open network system, or whether the network society is the result of the newly organised capitalist system. Former Marxists (Castells), it seems, favour the latter conclusion, while many, like Bernard Stiegler (1998), who have studied information technology in light of the history* of technology (rather than the history of capitalism), would say that technics* is prior

to capitalism, and that the history of network capitalism has to be understood first in terms of the history of networks, and that the latter is comprehensible only in light of the history of technics.

The overriding question has to do with the relationship of thought to the very idea of the openness of the labyrinth that is the network. Any attempt to characterise the network as capitalist, or even as global, tends to place a limit on it – as though, in an analogous way, one could distil, and characterise, an ideology* contained in the 'totality' of messages sent through the internet. The real point is that, as a network, the system has no character; capitalism has thus been superseded, unless capitalism, too, is that system which is open and free of ideology. But who would maintain that?

Castells, Manuel (2000) *The Rise of the Network Society*, 2nd edn, Oxford, UK and Malden, USA: Blackwell.
Stiegler, Bernard (1998) *Technics and Time I: The Fault of Epimetheus*, trans. Richard Beardsworth and George Collins, Stanford, CA: Stanford University Press.

See DICTIONARY–ENCYCLOPEDIA

NIHILISM

Nihilism – from the Latin *nihil*, meaning nothing – emerges initially in Russia and Germany in the late eighteenth century as a moral dilemma, or, as Nietzsche (1844–1900) says, in relation to values. With the growing secularisation of society, the highest values become devalued because the underlying basis of value* is weakened, if not destroyed, by the contradictions in the value system itself. The claim that 'God is dead' echoes throughout European culture in the latter half of the nineteenth century. 'God' stands for the basis, the foundation, or ultimate truth*, of all values.

Four works referring to the idea of the death of God, are Turgenev's *Fathers and Sons* (1973 [1861]), Dostoevsky's *The Devils* (1969 [1871]) and the *Brothers Karamazov* (1982 [1880]), and Nietzsche's *Thus Spoke Zarathustra* (1974 [1883–85]). Dostoevsky (1821–81) was a contemporary of Baudelaire (1821–1867), and a significant influence on Nietzsche.

In *Fathers and Sons* there is the rejection of the older generation's values by the sons; in *The Devils*, in a dialogue between Kirilov and Verkhervensky (Dostoevsky 1969: 610–613), it is claimed that 'man' invented God, and that therefore God does not really exist. *Thus Spoke Zarathustra* debates the existence of God and of good and evil, and poses the question of whether humanity could create a god. And in the chapter, 'The Grand Inquisitor' in *The Brothers Karamazov*, we read that it is only the instrumental, secular world that counts from now on – that material conditions take priority in the morality stakes:

'Do you know that ages will pass and mankind will proclaim in its wisdom and science that there is no crime and, therefore, no sin, but that there are only hungry people. "Feed them first and then demand virtue of them!" – that is what they will inscribe on their banner which they will raise against you and which will destroy your temple'…'You promised them bread from heaven, but, I repeat again, can it compare with earthly bread in the eyes of the weak, always vicious and always ignoble race of man? And if for the sake of the bread from heaven thousands and tens of thousands will follow you, what is to become of the millions and scores of millions of creatures who will not have the strength to give up earthly bread for the bread of heaven?'(Dostoevsky 1982: 296, 297).

The Inquisitor, who judges the heretic, is now judging Christ, and in so doing he gives a defence of his own life, which has been concerned with the physical welfare of humanity. It turns out that he has perpetuated a great deception: he was in league with the devil because the devil was concerned with the material well-being of people in this world: 'did you forget that a tranquil mind and even death is dearer to man than the free choice in the knowledge of good and evil? There is nothing more alluring to man than this freedom of conscience, but there is nothing more tormenting, either' (1982: 298).

For his part, Nietzsche argues that the 'highest values' devalue themselves. In the case of the Grand Inquisitor, there is a disjunction between the reality of the unequal physical suffering in the world, and the purity of God's moral commands. There is a disjunction between earthly bread, and heavenly bread. Purity of conscience is not enough in an impure world.

Nietzsche can be understood to mean, as Keith Ansell-Pearson says, that 'there is a disjunction between our experience of the world and the conceptual apparatus we have at our disposal' (Ansell-Pearson 1994: 35). This conceptual apparatus would include our moral precepts. Nihilism, then, is not the result of human recalcitrance, indiscipline or selfishness, but is the outcome of the (Christian) value system itself.

If we are intent on following the truth come what may, it could turn out that the truth is that, scientifically, God's existence cannot be proven. We thus find that a certain illusion is necessary for human beings to live in the world.

Or it could turn out that if one must love* everyone (Christian creed) that this entails loving the enemies of love, and that by loving the enemies of love, one furthers the cause of hate in the world.

Or it could happen that because someone loves 'man' so strongly, he feels impelled to tell him, as a matter of honesty, that 'God is dead'. This is the position of Nietzsche as expressed through the mouth of Zarathustra.

Yet again, it could be that if we follow the Christian principles of love, unselfishness and honesty absolutely, Christianity itself might suffer because it becomes vulnerable to those who are antagonistic towards it. In effect, it is often necessary to take a realist, or pragmatic approach to things in order to make progress towards achieving given moral aims in 'this' world.

Moral systems that stress purity of intentions, actions and innocence cannot deal easily with a world that is impure. An honest search for truth* seems to require us to recognise the world's impurity.

The moral dilemmas in relation to nihilism were invoked in a lecture given in 1918 by Max Weber (1967). There, Weber discusses the moral dilemmas that politicians in particular face, as representatives of secular goals. Weber speaks of an 'ethic of ultimate ends' and an 'ethic of responsibility'. 'The proponent of an ethic of absolute ends cannot stand up under the ethical irrationality of the world. He is a cosmic-ethical "rationalist"'. The proponent of an ethic of absolute ends cannot accept, under any circumstances, the principle that the end justifies the means. However, not to compromise here, is, given the state of the world, to be condemned to

political and moral impotence' (Weber 1967: 122). In other words, politics comes to dominate life* because the political realm is that which is interested only in what can be achieved in the material world. The essential core of politics is realist and pragmatic.

The development of a complex money* economy is also likely to contribute to nihilism. Money, as a means of exchange, shifts the emphasis from the intrinsic value of things to value as an entirely relative thing.

There are, then, two kinds of nihilism: the nihilism that derives from a conscious rejection of values (and which earns the epithet 'nihilist', as a term of abuse) and the structural nihilism that derives from science as an instrument in the secularisation of society. Structurally, too, science, which dominates secular society, has no goal of its own. It is thus not possible to believe in science as such, much as some might try to do so. This heightens the prospect of nihilism. It is this structural nihilism that Nietzsche is concerned about, even if he is also critical of the idealist residue in science itself. For example, in a famous passage, Nietzsche says: 'Against positivism, which halts at phenomena – "There are only *facts*" – I would say: No, facts is precisely what there is not, only interpretations. We cannot establish any fact "in itself": perhaps it is folly to want such a thing' (Nietzsche 1968: 267 sect. 481).

Ansell-Pearson, Keith (1994) *Nietzsche as Political Thinker. The Perfect Nihilist*, Cambridge: Cambridge University Press.

Dostoevsky, Fyodor (1969 [1871]) *The Devils*, trans. David Magarshack, Harmondsworth: Penguin.

Dostoevsky, Fyodor (1982 [1880]) *The Brothers Karamazov*, trans. David

Magarshack, Harmondsworth: Penguin.

Nietzsche, Friedrich (1968 [1901]) *Will to Power*, trans. Walter Kaufmann and R.J. Hollingsworth, New York: Vintage.

Nietzsche, Friedrich (1974 [1883–85]) *Thus Spoke Zarathustra*, trans. R.J. Hollingsworth, Harmondsworth: Penguin.

Turgenev, Ivan (1973 [1861]) *Fathers and Sons*, trans. Rosemary Edmonds, Harmondsworth: Penguin.

Weber, Max (1967 [1921]) 'Politics as a Vocation', in *From Max Weber: Essays in Sociology*, trans. H.H. Gerth and C. Wright Mills, London: Routledge & Kegan Paul.

See POWER

OBJECT

'Object' comes from the Latin, *objectum*, meaning something presented to sight or observed, an obstacle. It also has roots in *ob-* as forward or against, and *jacere* to throw. Object, verb, is linked to the idea of bringing forward in opposition (hence 'objection'), as well as something exhibited or exposed. As *objectiv* in nineteenth century German, object relates to 'what is external to the mind'.

Science, it is often said, studies a scientific object and aspires to be objective. That is, science implements a method to ensure that bias (e.g. subjective bias) does not become an obstacle to scientific truth*. For Newton (1642–1727), and science up until Einstein (1879–1955), nature was the privileged object of science. Humanity, through biology and medicine, also came to be viewed as essentially part of nature. In this context, humanity itself could be objectified by science.

In later, post-Newtonian, nuclear science, which studies the structure of matter, it was recognised that the study of light particles leads to a blurring of the difference between subject* and object. In effect, it becomes difficult to determine whether the movement of light observed is an effect of observation or of what is observed. Science's object becomes problematic. The concept of the object changes.

The question that social science has raised about the scientific object – especially if this is human action – is whether any method in the narrow sense can provide access to the object. Might it not be that the description of social action as the object in fact mirrors the observer's position in social space? The French sociologist, Pierre Bourdieu, has taken up this issue and has pointed out the need for a heightened reflexivity on the part of the social scientist (Bourdieu and Wacquant 1992). In short, the scientist him- or herself also has to become the object of scientific discourse.

In psychoanalysis, the concept of the object has been one of the most enduring domains of study, and a cornerstone of psychoanalytic theory. Thus the object, for Freud, involves castration trauma (Freud 1964a: 462–464). This occurs when the child, through the use of language, begins to separate itself from the external world and forms a discrete self. The mother, for instance, can be objectified. That is, she can be made an object through the symbolic order. To make an object is also to lose the mother as an inseparable part of one's self, the latter being characteristic of the infant's experience in the first year of life. To gain the mother symbolically – to know her as another being – is to lose her as a sensuous part of the self, but to find her as the mother evoked by the symbolic. Recognition of castration – of sexual difference – is to recognise the other as another human being who is not the self. This can often be a threatening difference, which is sometimes carried over into forms of racism, where, because the other is not (like) me, I hate the other; in fact I hate all otherness.

In a much-cited example, Freud's grandson endeavoured to master the actual presence and absence of his mother by using a reel attached to a length of cotton to represent her coming and going. So the reel would be cast out of the cot and the sound, '*fort*' (gone), would be uttered, while '*da*' (here) would be uttered when the reel was retrieved. Clearly, there are two objects here: the object represented (the mother) and the object used to represent (the cotton reel) (Freud 1964b: 284–285).

The French psychoanalyst, Jacques Lacan (1901–1981), developed a specific notation to represent the lost object: the lost object is the '*objet petit a*' ('a' stands for the 'a' in the French, *autre*, meaning other). This object is very much connected with fantasy and the imaginary* (Lacan 1977: 192–199). As such, it is a virtual object. It has no material existence. It is a product of the subject's imaginary world. But it is no less indispensable for all that. Working with such an object is related to desire. For, in the end, Lacan's theatre says, the object of desire is always lost. It becomes so when the infant enters the world of articulate language. In other words, when an object can be represented, it is also irretrievably lost.

In addition to the scientific object and the psychoanalytic object, there is the art object. As well as being the object the artist produces, the art object is the focus of the discourse of aesthetics*. In many non-European cultures such an object is not the concern of a particular discourse because art objects are an integral part of the everyday life of a culture*. The Australian Aborigine who carves the shaft of his spear might do so in order to be successful in hunting, not because of the beauty* of the design. The aesthetic object, then, is one that is not rooted in a given context. Or rather, a gallery context can be made for such an object anywhere in the world. The decontextualised object really only came fully into being in the eighteenth century. Renaissance art is still rooted in a religious context. The specific space for showing the aesthetic object is less important than the fact of a space for showing having been constructed.

From being a form of contemplation and an actual material entity, the art object is going through a transformation. For since the emergence of minimalism and conceptualism in the 1960s and 1970s, the art object has become the idea evoked by the materiality of the object, rather than the object itself. In effect, as in the cinema of montage, art, too, has (partly) become a discourse.

Bourdieu, Pierre and Wacquant, Loïc J.D. (1992) *An Invitation to Reflexive Sociology*, Chicago: University of Chicago Press.

Freud, Sigmund (1964a [1938]) 'Splitting of the Ego in the Process of Defence', trans. James Strachey, in *The Freud Pelican Library, Volume 11: On Metapsychology: The Theory of Psychoanalysis*, Harmondsworth: Penguin.

Freud, Sigmund (1964b [1920]) *Beyond the Pleasure Principle*, trans. James Strachey, in *The Freud Pelican Library, Volume 11: On Metapsychology: The Theory of Psychoanalysis*, Harmondsworth: Penguin.

Lacan, Jacques (1977 [1966]) *Écrits: A Selection*, trans. Alan Sheridan, London: Tavistock.

See FANTASY/PHANTASY, FANTASM

ONTOLOGY

The term 'ontology' derives from *ōn*, the present participle of the Greek, *einai*, meaning, to be. It is the inquiry into all aspects of being qua being. The word itself was coined in the early seventeenth century in order to avoid the ambiguities of the term, 'metaphysics'*. In more recent analytical philosophy, ontology refers to the study of what is. In Heidegger's (1889–1976) philosophy – where the theme of Being* assumes such central importance – the notion of what is, relates to existence (*Dasein*), or to particular beings or entities. For Heidegger, if ontology is to be profound, it has to look at the *being* of what is (Heidegger 1993).

Heidegger then distinguishes between ontology, which has Being as a whole as its focus, and ontic studies of existence, such as the sciences, which examine beings in particular contexts. The social and human sciences, then, are ontic, concerned with aspects of existence (facts) rather than Being. They study existence. Ontology seeks to bring out of unconcealment, the foundation of the ontic sciences, or the foundation of existence, the foundation of being at the level of particular beings.

Heidegger claimed that if the term 'ontology' led to confusion with ontic sciences of existence, it would be better to dispense with it. However, the issue is also about generating concern about foundations (therefore Being) in an era

when this question has been relegated to the bottom of the list in an economically rationalist society. The market, a single area of existence – the subject of an ontic science – has come to dominate the whole of the field where ontology should take up its place.

A final point about Heidegger's approach to ontology concerns the question of the priority of Being in relation to ontology. If Being is genuinely prior to ontology as a discourse, the result is an analytic of Being. The problem with an analytic of Being is that Being is already given in advance – it has already *been*. Heidegger demonstrates a profound ambivalence here. He recognises that Being is also the actual historical discourses which give a certain version of Being. In giving this version, the discourse is part of Being as becoming in a certain way. Heidegger, on this point, would thus link up with Nietzsche and Deleuze.

Nevertheless, in an environment in which foundational thought is becoming increasingly irrelevant, the questions which ontology can raise make it worth while to take a stand on its behalf. A society that looks at the world ontologically is a very different society from one that does not.

Heidegger, Martin (1993) *Basic Concepts*, trans. Gary E. Aylesworth, Bloomington and Indianapolis: Indiana University Press.

See ANALYTIC–SYNTHETIC

OTHER

'Other' is a term that came into currency in anthropology. It refers to the fact that encountering another culture* and its ways of doing things is often challenging, if not quite distressing. It is hard, for instance, not to wince at the way the Aztecs went about the grisly task of preparing for, then enacting, human sacrifice: 'for their last and very public hours, through the exhaustion of dance or simulated combat, through relentless excitation, or, more economically, through drink or drugs, [the victims] were relinquished to the sacred power their slow adorning and ritual preparation has invoked' (Clendinnen, 1993: 259). Then, 'a priest's arm rising, falling, rising again; the flaccid bodies rolling and bouncing down the pyramid's flanks' (1993: 261). This is death on a grand scale. The Aztecs 'killed humans almost exclusively in their sacrifices' (1993: 74). From a vaguely Christian and strongly Enlightenment perspective, the question arises as to how one is to deal with this, admittedly extreme, example of the other's culture, even from a totally relativist position, where all cultures have a place, and in taking account of the terrible atrocities committed by the Spaniards against the Mexica.

The idea of the other in anthropology has at least had the merit of inducing those of European origin to aspire to greater efforts of reflexivity. It is not that human sacrifice could ever be acceptable, or that the Aztecs can ever be fully understood, but that their example prompts a rethink of the anthropologist's own culture. Through an encounter with the extreme, one better learns what it is that counts as the field of normality – even if one is dissatisfied with the result. At least we are a small step forward in avoiding reducing the other to the order of the same.

Morally, the other has always been a crucial element in modern ethics. From Kant's dictum that the other must always be treated as an end, and never

as a means, to Emmanuel Levinas's (1905–1995) theory of the primacy of the other in the very formation of the self (Levinas 1979), the other has been writ large in morality. In morality, Levinas argues, the other precedes the self – precedes existence. More than this: otherness as morality precedes Being* – or is at least more primordial than Being. At the origin, there is the other – an other – who cannot be reduced to the order of the Same (Levinas 1989). The other, therefore, renders identity* as a primary category problematic. For the origin of the self becomes a certain dislocation (and not a homeliness). This is not to deny that a clear tendency exists in Western philosophy to universalise by reducing the other to the Same. This includes, quite fundamentally, reducing the other *in me* to the order of the Same. Levinas, then, is a rare kind of philosopher who takes the moral dimension as the dimension of the other as the key element in any philosophy.

Levinas has also been important for feminist thinking about the other and otherness, since, typically, the female has been rendered other in relation to the male as part of the order of the Same. As if to stress this, in French it is a question, when talking about male and female, of '*l'un et l'autre sexe*' – of 'the one and the other sex'. Man is the 'one', and woman is the 'other' sex.

In his psychoanalytic theory Jacques Lacan* showed that reducing the other sex to the order of the Same leads to real difficulties (Lacan 1982). It is to forget, for example, the role of fantasy in the constitution of sexual difference. Fantasy searches for 'woman' in the individual woman; but there is no woman in general. There are individual women. The latter are inaccessible, as the other qua other is inaccessible at the level of appearance, something illustrated by the error of assuming that it is always possible for an intelligent person to deduce the thinking of the other, or to know the other.

Where two individuals are locked in competition, there is the prospect of an infinite specular oscillation, since the smart move is to anticipate that the other is also intelligent and therefore is also anticipating moves in his, or her, turn. Eventually the game has to be given up in light of potentially infinite regress: I anticipate her anticipating that I am anticipating that she is anticipating…etc. The implication is that the other is a radical other, and that therefore a third, mediating element is necessary to avoid the two parties merging into one another. Or, more prosaically, the other, qua other, is an entity that can never be mastered; and this means that she can never be adequately represented; for representation is of the order of the Same.

Clendinnen, Inga (1993 [1991]) *Aztecs: An Interpretation*, Cambridge: Cambridge University Press.

Lacan, Jacques (1982 [1975]) 'A Love Letter' (Une Lettre d'Amour), trans. Jacqueline Rose, in *Feminine Sexuality*, ed. Juliet Mitchell and Jacqueline Rose, New York: Norton.

Levinas, Emmanuel (1979 [1947]) *Time and the Other*, trans. R. Cohen, Pittsburgh: Duquesne University Press.

Levinas, Emmanuel (1989) 'Ethics as First Philosophy' in *The Levinas Reader*, ed. Seán Hand, Oxford: Basil Blackwell, 76–87.

See FANTASY/PHANTASY, FANTASM

PANOPTICON

The Panopticon (from the Greek *panoptos*, seen by all, and *panoptēs*, all seeing) is the name of a prison that was envisaged in 1791 by the utilitarian philosopher, Jeremy Bentham (1748–1832). Since the features of this architectural structure emphasise a new technology of surveillance that would encourage self-discipline, the plans for the structure were re-examined in the 1970s by Michel Foucault (Foucault 1977). Foucault used the idea of the panopticon as the basis of a new theory of power*. In order to appreciate what Foucault took from Bentham, it is first necessary to indicate the prison's salient features.

The overall rationale for Bentham's Panopticon is based on the location of prison warders in a central tower surveying a series of cells surrounding the tower, each cell being home to a single prisoner. While at any time an inspector can see directly into the cell of a prisoner, the reverse is impossible. However, while a prison warder can look into a single cell at any one time, he cannot look into all cells. The prisoner knows this, but can never be sure when he is, or is not, under surveillance, Bentham's argument is that this uncertainty leads the prisoner to assume that he is continually under surveillance and to discipline himself accordingly. The body was thought to be the privileged point of discipline, since it was viewed as a mode of access to the soul.

The radical innovation that Foucault makes in relation to Bentham's idea is to claim that Bentham Panopticon is more than an architectural phenomenon: it has become a mechanism of thought, making explicit a new articulation of power. For the principle can be applied – as Bentham himself acknowledged – to factories, schools, hospitals, asylums, orphanages, the armed forces; in fact, to any situation where a relatively small number are responsible for managing a relatively large number of people. To the extent that these situations exist, the Panopticon is in operation.

Bentham also drew up plans for a school based on the same principle, and a model of this school was built in the colony of New South Wales in the 1830s. The school was called *Chrestomathia*, a word meaning 'conducive to useful learning'. The rationale was to inculcate discipline without resort to corporal punishment. The child's mind would belong to the schoolmaster as his body belonged to the father. In terms of physical layout the master's central position in the school was analogous to the warder's in the Panopticon tower. The position was covered and each pupil was divided from others by a system of screens. Every student, every 'human object' was kept within the master's gaze.

A single inspector in his tower, a single master in his covered situation, would suffice to control the bodies, and therefore the minds, of a prolific number in his charge. This, according to Foucault, is the sign* of a new configuration of power. Rather than power being public and administered from on high – rather than the subject* of power being the subject of external physical coercion – power was now infused throughout the social body by way of intricate disciplinary practices that the subject would ultimately make his, or her, own. Power is now as much internal as external.

Many have criticised Foucault's theory of power as totalising and absolute, even if it is personalised and detailed in its articulation. And in the end, this may be true. But it is important not to be mistaken about Foucault's project. A surveillance society is not one that constantly watches its citizens, waiting for a wrong move so that it can mete out punishment. Panopticon power is not the repressive power described in Orwell's *Nineteen-Eighty-Four*, where Big Brother is watching the thoughts and every act – including writing – however personal. No one in Oceania is allowed to keep a journal, for example.

By contrast, the power that Foucault describes is efficient in its enactment before it is sinister. If it is totalising, it is so through the agency of those over whom it is wielded. It raises the question of where the polity at large stands in the field of power, not just where the governors stand. The polity as a whole participates in the implementation of power. If there is a contestable element

of Foucault's theory it is precisely here. This, then, is the point to which questions should be directed.

Foucault, Michel (1977 [1975]) *Discipline and Punish: The Birth of the Prison*, trans. Alan Sheridan, London: Allen Lane.

PHANTASY-PHANTASM (see FANTASY PHANTASY)

PIXEL A pixel is a digital* product of imaging technology. This implies that it is a discrete, discontinuous entity, not continuous, as is the case with analogue* processes.

In photography, upon which we shall concentrate, a digitally produced image differs profoundly from one produced using analogue techniques, where physical light hits a photosensitive surface in a continuous fashion. Light and dark in the analogue photograph are thus continuously graded; borders are entirely fluid. Digital images, by contrast, are turned into discrete cells, known as pixels, which are then encoded into numbers representing the intensity of the colour. The two-dimensional array of numbers can then be stored on a computer. As Mitchell points out: 'in such images... fine details and smooth curves are approximated to the grid, and continuous tonal gradients are broken up into discrete steps' (Mitchell 1994: 5).

As Mitchell also says, when digital photographs are enlarged no more information is available, the opposite is true with a continuous tone, analogue photograph. This point is illustrated by Michelangelo Antonioni's film, *Blow-Up* (1966) where the photographer, played by David Hemmings, continually enlarges parts of a negative of a shot taken of a park bench, beneath which there could be a previously unnoticed body. Each enlargement is more suggestive, revealing a face with a gun concealed in the foliage. Police forensics could work with an analogue photograph in this way, but not with a digital shot.

While almost all newspaper images are digital and thus susceptible to manipulation by computer collage, most of the general public do not appreciate this. The worry is that altered images might give a completely fabricated version of events, particularly if there are political or economic interests involved. When people look at a photograph they still tend to assume that it has not been reworked. This is the source of the doctored photograph's power.

Mitchell, William J. (1994) *The Reconfigured Eye: Visual Truth in the Post-Photographic Era*, Cambridge, Ma and London: MIT Press.

See IMAGE; TRUTH

POSTMODERNITY
The difficulty with the term 'postmodernity' is that it is has been understood in so many different ways. It is almost true to say that there is no consensus: its meaning is relative to the interests of the inquirer. And indeed, 'relativism' and 'nihilism*' are sometimes said by its opponents to be the key characteristics of postmodernity.

Taken literally, the 'post-' in 'postmodernity', meaning 'after', implies that postmodernity should, chronologically speaking, be the era after modernity*. But chronology itself is not entirely innocent. A chronological view of time is often thought of as time* as a succession of 'nows' – of present moments which, in themselves, are timeless. Zeno's story of Achilles and the tortoise illustrates the logical impasses involved in the chronological, and purely quantitative, view of time (see Zeno's Paradox). A chronological view of postmodernity seems then to be tied to a view of time that is also dominant in modernity. Maybe it is a question of a qualitative change.

Some argue that postmodernity is simply the post-industrial – the move from technologies of thermodynamics* to informational technologies. However, this move could also be seen as exemplary of the very kind of fundamental change which modernity as a cultural and political phenomenon stood for – and still stands for.

In his influential work, *The Postmodern Condition* (1984), Jean-François Lyotard sees postmodernity as the demise of grand narratives, of those frameworks of understanding and faith which interpreted the world in global terms – whether the search for truth*, the realisation of liberty or of social and political equality, the pursuit of knowledge for its own sake or the establishment of a socialist society. In effect, these are legitimising narratives (see legitimacy) in politics and science, narratives that would give an indication of the essence of these domains. Now, since the Second World War and the emergence of cybernetics*, belief in legitimising narratives has given way to a radical pragmatism best illustrated by the idea of a language game. 'Language game' refers to the fact that every discipline has a form of rule-based discourse – or a language – which is specific to it, and which has to be followed in order that an acceptable statement can be made within it. The world of science has its language games, as does the worlds of literature, philosophy, theology, economics, politics and morality. To speak in each of these worlds in the postmodern era entails invoking the language that is specific to each. There is no credible, absolute end that would fuel a common language, as was still the case in modernity.

Science offers, according to Lyotard, another chapter in postmodern pragmatics – a pragmatics brought about by the performativity equation and the dominance of market relations. The performativity equation – minimum input for maximum output – has come into prominence because of the incredulity towards the metanarratives typical of the postmodern experience. Now, funding science projects is simply based on efficiency: who can do more with less? Those who 'win' in the competitive grants system are those who can set a track record of success with finite funding; the issue turns around questions of quantity, not quality. The same principle affects the whole of the education system where market forces have intervened on a grand scale and the liberal arts are in decline (What's a liberal arts degree worth? – this is now the question). Little that is inventive will be funded or encouraged, as it is too difficult to justify it and to manage its realisation.

In the end, postmodern science gestures towards a state of affairs beyond the ideology* of market pragmatism. This is because true performativity is more than the calculable state of affairs represented by market relations. An entirely calculable system, over which there can be total control, risks running down, risks imploding. The

paradoxical sciences of fractal* geometry and quantum mechanics force the system to deal with what is entirely new and unanticipated. Inventiveness is not, therefore, foreign to performativity, whatever the claims made by the apologists of market-driven science. Rather than consensus – which keeps things the same – it is necessary to accept paralogy ('illogical' claims) in order to enrich the system.

In *The Condition of Postmodernity* (1990), David Harvey has described postmodernity as emergence of such things as flexible labour markets and capitalist accumulation, the compression of space and time, the loss of community and the rise of individualism, the emergence of avant-garde art, the rise of an uninspiring pragmatism and nihilism in morality and politics. In effect, Harvey puts a negative spin on what he sees as the rise of postmodernity; for, to him, this era signals an intensification of capitalist domination.

For some commentators, neither Lyotard nor Harvey can be relied upon to give a true insight into postmodernity because they see the world in high, or late-modernist terms. This is indicated by the fact that both thinkers are still focused on the 'shock of new', something typical of modernism, if not modernity. The real change brought by the postmodern turn is in the challenge phenomena like multi- or transcultural polities make to the dominance of the European Enlightenment polity. A certain kind of revival of tradition thus puts Reason in question. This revival of tradition aims in fact to reveal the tradition in the Enlightenment itself. That is, Reason now comes to be seen as interested, not neutral, and based in its own version of ethnicity. Or again: Europe is ethnocentric. As such, Europe's view of the other is as much prejudiced as scientific. 'True' postmodernity would be about otherness (other cultures) gaining recognition within an Enlightenment framework. This would be real progress, as opposed to the Enlightenment's pseudo-progress.

Still another view of postmodernity sees it essentially as a movement in art, and especially architecture, where quotation and decoration become the key elements. Charles Jenks points to the initial postmodern moment as being the dynamiting, in July 1972, of the functionalist, modernist, Pruitt-Igoe modernist tower-block housing development in St Louis in the state of Missouri, and the re-emergence of decoration as a key dimension of the architectural imagination* (Jenks 1986: 15). Similarly, in painting and other arts, the notion of modernist originality is challenged by artists quoting the work of others – to the point of exact replication – in an effort to redefine the very meaning of a work of art. Henceforth, the significance of the postmodern work of art lies not in what the work is, but on what it says, or signifies.

More generally, postmodernity is seen by some as an as yet unknown era occurring after modernity. For these commentators, postmodernity does not have an identity* and may even be opposed to the very idea of identity (modernist idea) in the wake of difference. Whatever the case, the term itself has been at the centre of debates between those who think that postmodernity stands for relativism, the blurring of the difference between high and popular culture*, the notion that 'anything goes', and a devaluing of history*, and those who see it as the basis of new forms of innovation which no longer depend on Romantic notions of genius and individuality,

and which open the way to broader forms of participation in the arts and politics.

Harvey, David (1990) *The Condition of Postmodernity*, Oxford: Basil Blackwell.
Jenks, Charles (1986) *What is Postmodernism?* London: Academy Editions; New York: St Martin's Press.
Lyotard, Jean-François (1984 [1979]) *The Postmodern Condition*, trans. Geoffrey Benington and Brian Massumi, Minneapolis: Minnesota University Press.

See DIFFERENCE–INDIVIDUALITY

POWER 'Power' derives in part from the Middle English (1100–1500) word, *poër*, from which evolved *pouer*, direct root of the modern French, *pouvoir*, to be able to, to have the ability to do something. Also related to *pouer* is 'potent' deriving from the Latin, *potens* and *potentis* meaning able and mighty.

In the sphere of politics, the concept of power has evolved to the point where it has a positive as well as a negative meaning. To take the negative meaning first, power has been defined as that actual or virtual force which says, 'no', which is prohibitive. Both the father's interdiction in the family and the law as a negative force for preventing crime, instead of taking the lead in making things happen, are indicative of power as a negative phenomenon. This view of power dominates the institutional versions of it as articulated by the legal system – at least in the West.

The idea of power as a destructive force was first presented in a systematic way in Hobbes's *Leviathan* (1968, first published in 1651). For Hobbes, the people as an aggregate, left to their own devices in the state of nature, will soon find themselves in a state of war. For war and conflict are the natural tendency of a human nature bent on the pursuit of self-interest. While each individual has a modicum of power as force, this has no effect against the power of the rest. Such is the logic of the Social Contract. Power is thus institutionalised in society in the figure of the leader and his entourage. The leader has to maintain order in society. If the leader has no legitimacy* (no right to wield power) the articulation of power becomes tyranny; but even though there may be a legitimate process for appointing a leader, the existence of inequalities in society can result in domination: the domination of one class over another, for example. But is power as embodied in the law and invested in the leader the same thing as maintaining order, whether or not through fear? Is power inevitably centralised in the figure of the leader or party? Is power always a negative, if not destructive force in society?

The work of Michel Foucault on the prison and the panopticon*, on governmentality*, and on sexuality (Foucault 1979), attempts to give a partial answer to these questions. For Foucault, power is not an essentially negative force, but can also enable things to happen. Power is more than the juridical definition of it, a definition that has been with the West for more than four hundred years. Such a definition is applicable to kingly power. When it comes to understanding the nature of

power, the king's head, according to Foucault, still remains to be cut off (Foucault 1980: 121). Power is instead to be understood as dispersed. It becomes visible when there is resistance in society – when force meets force.

Secondly, law is not equivalent to order. A police state can maintain order. The law should rather concern itself with evidence and justice*.

Thirdly, power is also internal to the subject, or indeed forms the subject*. Power, knowledge and subjectivity thus go together; they are not alien to each other, as the humanist notion of power suggests.

Fourthly, power can be harnessed, or implemented, by any entity or group, as it is not something that can be possessed, but is a play of forces in a virtual network* of forces. In this sense, power is synthetic rather than analytical. It is from this that it derives its positive and creative force, despite Foucault's terminology of an analytic of power.

Foucault, Michel (1979 [1976]) *The History of Sexuality, Volume I*, trans. Robert Hurley, London: Allen Lane.
Foucault, Michel (1980) *Power/Knowledge*, ed. Colin Gordon, Brighton: Harvester.
Hobbes, Thomas (1968 [1651]) *Leviathan*, London: Penguin.

See ANALYTIC–SYNTHETIC

PROFANE (See SACRED–PROFANE)

Q

QUANTUM

Quantum is a Latin term meaning, 'as much as', or how much?' Quantum theory, developed by Max Planck (1858–1947) in 1900, proposes that energy is emitted and absorbed in quanta, or discrete units, rather than being continuous. Initially this idea was so radical that it seemed to put into question the whole framework of physics, especially with regard to the older laws of radiation. It should be said, however, that nineteenth-century British scientists (Faraday, Kelvin, Maxwell and Fitzgerald) tended to favour a view of energy as continuous, while the Germans (Fechner, Weber, Riemann, Kirchhorff and Clausius) were more predisposed to a particle view of energy.

Quantum theory found its most important application in relation to the investigation of the structure of the atom. It was discovered, for example, that when electrons circulated the nucleus of the atom, no energy was lost, but that when an electron changed orbit, it radiated energy in accordance with quantum predictions.

In another key development, Heisenberg showed in 1927 that electrons could not be located with accuracy because the high and low quanta of energy used in the observation caused an alteration in the behaviour of the observed electron. Much has been made of the 'Uncertainty Principle' which was formulated by Heisenberg in the wake of this problem.

In view of all this, the word 'quantum' has entered more popular parlance to signify a radical change in a framework of thinking that had not been anticipated by existing frameworks. Hence, people speak of 'quantum leaps' in relation to ideas of a highly novel nature. Secondly, quantum theory signifies the potential interpenetrability of the observer and the observed in scientific work. Although this occurs under unique and special conditions in relation to the study of the structure of the atom, the idea has been taken into the broader planes of science in order to quell a certain positivist rigidity regarding the status of subjectivity in science.

See EPISTEMOLOGY

RESPONSIBILITY

'Responsibility', which arrives with the idea of the individual in the eighteenth century, is a term that has an everyday as well as a deeper, often moral significance. In the everyday sense, responsibility refers to the point in the hierarchy where 'the buck stops' – the point where some person, or persons, can be assumed to be the equivalent of the cause of something, or are authorised to act on their own account in a given matter or matters. Increasingly, however, there is no point seeking restitution for damages or for an injury done from the sales person, the public official, the bank officer, or, frequently, the lawyer or doctor, for they are not responsible; they are just doing their job. A bureaucratic mentality is in evidence: the office speaks, not the person.

Adults, the law says, are, with notable exceptions, responsible for their actions. They have to suffer the consequences of their actions in a way that a child does not. The worry for some here is that adults are becoming increasingly traumatised at the prospect of suffering such consequences. However, this is a value judgement and subject to debate.

In debating the issue of responsibility, social scientists have sometimes taken the view that economic, political and cultural circumstances militate against the responsibility which can, or should, be attributed for unacceptable action, in whatever context. Thus, individuals who have been abused as children, as well as members of ethnic minorities who have suffered discrimination, have been thought to be less stringently tied to responsibility for their actions. The extent to which this is accepted is the key question and requires deep thought. Put in its simplest form, to what extent should victims accept responsibility for their actions at a later date? This question must be asked of Israelis, of Palestinians, of oppressed women, of postcolonial peoples, of African Americans, of Australian Aborigines, and others. If Israelis commit acts of atrocity against others, to what extent can the Jewish experience of the Holocaust be used as a reason for shifting responsibility for such action? If Palestinians commit acts of terror against innocent victims, to what extent should their situation of oppression be accepted as a reason for their not assuming responsibility for the death of the innocent? If acts of domestic violence and rape are rife in certain Australian Aboriginal communities, to what extent does unjust colonial oppression excuse such behaviour?

People with certain mental illnesses, or with deteriorating mental faculties caused by old age, as well as children under a certain age, are not legally responsible for their actions. However, responsibility can also be enshrined in institutional procedures, as is the case with the Westminster system of ministerial responsibility.

The Westminster system opens up the question of the responsibility of a minister for the actions of his or her department. In recent times, especially in Australia, the relevant minister has behaved as though s/he were not responsible if s/he did not actually do the act. Responsibility is thus denuded of symbolic force. Such a use of responsibility removes it from its classical meaning and turns it into a form of immediate cause and effect action. The question to be answered is now a straightforward empirical question worthy of the detective story: 'who dunnit?'. Ministerial responsibility used to contain the important element of moral courage that is always present in the assumption of responsibility in the deepest sense, particularly when parents assume responsibility for the actions of their children, a family member for the family as a whole, an individual, or individuals, for the past actions of the nation. For example it is often said in Australia that since the present generation did not commit the acts of cultural destruction against the Aborigines, the present generation cannot be held responsible. However, it is a key aspect of the meaning of responsibility that it can be assumed, and that simple cause and effect logic is not relevant. Responsibility has both a legal and a moral dimension, and this is what gives it a symbolic as well as a descriptive status.

The symbolic aspect of responsibility can also be seen in the various forms of representative democracy. In this context, the representatives are essentially chosen, through the ballot box, by the people. It may be said, however, that such representatives represent themselves, that they are self-interested, are often as not corrupt, and so on. Also, the framework of representation is a very rough instrument, and the people as a whole have very little say in which candidate will be presented for election. Without denying that there may be historical factors which confirm part of this claim, it could also be said that responsibility means that people assume responsibility for their candidates, that the people are also imperfect, and that it is a question of recognising and fighting against such imperfection. Rarely these days could such a view of responsibility gain a hearing. For the political system is increasingly dominated by *realpolitik* – a phenomenon which *includes* the people.

Finally, responsibility can be thought of as essentially moral identity, as found in the work of Emmanuel Levinas (1905–1995), where responsibility underpins the other as the basis of the self. Thus Levinas speaks of a 'responsibility that goes beyond what I may or may not have done to the Other or whatever acts I may or may not have committed, as if I were devoted to the other man before being devoted to myself. Or more exactly, as if I had to answer for the other's death even before *being*' (Levinas 1989: 83. Levinas's emphasis). This is not a responsibility that originates in guilt, but one embedded in the person one is as a moral being.

Levinas, Emmanuel (1989) 'Ethics as First Philosophy', in *The Levinas Reader*, ed. Seán Hand, Oxford: Basil Blackwell, 76–87.

See OTHER

RESSENTIMENT

'Ressentiment' comes from the French, *sentire*, 'to feel', and *ressentir*, to feel acutely over again. It is a term that became known through Nietzsche's *On the Genealogy of Morals* (1989), an essay intended in part as a critique of Christian morality.

According to Nietzsche (1844–1900), Christian morality rewrites the history of morals so that the meek, the gentle – those who say 'no' to action – come out on the side of the good, while the strong and the affirmative spirits are categorised as evil. In Nietzsche's terms, 'good and bad' are replaced by 'good and evil'. Nietzsche puts things even more strongly: *ressentiment* is the outcome of a slave revolt in morality. Not being able to match the master in actions, the slave uses guilt as a weapon. Nietzsche's description and explanation is as follows:

> The slave revolt in morality begins when *ressentiment* itself becomes creative and gives birth to values: the *ressentiment* of natures that are denied the true reaction, that of deeds, and compensate themselves with an imaginary revenge. While every noble morality develops from a triumphant affirmation of itself, slave morality from the outset says No to what is 'outside', what is 'different', what is 'not itself'; and *this* No is its creative deed. (Nietzsche 1989: 36 sect. 10. Nietzsche's emphasis)

Nietzsche thus sees *ressentiment* as emanating from a position of actual weakness. In other words, Christianity glorifies weakness because it arises out of a people who are oppressed. And although he attempts to provide a historical basis to his theory, it is the psychological disposition identified in Nietzsche's essay that has given rise to its fame. This disposition is marked by a lack of generosity of spirit, of being unable to say that the other is worthy, and indeed even better than oneself. The people of *ressentiment* cannot say this because, in their eyes, to praise the other is to revile oneself. Yet, to be able to praise another can be the mark of a noble bearing. The person of *ressentiment* is unable to see this. All he or she can believe is that self-worth comes from equalling the feats, or personal bearing, of the one (secretly) admired. Being unable to match up leaves no alternative: the feat itself – the person him or herself – must be reduced through moral criticism.

Ressentiment, then, through its negativity, is reactive. It does not create or affirm. It is a response to those who do create and affirm. As others have pointed out (cf. Wolf cited in Stringer 2000: 249), the issue for political action is twofold: reacting as a victim (because one is a victim), and using victimage as a mode of identity* itself – as feminism has sometimes been accused of doing. There is then the risk of *ressentiment*, in being a victim, that one will wallow in victimage, and there is an affirming attitude, where one uses oppression as a springboard for attempting to overcome oppression. A similar point would apply to minorities (such as African Americans or Australian Aborigines): their victimage can be worn affirmatively or resentfully. In the latter case, those who committed the injustice are seen as without merit and as entirely responsible for the victim's plight. In other words, the victim is morally virtuous, while the victor is morally vile.

If negative *ressentiment* is to be avoided, the question remains as to its psychic rationale. What is the basis of its emergence? Why should there be such deep self-hatred? Freud must be read in detail in order to gain the profound insights needed to give an answer here. But maybe the intensity of oppression and the accompanying violence imposed on the self by the victor should lead us to wonder whether *ressentiment* is as much a political weapon as it is – in Nietzsche's terms – an 'instinct'.

The question arises as to why Nietzsche uses the word, *ressentiment*, and why this French version, rather than the English, resentment, continues to be used. Part of the answer, as pointed out in the Editor's Introduction to the Vintage edition of *On the Genealogy of Morals*, is that Nietzsche used French because there is no exact German equivalent, and because he wanted to strike a blow against German cultural complacency.

Nietzsche, Friedrich (1989 [1887]) *On the Genealogy of Morals*, trans. Walter Kaufmann and R.J. Hollingdale, New York: Vintage.
Stringer, Rebecca (2000) '"A Nietzschean Breed": Feminism, Victimology, *Ressentiment*', in *Why Nietzsche Still? Reflections on Drama, Culture, and Politics*, ed. Alan D. Schrift, Berkeley, Los Angeles and London: University of California Press.

RHIZOME

'Rhizome' has been made famous by the work of Gilles Deleuze and Félix Guattari (1987), where it is used as an invocation of horizontal connections in thought and philosophy. Literally, rhizomes are bulbs that spread out horizontally rather than growing vertically in a tree-like fashion. Tree-like thought approximates the structure of the dictionary, where everything refers back, in principle, to an original point. Psychoanalysis, it is claimed, is one example of tree-like thought, with everything referring back to childhood and other experiences – experiences and fantasies of the parents, for example, and their experiences of their parents, and so on *ad infinitum*. The advocates of rhizomatic thought find tree-like thought restrictive because it is seen as closed. The rhizome evokes openness, and a non-totalising whole, much as represented in principle by the encyclopedia.

A rhizome is a network*-like structure where every point, or node, can be connected with every other point – or where there is no fixed format about the direction in which one should proceed. Connecting different points is part of the creative, synthetic aspect of the structure of the rhizome. Tree-like thought, by comparison is analytical. There are no fixed points in a rhizome structure, only continual drawing of lines. A rhizomatic whole has no inside or outside. This can be illustrated by the specific articulation of the internet. As soon as there is a point outside the net, another connection is there waiting to be made. The outside quickly becomes the inside. Since the rhizomatic whole is synthetic, it is also open and multidimensional; no global and complete description of a rhizomatic structure is possible. Only a whole which is closed can be fully described. As a result of the impossibility of global description, a rhizomatic structure is a collection of local* descriptions. The local returns, or is rediscovered, with rhizome, just as it was lost with the 'tree'.

The rhizome, then, gives rise to heterogeneous assemblages. It is machine-like in the sense that it is the arrangement of elements (the actual connections made) which is fundamental, not the nature of the elements themselves. Artistically, this can give rise to bizarre structures composed of a wide variety of materials taken from different contexts.

Politically, a rhizomatic approach would emphasise the creative spark that can arise from new alliances, rather than the old traditions of solidarity. What sort of political structure is desirable in relation to this approach is less clear due to the heavily pragmatic, non-idealist, orientation of rhizome-inspired politics. As Eco says, when discussing the rhizome: 'thinking means to *grope one's way*' (Eco 1984: 82. Eco's emphasis).

The problem with rhizomatic thought is that it tends to generate scorn for all historically determined formations, unless history* is itself based in a multiplicity of times. It is therefore easy to privilege a superficial view of the present moment, even if this is not the intention of the inventors of the term. In addition, it has to be recognised that to privilege the rhizome to the exclusion of analytical thought is to risk being sucked into a network of excessively pragmatic moves in politics and morality, as well as in art and philosophy. Creativity has, in short, to be distinguished from the privileging of a certain immediacy.

Deleuze, Gilles and Guattari, Félix (1987 [1980]) 'Introduction: Rhizome', in *Capitalism and Schizophrenia*, trans. Brian Massumi, Minneapolis: University of Minnesota Press.
Eco, Umberto (1984) *Semiotics and the Philosophy of Language*, London: Macmillan.

See ANALYTIC–SYNTHETIC; DICTIONARY–ENCYCLOPEDIA; LOCAL

RISK SOCIETY

The theory of the risk society was developed by the German sociologist Ulrick Beck (1992). Beck defines this society as one where risk has ceased to be contingent and has become a structural feature. Risk in the nineteenth century, at the height of steam-driven industrialisation, as a phenomenon is very different to risk in the late twentieth century.

In the former case, risk derives from dangerous working conditions in mines and factories, from insufficient wages, local pollution of air and water, long working hours, poor sanitation, and the like. The risk to health and life is not shared evenly, a fact consistent with the uneven distribution of wealth and power. The factory owner is able to insulate himself from the stench and pollution of the smokestack in industrial England, whereas the worker cannot do so. All of this is well known and analysed by Marx (1818–83).

What has changed by the end of the twentieth century is that risk has become increasingly intractable and global. The consequences of a nuclear accident can no longer be isolated and localised like a mine disaster, and, as occurred after the explosion at Chernobyl in 1986, these consequences affect a wide geographical area, if not the rest of the world. Similarly, the effects of global warming and climate change, to the extent that these are real, are global, not local* in scope. The loss of animal species, the pollution of air and the poisoning of waterways leave little chance that some will escape the burden while others bear it.

The very nature of risk has changed, Beck argues, so that although privileged groups still exist, in principle, no one can escape the kind of risk which is now in play. It is therefore necessary now to draw up – in a figurative sense – a 'natural contract' that would exist in parallel with the 'social contract'.

The risk society exists in another sense as well. For the risk of certain diseases related to 'lifestyle' (cancer, heart trauma) no longer affect just one group in society; they affect all people to the extent that the higher standard of living which provokes such diseases is universal. In fact, susceptibility to heart attack and cancer may still have a class basis; in principle, though, all will eventually be affected equally. Health funds, insurance companies and banks are all in the business of calculating the relative risk to people. They are an integral part of the risk society in the sense that, with the broadening of the shareholder base and the promise that this will continue into the future, the failure of a particular company can no longer be seen as a local matter. The whole of the economy* is likely to be affected. This is why governments often intervene in the wake of corporate failures.

Now that risk cannot be eliminated, the practice of 'risk management' has arisen: here probability estimates govern the kinds of action that become viable in light of the degree of risk involved.

The concept of the change in the nature of risk is enlightening. However, why precisely do we need to speak of the 'risk society'? That all societies face risks does not turn them into risk societies – societies whose nature and activities can be described solely in relation to risk. Action to combat risk may be a small part of activity without there being a society whose nature is determined by its attitude towards risk. Beck overdoes it here. Risk, yes; but risk society, no.

Beck, Ulrich (1992 [1986]) *The Risk-society*, trans. Mark Ritter, London: Sage.

See GOVERNMENTALITY

SACRED–PROFANE The father of anthropology, Émile Durkheim (1858–1917), perhaps unsurprisingly, saw the sacred as the foundation of society. At least this is unsurprising if we are referring to the significant non-secular cultures still extant in the world. But Durkheim also saw the sacred as being the foundation of modern society. Even with the latter's highly differentiated division of labour and up-to-the-moment transport and communications systems, various times are still set aside for collective ceremonies, festivals and religious celebrations. The French Revolution, for example, 'established a whole cycle of holidays to keep the principles with which it was inspired' (Durkheim 1984: 442). Even if these holidays have fallen into desuetude, it indicates, according to Durkheim, that new religious and sacred moments can be created and re-created; these are moments in which collective representations give access to the collective consciousness at the heart of every society – including modern, industrial society. This implies that, at its foundation, every society is also a community* a community in which the sacred lives.

The profane world, then, is the world of difference and diversity, of science and bureaucracy, where individuals are competitive and live in anomie, or a state of rootlessness. Indeed, for a long time, says Durkheim, submission to scientific thought seemed to many to be equivalent to profanation (Durkheim 1984: 444). Thus, it is somewhat ironical that Durkheim sees the gap between tradition and modernity* as being bridged by religion. Religious sensibility signals that, despite all, the sacred is also at the heart of secular society, as it is of traditional societies.

In Weber's (1864–1920) influential notion that the *differentia specifica* of modern society is its secular character as evidenced in means-ends nationality (see Weber 1948: 77–128), the sacred disappears from view. It has, however, re-emerged as an issue for modern polities, but not directly. The reawakening of interest in the sacred came through the work of anthropologists like Mary Douglas (1969), who saw the sacred as a way of dealing with ambiguity. All liminal states thus tend to be the subject of taboos that evoke the sacred. The taboo removes the ambiguity that would put the social order in question. These taboos involve pollution in relation to: the borders of the body – hair, nails, saliva and excrement, tears, milk, menstrual blood – as well as borders in relation to the sick body, and the dead body; borders between inside and outside (threshold of the house, etc.); boundaries between childhood and adulthood (hence initiation rites); borders between self and other, between the gods and society, and many more. Because of their ambiguity, all of these domains are the subject of purification rites and rituals.

With regard to the cadaver, it appears to be universally true that, poised as it is between life* and death, nature and culture, the cadaver is subject to mourning and purification rituals. The dead body both is and is not the person whose body it is. Only ritual can make it right – that is, only ritual can enable the cadaver to find a place within the symbolic order.

In light of Mary Douglas's insights, Julia Kristeva has linked the ambiguity of objects and conditions that are subject to sacred rites to her notion of abjection* (Kristeva 1982). The abject thing or action is one that does not fit into any prevailing profane classification, and which is excluded from the symbolic order for this reason. It is the abject, then, which is the subject of prohibition.

In psychoanalytic terms, the abject is between separation from, and fusion with, the mother. As a certain degree of separation is necessary for a rich cultural and social life (language, for example, would be compromised without it), Kristeva proposes that certain cultures – such as the Indian – with a weak state apparatus, displace the work of the formal state on to a rich and complex system of substantive actions, or rituals. Without such rituals of separation, there is a risk of social disintegration. Not to carry out the ritual in the face of the polluting thing often gives rise to intense anxiety. Ritual thereby takes the place of a strong state and a highly abstract symbolic order in maintaining the social order. As Kristeva says, it is a

kind of 'writing of the real', where societies without writing, in the conventional sense, use the opposition between 'purity and danger' as a mechanism for constituting the general order of society.

From another angle, Georges Bataille connects the sacred to sacrifice and to what he calls 'inner experience'. If the profane world is the world of individuality and separation (one from another), the sacred world is one that encourages ecstatic fusion: the sacred is involved in the violation of boundaries. At least this is true of the destructive and non-contemplative form of the sacred. Thus states of intoxication and identification with the victim in sacrifice become the markers of the sacred. As Bataille says: 'this sacredness is the revelation of continuity through death of a discontinuous being' (Bataille 1987: 22). Here, then, the sacred gives rise to a continuity of being, as opposed to its discontinuity in the profane world. Continuity, says Bataille, calls into question the very being of the human (Bataille 1987: 29). It opens up a disequilibrium that has no utilitarian correlate. Utility is the mark *par excellence* of the profane world.

Through drawing together the sacred and violence, Bataille is able to open a face on the sacred which many had not seen, or would not see. Just as the mere possibility of the return of human sacrifice as part of this aspect of the sacred is unimaginable, so the presence of the sacred in its fullness must no doubt remain secretive, in obscurity, displaced in experiences such as eroticism, violence, mysticism and intoxication. Despite Christianity's counselling of passivity and gentleness, the sacred may have more to do with violence and sacrifice than was ever envisaged. Or, to put it another way: violence and death are the source of both horror and fascination. In relation to this, the taboo is instituted. But the taboo is the limit in relation to which transgression has a meaning. Abolishing the taboo, as a libertarian might suggest, is also to abolish the transgression. For this reason, taboos – such as the one against sexual intercourse – are frequently transgressed legitimately, as occurs with sex in marriage. It is, above all, the work of Bataille which has brought this insight; it is an insight which refines and deepens an understanding of the sacred and the profane.

Bataille, Georges (1987 [1957]) *Eroticism*, trans. Mary Dalwood, London and New York: Marion Boyars.

Douglas, Mary (1969) *Purity and Danger*, London, Boston and Henley: Routledge & Kegan Paul.

Durkheim, Emile (1984 [1912]) 'On the Future of Religion', in *Sociological Perspectives: Selected Readings*, ed. Kenneth Thompson and Jereny Tunstall, Harmondsworth: Penguin.

Kristeva, Julia (1982) *Powers of Horror: An Essay on Abjection*, trans. Leon S. Roudiez, New York: Columbia University Press.

Weber, Max (1948) 'Politics as a Vocation', in *From Max Weber: Essays in Sociology*, trans. H.H. Gerth and C. Wright Mills, London: Routledge & Kegan Paul.

SEMIOTIC

The word 'semiotic', derives from *sēmeîon*, the Greek word for sign. From this origin has arisen the modern disciplines of semiotics, invented by Charles Sanders Peirce (1839–1914), and semiology, in the terminology of Ferdinand de Saussure (1857–1913). Specialised research in the study of signs and significations has now been under way

for over forty years. A key principle of such research, and of semiotics in general, is that the sign exists within a system of differences. In other words, a sign – through its division into signifier and signified – is part of a code*, which permeates the whole of social life. As Eco points out, a 'general semiotics studies the whole of the human signifying activity' (Eco 1984: 12).

To see the sign as a code, however, is to render it entirely formal and abstract, whereas, in its incarnation, the sign is also informal and charged with emotion. The question has been whether or not semiotics can do justice to the passion and emotion in language, the subjective dimension of language, in effect.

A key field of study here relates to the text, defined in its broadest sense as a system of writing, but including consideration of drive activity (based in affect) enacted in the modernist avant-garde text, as exemplified by James Joyce (1882–1941) and Stéphane Mallarmé (1842–98). The principal theorist of such writing is Julia Kristeva, who has married Freud's insights to those of semiotics. In effect, Freudian psychoanalysis links up with a theory of the sign from a semiotic point of view (Kristeva 1984).

For Kristeva, the semiotic (*le sémiotique*) appears in the subject – or is constitutive of a phase of subjectivity – in the period prior to the formation of articulate language. However, its chronological status is less important than the way it is enacted in the concrete instance. At the level of the semiotic, the musicality and rhythm of the signifying process become evident. Thus, in repeated cries, singing and gestures, in rhythm and word-play, or in laughter, the raw material for the avant-garde text is found. Although this process is also present in non-poetic language – and indeed, in every linguistic instance – the semiotic is most clearly visible in the poetic act. Musically, the semiotic closely approximates the tone colour of *Klangfarbenmelodie** as developed by Schoenberg and Webern. It is here that the timbre of musical sound becomes accentuated.

The philosophical figure Kristeva uses in order to specify the semiotic is the Greek *Khora*, which is mentioned by Plato in the *Timaeus*. The figure of the *Khora* is an original container (it connotes, psychoanalytically, the position of the mother) that can be signified only through the rhymical instantiation of space. There is no science, no philosophy, which can, strictly speaking, gain access to *Khora* as such. Even the presence of the definite article is misleading; for *Khora* is not a space that can be named; it is rather an invocation of the unnameable and inexpressible.

Through Kristeva's initiative in this area, the semiotic has opened the way to an appreciation of the material incarnation of language. As such, language is seen as being enacted in a specific space and time – in a given context. A strictly formal approach to language cannot do justice to this enactment of language.

Kristeva's work with the semiotic also has implications for a conception of subjectivity. Now it is possible to appreciate that the subject is not fixed and static, as phenomenology would have it, but is always in process because the subject is nothing other than the material enactments of itself. In other words, it is not eternally given. Now, too, it is also possible to appreciate a text at the level of the materiality – the rhythm – of words, as well at the semantic level. This has

opened the way for avant-garde texts to gain a wider audience.

Eco, Umberto (1984) *Semiotics and the Philosophy of Language*, London: Macmillan.
Kristeva, Julia (1984 [1974]) *Revolution in Poetic Language*, trans. Margaret Waller, New York, Columbia University Press.

See SIGN: SIGNIFIER/SIGNIFIED

SIGN:SIGNIFIER/SIGNIFIED The idea of the sign has gone through a number of variations since the time of the Ancient Greeks. For the Greeks the sign was *sémêïon*, and this constitutes the origin of semiotics, the discipline that studies signs and significations in society. In the Greek context – if we take Plato and Aristotle as examples – the sign is not reducible to a word but refers to phenomena that indicate something hidden. That is, signs are symptoms of something that is not itself manifest. Words would be signs in this sense only when they indicate 'affections of the soul', or the state of something hitherto invisible (Eco 1984: 28).

The Greek notion of the sign thus institutes a substantive, as opposed to an arbitrary*, relationship between the sign and what it signifies. With the Stoic conception of the sign (300–200 BC), there emerges, in addition, the first clear distinction between signifier (*signans*) and signified (*signatum*). This distinction, which came to be so influential in the work of the father of modern linguistics, Ferdinand de Saussure (1857–1913), has given rise to the movement of structuralism, where a semiotic approach to culture and society has come to emphasise the conventional, as opposed to essential, nature of these realities.

For Saussure, then, a sign can be either motivated or unmotivated. A motivated sign is like the object it signifies: a picture of a glass of beer signifying beer is a motivated sign, as onomatopoeic sounds are similar to the sounds they signify ('bow-wow' = a bark). Unmotivated signs, on the other hand, and the linguistic sign in particular, divide up into signifier and signified (Saussure 1993: 65–70). The signifier is the vehicle and the signified the meaning. The key aspect here is that the relationship between the signifier and the signified is arbitrary and differential. This means that it is the relationship between, and not the nature of, signifiers, which gives meaning. Differential, arbitrary and systemic – such are the terms describing the Saussurean, unmotivated sign. As an illustration, Saussure points out that 't' can be written in ways that barely approximate an ideal model, but that the relation of the mark to other letters determines its meaning. Or again: 'There is no internal connection …between the idea "siste" and the French sequence of sounds s-ö-r' (Saussure 1993: 67).

In his theory, the inaugurator of semiotics, Charles Sanders Peirce (1839–1914) said, in one of his many definitions, that a sign is 'something which replaces something for someone', and is determined by its object (Peirce 1991: 251). For Peirce there were multiple types of sign, for which he attempted to provide an exhaustive table of classifications. Three key types stand out. These are: the *icon**, or a sign which is similar to what it signifies; the *index**, which is affected by what it represents; and the *symbol*, a sign that is connected to what it signifies by a law, or convention. It is Peirce's symbol that most clearly approximates Saussure's signifier–signified dyad.

Two significant points should be made regarding Peirce's approach to signs and, therefore, to semiotics. These are that all dimensions of human experience involve signs, including thought and logic. And that the task of classifying signs is an endless one because signs emerge through the inventiveness of human beings.

Eco, Umberto (1984) *Semiotics and the Philosophy of Language*, London and Basingstoke: Macmillan.
Peirce, Charles Sanders (1991) *Peirce on Signs*, ed. James Hooper, Chapel Hill and London: University of North Carolina Press.
Saussure, Ferdinand de (1993) *Course in General Linguistics*, trans. Roy Harris, London: Duckworth.

See SEMIOTIC

SIMULACRUM
The simulacrum is a form of image*. In Plato's language, it is an *eidolon*, or idol, compared to an *eikōn*, or authentic image. If the *eidos*, for Plato, is the true, original and totally self-contained reality, the *eidolon*, also self-contained, is the totally false reality. Worse than this: a simulacrum can have the appearance (be the counterfeit) of an *eikōn*, and yet be quite removed from the true reality the *eikon* evokes. In the relationship between the original and the copy, the simulacrum does not even qualify at being a bad copy; it is instead a 'false claimant', as Deleuze (1925–1995) says (Deleuze 1994: 60), aspiring to the mantle of truth* equivalent to that of the *eidos*.

All of this is familiar territory for those brought up in the Western, European tradition of thought and morality (Greek and Judaeo-Christian).

It is always a matter here of distinguishing between the appearance and the reality – especially in advertising. Art plays games with *trompe-l'oeil* images – which still qualify as *eikons* to the extent that the game is evident, but would constitute simulacra if the painting of a veil led someone to mistake the painted image for a real veil. Simulacra can then be used as tools of deception. The whole thing becomes more complicated when the imitation involved might be another work of art, or imitation. In this regard, the original Lascaux caves in France have been reproduced some distance away. For the visitors to the replicated caves, the Palaeolithic images on the walls are indistinguishable from the originals. So that although the visitor does not believe the replicas to *be* the original, he or she does believe that the experience of seeing the replica is identical to seeing the original. Such is precisely the intention behind the new caves' existence. The replicas thus seem to be part image and part simulacrum.

In Deleuze's thinking, the simulacrum is anything that overturns the hierarchy between original and copy, appearance and reality, superficiality and profundity, so that it ceases to be possible to distinguish between the levels. There is no longer a prior identity (original) with which the image can be compared. The simulacrum itself might even be the means through which identity is constituted.

More sociologically, the work of Baudrillard has taken the notion of simulacrum and linked it to simulation (Baudrillard 1983). Through the code*, simulacra simulate reality to produce hyperreality. In other words the ultimate ground of reality ceases to have a material incarnation and becomes virtual. Simulacra, therefore, are ultimately virtual. The situation can be understood historically in light of different forms of simulation corresponding to three kinds of counterfeit.

Simulation in the Renaissance and Classical era (fifteenth to eighteenth centuries in Europe) is based on the difference between the natural object and its imitation; in the industrial era (nineteenth to mid-twentieth centuries), counterfeit is based on the difference between the true and false product (e.g. between an authentic and a fake Cartier watch); finally, in the era of reproduction and the code (Second World War onwards), the difference between the real and its representation is erased. Or, as was signalled by Deleuze, the question of the relation between the original and the copy ceases to matter.

From a social point of view, the dominance of the code has profound implications if, as seems likely, all traditional forms of truth and authenticity begin to break down – not necessarily because society has become more permissive or nihilist, but because the idea of an origin, whether natural or cultural, as preceding the present is no longer so plausible in scientific or philosophical terms. Consequently, opposites begin to collapse and become potentially interchangeable, and the undecidable reigns – in fashion, in relation to the beautiful and the ugly; in politics, in relation to left and right; in the media, in relation to truth and fiction; at the level of objects, in relation to the useful and the useless; in nature, in relation to culture, in the imaginary* in relation to the real.

As with Lascaux, other entire cities have been reproduced (colonial Williamsburg), initially in the interest of preservation or leisure; subsequently, the imitation itself has come to assume an importance equal to a hypothetical reality. The claim is that, very soon, the majority of people will have forgotten the original of which the simulacrum is a reminder. At that point, we are truly in the world of hyperreality.

Another dimension of the simulacrum concerns signification. In light of structuralist semiotics, everything signifies: there is no pure object in itself, as the grand hope of science led the early twentieth century to believe. Or at least, were there to be an ultimate reality, it is not conventional systems of signs that will lead us there. The disposition of buildings in a city might symbolise a way of life* and a history, as well as the presence of wealth or poverty. Or, buildings, such as are found in New York, might signify the high point of modernity*. Again, the way that fields are ploughed (or not) signifies the type of technology used and therefore whether or not we are dealing with an agricultural community or a collection of farms producing goods for the international market. Everything that is extant signifies. The era of the signifier (see sign: signifier/signified) thus joins that of the simulacrum.

In this light, it is only a small step to ask about the 'reality' of the signifier: the difference between appearance (signifier) and reality then becomes undecidable and the simulacrum appears. Because every signifier is essentially conventional, or arbitrary*, the simulacrum also ushers in the dominance of the code, or hyperreality. Like the code, the simulacrum signals that we are in the era of reproduction, the essential principle of the code being reproduction. Clearly, because it is driven by the digital* code, the computer world, and, more generally, cybernetics* and cyberspace*, is the field of reproduction *par excellence*. The field of molecular biology and DNA manipulation is also to be understood as dominated by the code. The reproduction of cells in cloning (see clone) assumes that the material incarnation of bodies is less important than the ultimate cell structure, which if it cannot be reproduced itself can be treated as a mechanism of reproduction pure and simple.

The issue with all of this is that the sacred – the true origin which cannot be reproduced – will also be erased. When war comes, everyone can be a target; terror can be the order of the day. The difference between enemy and friend cannot be determined in any absolute sense. Now, there is no longer an authentic, non-innocent target. If everyone is guilty, no one is; but if no one is guilty, everyone can be guilty. In effect, a sense of responsibility is needed in relation to these issues and not just the glib discourse of jaundiced intellectuals.

Baudrillard, Jean (1983 [1981]) *Simularcra and Simulations*, trans. Paul Foss, Paul Patton and Philip Beitchman, New York: Sémiotext(e).
Deleuze, Gilles (1994 [1968]) *Difference and Repetition*, trans. Paul Patton, New York: Columbia University Press.

See CLONE; NIHILISM TECHNICS; TRUTH

SPECTACLE
The origin of 'spectacle' comes from the French, *spectacle*, meaning, play, in the theatrical sense. This is the context in which Jean–Jacques Rousseau (1712–78) published a treatise against theatre entitled, *Lettre sur les spectacles* (Letter on the Theatre: 1758). From the Greek, *theoria*, theory is a way of viewing the spectacle – of seeing at a

distance. According to the French sociologist, Pierre Bourdieu, this gives rise to the objectivist illusion which amounts to treating the world as a spectacle to be observed and forgetting that the objectifying gaze is itself a part of the world (Bourdieu 1990: 27).

In the 1960s, the French situationist, Guy Debord (1931–1994), gave the idea of spectacle a modern twist when he coined the phrase, 'society of the spectacle' (Debord 1994). According to Debord, modern, capitalist society has become a society of spectacles and of the image. In fact, the spectacle is mediated by the image. Here we could think of the media itself as dominating all other institutions, so that everything turns into a representation – or even into a simulacrum*. There is no reality any more, no profundity; everything deemed to be important has entered the world of appearances. Needless to say, perhaps, everything has been turned into a commodity. Exchange-value and the market have taken over from use-value and the gift*, and now dominate all forms of social and political life.

With the commodification of society comes the total professionalisation of life. Sport as much as teaching has become professional. The upshot of professionalisation is that the life of the amateur has receded into the background. Non-professionals in the sporting domain are forced – and now want – to watch from the side. The aim is to mount the most spectacular show possible; club loyalties are on the wane, as spectators go for the biggest spectacle. Headlines say: 'The two greatest teams of all time in a head to head clash!' But most people, the spectacle theory points out, are passive bystanders. They are not physically involved in the proceedings on the ground.

Daniel Boorstin's 1962 book on the image presents a similar argument: once there were heroes who truly achieved things, now there are celebrities created by the media; once there were travellers who endeavoured to know the lands they visited, now there are tourists who stay within the cultural capsule of their own culture even when they are outside that culture, and so it goes on (Boorstin 1971). For Boorstin, as for Debord, the image* is superficial. Only reality is profound.

Despite the retrospective nostalgia such views might seem to represent, they have received a new lease of life in the work of French intellectuals like Julia Kristeva and Philippe Sollers. For these thinkers, new technologies (the internet, genetic engineering), which tear everything from its context, along with the mediatisation of reality, have resulted in the atrophying of psychic space. One index of this is the extent to which 'borderline' psychological disorders are noticeably on the increase. Such disorders deform the capacity to fantasise and imagine*, as they also inhibit the capacity to interpret reality.

These deficits reduce the capacity to develop individuality because the opportunity for revolt is inhibited (see difference–individuality). Revolt does not have to be transgressive in the Romantic, early nineteenth-century sense of the term; it simply has to be an obstacle to being swallowed up by the standardised behaviour represented in the media. Revolt can be eminently personal, if need be. Writing* a novel, or engaging in psychoanalysis (which aims to liberate the individual's unconscious) can constitute revolt in this sense.

No doubt some critics will remain dissatisfied with the critique of the society of the spectacle as here outlined. They will say that the democratisation of culture increasingly brings the high culture of the canon into contact with the popular culture of the media. And politically, this must be a good thing. On the other hand, there is the issue of judgement and the implications for quality that this entails. Not to be able to face this raises the prospect of *ressentiment** – to the extent that the popularisation of culture can also be a way of levelling those whose talents are greater than one's own.

Boorstin, Daniel J. (1971 [1962]) *The Image: A Guide to Pseudo-Events in America*, New York: Atheneum.
Bourdieu, Pierre (1990 [1980]) *The Logic of Practice*, trans. Richard Nice, Cambridge: Polity Press in association with Basil Blackwell.
Debord, Guy (1994 [1967]) *Society of the Spectacle*, trans. Donald Nicholson-Smith, New York: Zone Books.

See DIFFERENCE–INDIVIDUALITY

SUBJECT

'Subject' derives from the Latin, *subjectum*, meaning, 'something put underneath', and corresponds to the Greek, *hypokeimenon*, connoting the ideal of a substratum. Subject, in this indirect way, is close to 'substance'. Before looking at the main social and philosophical issues concerning the concept of 'subject', there are a number of relatively common meanings of the term. These are:

1   the subject of a dissertation or book, which is what the text in question is about – its central theme and field of inquiry;

2   'subject' used as a verb meaning being 'subjected to', or constrained and directed by, as with the notion of being subject to law, or subject to someone's beck and call;

3   the subject of a sentence: this can refer to the topic of the sentence, or it can mean the subject in language through the use of first, second or third person: the grammatical subject.

The idea of the linguistic subject has been a particularly important inspiration in the version of psychoanalysis presented by Jacques Lacan (1901–1981). Lacan famously said, for instance, that the 'signifier represents the subject for another signifier' (Lacan 1977: 316). Here the subject is to be understood as being much more than the grammatical subject of the sentence, but much less than a fully sensuous, psychological subject. The point is less that the latter does not exist, than that access to the subject is always via a signifier, that is, through the symbolic order.

In a further move, Lacan locates the subject in the defiles of desire. For desire, too, is essentially symbolic. Desire, like the sign*, evokes the absence of the object. This includes the absence, or lack, of the phallus/penis in the experience of castration. The subject is the subject of this lack: that is, the subject is the one who continually fails to unite with the object of desire, since to do so would entail the end of desire as such. This is perhaps why desire is essentially unconscious*. For the consciousness subject can only imagine uniting with the object, and of overcoming the separation which in fact keeps desire alive.

Psychoanalysis has then supplied a good deal of the impetus for the revival of interest in the subject. In doing so, it has emphasised the symbolic dimension of human experience in relation to sexuality and identity*, including fantasy, over the biological dimension, even though the language of Freud's early work can sometimes be misleading on this front. Psychoanalysis, after all, is charged with being concerned with psychic space, and this brings it into immediate contact with the subject. Even the object* in psychoanalysis matters only because of its symbolic status and thus because of its importance in the formation of the subject. The subject, to give a definition in this light, is that entity which constitutes itself in and through its objects.

Also in the psychoanalytic tradition is Julia Kristeva's concept of the 'subject-in-process' (Kristeva 1984: 22). The latter continually restructures itself in the dialectic between the semiotic* (or drive element) and the symbolic (the domain of language and signs). The dynamic drive dimension continually challenges the more static symbolic order. In the symbolic, the law takes over; the subject-in-process is a challenge to the law.

In a more political sense, there is a difference between being a subject and being an object – being objectified. Here, the issue concerns the assumption that the other* (object) is already known and can be subjected to the idea or rule of the one who posits the other as object. By contrast, to approach the other as subject is to recognise the other's autonomy, and to acknowledge that there may be no idea or rule adequate to this autonomy. Women, obviously, and ethnic minorities, have often been treated as objects rather than subjects.

Even though Kant (1724–1804) posited the transcendental 'I' subject as a noumenal idea (no experience can access it because this 'I' does not belong to the phenomenal world), in 1781, philosophically, Nietzsche (1844–1900) is the thinker who possibly attributes most importance to the subject. For Nietzsche the 'will to power' is at bottom a subjective, purposeless will, a will of nihilism* (Nietzsche 1968). This subject as will to power is open ended, yet Heidegger (1889–1976) saw in it a reductionism: everything becomes *subjectum* (Heidegger 1977: 88–112). Nietzsche is thus characterised as the last metaphysical thinker, the last thinker to propose a general answer to questions about human nature and the nature of the world.

Heidegger's positing of Nietzsche as a metaphysician, in spite of his nihilism, corresponds to the reservations some philosophers have about the concept of the subject, due to its metaphysical aspects. That is to say, 'subject', like 'object' seems to be already given before the task of establishing its nature has even begun. One way round this is represented by Foucault. In nearly all of his works, he attempts to write a history of subjectivity, if not of the subject (cf. Foucault 1973, 1986). For Foucault, the responses to marginal states such as madness and sexual perversions, the psychological characterisations involved in classifying criminals, can offer insights into the highly complex and differentiated possibilities which lie behind 'subject': a term so often used but so little understood.

Foucault, Michel (1973 [1961]) *Madness and Civilization: A History of Insanity in the Age of Reason* (abridged), trans. Richard Howard, New York: Vintage.
Foucault, Michel (1986 [1984]) *The History of Sexuality, Volume 3: The Care*

of the Self, trans. Robert Hurley, New York: Pantheon.

Heidegger, Martin (1977) 'The Word of Nietzsche: "God is Dead"', in *The Question of Technology and Other Essays*, trans. William Lovitt, New York: Harper & Row (Harper Torchbooks).

Kristeva, Julia (1984 [1974]) *Revolution in Poetic Language*, trans. Margaret Waller, New York: Columbia UniversityPress.

Lacan, Jacques (1977 [1966]) *Écrits: A Selection*, trans. Alan Sheridan, London: Tavistock.

Nietzsche, Friedrich (1968 [1901]) *Will to Power*, trans. Walter Kaufmann and R.J. Hollingsworth, New York: Vintage.

See FANTASY/PHANTASY, FANTASM

SYNTHETIC (See ANALYTIC–SYNTHETIC)

TECHNICS

Strictly speaking, technics is the practice of technical procedures of all kinds. Its origin goes back to the Greek, *tekhnē*, meaning art. 'Art' here has now come to refer to applied technical procedures, or skills. The more usual term for these procedures and programmes is of course, technology. But this literally means the discourse or science of technics, rather than the procedures themselves. As key technical advances are the usual focus of those who use the term 'technology', technics is a more appropriate term. 'Technics' also alerts us to how overused 'technology' is becoming in a climate of apparently endless technical advances – as seen in the domain of technoscience (e.g. biotechnology*) and cybernetics*.

Technics is often defined, in its most general sense, as a means which can be applied to a multiplicity of ends. The proliferation of this means-ends rationality, as the essence of technics, is frequently invoked to show that technics has become a force dominating humanity, rather than a force for liberation. Marx would call this an alienating force (see alienation*). Here, the user of the technics is put on one side of the equation, and the technics itself on the other. Recently, however, the validity of this separation has been brought into question – first of all by Simondon (1964: 18–19) with the idea of 'transduction', then by Stiegler (1998: 21–27) – so that the human and the tool become inseparably intertwined. 'Man' is not only a 'tool making animal', he is also constituted in his very being by what is 'outside' him – almost to the point where his outside 'is' his inside. The essentially human can no longer be understood, on this account, as alienated from technics. The term that describes this close relationship between the human and the technical sphere, 'transduction', means that one term or element cannot be without the other. The subject, or 'who', of humanity is thus inseparable from the object, or the 'what' of technics. They are joined in a transductive relation. We must elaborate on this, but first it is useful to consider the notion of techniques.

It is not only the development of explicitly external tools and technics that makes humanity what it is, but also the use of the body. In the first place, the human hand can be conceived as a tool for grasping and for doing many other things: carrying, digging, manipulating, scraping, hitting, pulling, levering, and so on. Other parts of the human body are similarly used in a host of both everyday and exceptional tasks and projects. The gap between technics and the human is thus gradually reduced. And this is even more the case in light of Mauss's (1872–1950) description of techniques of the body (Mauss 1973). Mauss shows that many everyday activities – from spitting to squatting – are techniques, which means that they are learned and perfected. An indication of this is given by cases in which the subject is unable to perform what seem to be the most elementary tasks. To be a technique, at least two conditions must pertain: the technique must be efficacious and so capable of producing the desired result, and it must be transmissible, that is, for Mauss, it must be inscribed within a tradition. Bodily techniques, as techniques, are not spontaneous but are learned. It is also because they are learned, that they are transmissible, that is to say, reproducible. Bodily techniques are thus like technics without an instrument.

From the idea that technics is only instrumental – a mere means – and separate and distinct from what is essentially human, we now have the idea that the human and the technical go together; for all learning is grounded in technique, in the sense that all learning enables the repetition, if not the reproduction, of something. Even the act of spitting entails a minimal amount of practice in order to get it right. Memorising, too, requires technique – either the practice of movements of the body in a particular way (as in sports), or intellectual procedures, the most spectacular of these being the Roman use of imagination* in order to represent walking around a house (usually the childhood abode) and depositing information that one wishes to recall. Probably there are also memories which bypass all technique; but at least there is a vast array of information which does not.

When technics (technology) is defined as the application of ideas produced in pure research, it is again placed on the applied side, while scientific ideas are theoretical, and essentially different from their application. Maybe this is so. What is less certain is that the production of ideas is independent from technique. This is implied when people speak about strategies for invention, for being creative – such as having a break from a task in order that one can come at it with a fresh mind.

In Bernard Stiegler's recent work on the nature of technics, we see that technics is also a process of disorientation: technics – the revolutions in technics – uproots humanity from community and context. Community*, from this point of view, can only ever be provisional – established for the duration of a prevailing framework of technics. Thus does the Agricultural Revolution give way to the Industrial Revolution, and the latter to the information* age, based in computer technology. More particularly, every form of 'know-how' produces something; every new form of 'know-how' produces something new. The marriage of technics and 'know-how' produces constant disorientations in human history*. In fact, history is driven by these disorientations. Even the most so-called traditional societies and cultures will be affected by them; for if they do not produce them themselves, they cannot escape being affected by the forces that do produce them. No culture* can reinvent itself as an island. This is Stiegler's central and most provocative thesis. It gives little enduring weight to the impact of context, preferring to emphasise the continual decontextualisations technics brings in its wake. Ultimately the 'what' signals the decontextualisation of the 'who'.

Stiegler goes further. Even if memory* relies on techniques for its enactment, as a relation to a body of information* and knowledge* – to a heritage, indeed – memory is finite. This is what ties humanity to technics. Even more, says Stiegler: memory is technics. For only God has perfect recall; only God forgets nothing. In this sense, the new data retrieval systems of CD-ROMs and other storage forms serve to bind humanity ever more surely to its destiny in technics.

If there is a response to Stiegler, it may be that of Heidegger, even though Stiegler also mounts a strong case against Heidegger's approach to technics. For Heidegger, the key to technics is inaccessible: technics is conceived solely as a means (Heidegger 1977: 21). The resonances of the Greek, *tekhne* offer the possibility also of thinking technics as *poiesis*, or the unveiling of what is concealed. What prevents technics being appreciated as poiesis is the dominance of the instrumental view of technics as a means and the dominance in science of the *causa efficiens*, the efficient cause. Little thinking is possible when technics is conceived in this way. Technics (technology) rather has to be linked up with the idea of revealing – of revealing the truth* of Being*, in fact. Thus, *tekhne* becomes a 'bringing-forth' linked to poiesis. Instead of an instrumental version of technics, which would enable humanity to do things in its own interest, Heidegger wants to poeticise technics and in so doing claim it for a thought which allows Being to come into unconcealment. This, for Heidegger, is the ultimate truth (*aletheia*). Is there anyone – other than the specialist – who is willing to lend an ear to this argument for a poetic view of technics?

Heidegger, Martin (1977) 'The Question of Technology', in *The Question of Technology and Other Essays*, trans. William Lovitt, New York: Harper & Row (Harper Torchbooks).

Mauss, Marcel (1973 [1935]) 'Techniques of the Body', trans. Ben Brewster, *Economy and Society*, 2, 1: 70–88.

Simondon, Gilbert (1964) *L'Individu et sa genèse physico-biologique*, Paris: Presses Universitaires de France.

Stiegler, Bernard (1998 [1994]) *Technics and Time, 1: The Fault of Epimetheus*, trans. Richard Beardsworth and George Collins, Stanford, CA: Stanford University Press.

THEORY

In its popular form, theory is often contrasted with practice, or with reality, or with the body (as opposed to the intellect). There is often a negative connotation here, to the effect that theory does not have much practical use. That is, theory can become an end in itself rather than leading to a utilitarian outcome.

Theory, however, originated in the Greek, *theōria*, as that which enabled one to see the spectacle*. Other connotations include speculation and contemplation. Theoretical work would allow a certain detachment, in relation to a body of information*, so that the underlying coherence or logic of it could be revealed.

In physics, in the field of quantum* theory, observation of the orbit of electrons around the nucleus of an atom can only be known theoretically, through the use of probability theory. And Einstein's work involved the *theory* of relativity before it could be proven in practice.

In Marxism, theory came to be the guiding tool for political practice. Without such theory, Lenin and others thought, there could be no revolutionary practice. This could be called the 'blueprint' notion of theory. It is intellectualist in that it presupposes that ideas precede action. It is analytical in that it assumes that the object can, in theory, be broken down into its essential elements before it is used in an application (see analytic–synthetic).

Overall, though, theory has developed into a quasi-discipline in humanities and social science departments in Anglo-American universities. Here, theory questions the basis of discipline areas, searching out ideological encrustations – as in feminist theory, queer theory, postcolonial, or postmodern theory; it also attempts to make discoveries by engaging in particular types of readings of a variety of texts. French thinkers, such as Foucault, Derrida and Deleuze, have also been called in to assist with the project of gaining theoretical insights (an evocation – not always recognised – of *theoria*).

One limitation of much of the work done in theory concerns the privileging of subjectivity. This is perhaps most marked in the idea of 'situated knowledges' as proposed by Donna Haraway (1990). All knowledge, says Haraway, contains the mark of position of the observer theorist. A further, reflexive, step, however, would suggest that the possibility of knowing the situatedness of all knowledge is one which speaks from a position of objectivity, where position is not an issue. It is as though there can be no theoretical position that would enable a true insight into the situated nature of knowledge as such.

Theory has also been invoked with a certain political intent against empirical work claiming to show eternal verities. The domain of IQ studies is one such notorious domain; class stratification studies is another. Here, empirical work claims to reduce theory

to a minimum, if it does not eliminate it altogether. The counter-argument is that empirical research depends on a philosophical framework, whether this is explicit or not. A particularly influential framework here is that of the correspondence theory of truth*, which says that good scientific work is, in some profound sense, a reflection of the reality it studies.

At the other extreme is the notion that, in science, there is ultimately only a theoretical reality, since the scientific object is produced by science itself, and that, therefore, all empiricist claims that a knowledge of the object is equivalent to the (external) object itself are misplaced.

An additional issue surrounding theory is that it is not 'popular' – that is, it does not have the transparency and immediacy of common sense and often demands some effort in order to be understood. This puts theory in a problematic relationship with a society where results tend to count more than the effort needed to achieve them.

Haraway, Donna (1990) 'Situated Knowledges: The Science Question in Feminism and the Privilege of Partial Perspective', in *Simians Cyborgs and Women: The Reinvention of Nature* New York: Routledge, 183–202.

See ANALYTIC–SYNTHETIC; EPISTEMOLOGY; POSTMODERNITY

THERMODYNAMICS

Literally meaning the study of the behaviour, or force, of heat, 'thermodynamics' (from the Greek, *dúnamis*, force, and *thérmē*, heat) came into being in the nineteenth century, in the 'age of steam' and, therefore, of energy. In 1824, a French army engineer, Sadi Carnot (1796–1832) found that in a steam engine heat flowed from warmer to cooler regions – from the hot boiler to the cooler condenser. Although Carnot was incorrect to think that no heat was lost from the system, he did recognise that the more efficient the system, the less the energy required for its operation – a not insignificant fact for the growing capitalist economy of the nineteenth century.

Following Carnot, Rudolph Clausius (1822–88) in Germany in 1865 coined the term 'entropy'* and the age of thermodynamics had arrived. While the first law is that the quantity of available energy remains constant, 'entropy' is the second law of thermodynamics and it states that energy will be lost from every mechanical system, and will tend towards a maximum. Another way of putting this is to say that, from a thermodynamic perspective, disorder affects every system. As a result, each has a 'use by' date; none can go on for ever – whether these systems be biological, mechanical or informational. Thus, individuals, or communities, that want to find the secret of eternal life are, at the same time, seeking a way of countering entropy.

Prior to the Industrial Revolution and the age of steam, the Newtonian era of wind and sail, of wheels, pulleys and winches, did not recognise entropy as an essential dimension of life. For this era time was, in principle, reversible. Only the contingent limitedness of human knowledge* caused time* to be irreversible. For God, time was perfectly reversible.

Apart from its place in the history* of science, thermodynamics has a more general place in nineteenth century and contemporary European thought. Marx (1818–83), for example, saw society as being in constant need of renewing itself, both economically and

politically. Without finding new ways to produce more energy (including resources necessary to maintain the labour-power* of the proletariat) the capitalist economic system was bound to break down. The very internal logic of capitalism, Marx thought, was to maintain an endless cycle of production, whether what was produced was needed or not. In the end, this was impossible. As if he had read Clausius in great detail, Marx says that, eventually, the capitalist system, because of its internal contradictions, must break down into the disorder of revolution.

In his early, and in some of his later, work Freud (1856–1939), too, was influenced by the thermodynamic paradigm (Freud 1961, 1966). In his posthumously published text of 1895, Freud famously refers to psychical energy as bound (order) and unbound (disorder). And in his 1920 work *Beyond the Pleasure Principle* Freud evokes thermodynamics in his description of the death drive as a drive towards complete satisfaction brought by a complete dissipation of psychic energy, and a concomitant absence of the excitation typical of the sexual, or life, drive. Life, in short, here equals more psychic energy; death is equivalent to a complete absence of energy. In effect, complete satisfaction is also the equivalent of the thermodynamic idea of homeostasis, or equilibrium, while the life drive is a build-up of energy that brings about a disequilibrium in psychic space. Disequilibrium implies a certain disorder, or randomness, in the organisation of the psyche.

In an article on change from the age of mechanics to that of thermodynamics, Michel Serres (1982) makes the following points, which he illustrates, in part, by looking at the painting *A Wharf on the Thames* (1796) by the late eighteenth-century artist, George Garrard and works by J.M.W. Turner (1775–1851), the precursor of Impressionism.

Garrard's works are dominated by drawing and outline, that is: 'lines, points and circles', volume, balance and equilibrium illustrated by a world of 'levers, balances, winches, pulleys, hoists, ropes, weights and blocks', where 'geometry alone rules', while in Turner's works, by contrast (e.g. *The Burning of the Houses of Lords and Commons*, 1835), paint and colour dominate, and line and point give way to volume, random shapes and the fragmentation of clouds, ice, snow, fire and smoke, mist and fog – elements typical of stochastic series of random events. Turner, then, attempts to capture disorder, or irreversible time, on canvas.

Turner is a painter, Serres shows us, who is marked by the thermodynamic notions that were to become so integral to the Industrial Revolution and the age of the steam engine.

With the new information* technologies in computing and the internet, the question now arises as to whether thermodynamics and the energy model used for interpreting the period of the Industrial Revolution and large-scale production that this entailed, is now giving over to an age of reproduction and 'cool' technologies, which no longer depend on the dynamic relationship between disorder and equilibrium, input and output, conservation and dissipation. According to some scientists, entropy is still a feature of information systems, but it can serve positive, survival ends when it is recognised that unexpected disorder is the information message that a system needs in order to renew itself. In other words, information has become an otherness necessary to the identity of the system itself.

Freud, Sigmund (1961 [1920]) *Beyond the Pleasure Principle*, trans. James Strachey, New York: W.W. Norton.

Freud, Sigmund (1966) 'Project for a Scientific Psychology [1895]' (posthumous), trans. James Strachey, in *The Standard Edition of the Complete Psychological Works of Sigmund Freud Volume I* (1886–1899), London: The Hogarth Press.

Serres, Michel (1982) 'Turner Translates Carnot', trans. Mike Shortland, in *Block 6*. 46–55.

TIME

'Time' derives from Old English, *tima*, and Swedish, *timme*, meaning an hour. Also from the same base comes 'tide', which was superseded by 'time'. There is no dimension of life that does not include time. This is true whether the focus is history*, as the *longue durée* (long term), or whether the focus is memory. Time in the everyday sense is the time of clocks. This is intellectual time which measures the duration of instants. The weakness of this view of time is that it presupposes, as Bergson showed (Bergson 1991), a durationless moment, or a moment outside time in order to found the temporal domain. In a calculating society dominated by the market, this is the version of time that prevails. Or, to put it another way: time as pure presence prevails. This, however, is, in a certain sense, also a denial of time. Under such circumstances time has to remain unconscious* (even though Freud said that the unconscious does not recognise time).

There is also qualitative time, time as subjective, based in emotional experiences, which has nothing to do with measurement. This is time as difference. Within such a framework, we have time as timeliness, time as the 'untimely' in Nietzsche's sense, where what is presented (ideas, art) cannot yet be understood or accepted, or where a person is ahead of his or her time. These are all qualitative expressions of time.

Further thought reveals that subjective notions of time, as encapsulated in 'early', 'late', 'up to the moment', or the sense that 'one's time has come', are also experiences of time, rather than measurements of it. Here, time has a meaning.

A further development along the lines of time as subjective is contained in Gilles Deleuze's (1925–1995) reworking of Bergson's notion of time in relation to cinema (Deleuze 1986, 1989). Thus if photography embodies for many the notion of time as a series of static moments – time as spatialised – cinema, in Deleuze's hands, brings a dynamic aspect to time. Initially through movement in the films of the period before the First World War, then as a direct presentation of a time image, cinema comes to constitute a real innovation in relation to the experience of memory* and time. Memory is no longer a weaker version of perception and has its own autonomy.

In the work of Bergson and Deleuze, cinema is to time what photography is to space. For photography, in having, as its essential task, the presentation – or re-presentation – of the moment of the past frozen for eternity – in recapturing the present – gives a perception version of time based in representation, time as space, not time as memory, as subjective and affective experience. The latter, made explicit in Italian neo-realism and French New Wave films, is what cinema brings.

Bergson, Henri (1991 [1939]) *Matter and Memory*, trans. Nancy Margaret Paul and W. Scott Palmer, New York: Zone Books.

Deleuze, Gilles (1986 [1983]) *Cinema 1: The Movement Image*, trans. Hugh Tomlinson and Barbara Haberjam, Minneapolis: University of Minnesota Press.

Deleuze, Gilles (1989 [1985]) *Cinema 2: The Time Image*, trans. Hugh Tomlinson and Robert Galeta, Minneapolis: University of Minnesota Press.

See DIFFERENCE–INDIVIDUALITY; IMAGE; ZENO'S PARADOX

TRANSCENDENCE (see IMMANENT / IMMANENCE-TRANSCENDENT / TRANSCENDENCE)

TRUTH

Although the root of the English word, 'truth', derives from Old English, *trīewth*, and *trēowth*, meaning 'as truth', the philosophical idea is more significant, and so it this, rather than the word itself, which will be addressed in what follows.

In the wake of Nietzsche's (1844–1900) claim that truth is an error (Nietzsche 1968: sect. 535) and part of the will to power* – where truth would be relative to the interests involved (ibid.: sect. 455) – some would say that truth in itself is no longer a valid category. On the other hand, life* holds such importance in Nietzsche's philosophy that it assumes a quasi-truth for him. In the wake of the terrible as well as the positive qualities of life, Nietzsche asks how much truth a spirit can stand (ibid.: sect. 1041).

More generally, though, 'the true' might be as close as one can get to truth in a pragmatic age. A proposition is true if it accords with the reality to which it claims to refer. This is truth as adequation, or the correspondence theory of truth. For Heidegger, this philosophical meaning derives from the Latin term, *veritas*. In the Greek version, truth was *aletheia*, or the coming into unconcealment of that which was concealed. It is very different from *veritas*, as it is not related to error, but concerns the appearance of Being as such. *Veritas*, or truth as correspondence, can only be concerned with particular beings and natural reality; in other words, it is concerned with existence rather than with Being as such (cf. Heidegger 1994: 95–107).

The dominance of truth as adequation would be fine were it not for the fact that it ties in with an excessively calculating and technocratic approach to life: that is, truth as *veritas* is excessively pragmatic.

Truth can also be an ideal, a transcendent domain, which locks into a religious doctrine and disposition. Christ, for example, said: 'I am the way the truth and the light'. 'Light' reminds us that in the Platonic schema, truth was equated with the sun, or light in the strongest sense. However, if the sun is a metaphor for truth, is truth thereby devalued? For truth cannot be metaphorical without paradox. This would be like saying that the truth is figurative, or is even a fiction. The Enlightenment, too, in the eighteenth century is caught in the dilemma of truth as metaphor, where truth is the light, retrieving an entity or object from obscurity.

Nihilism* says that truth has no absolute foundation, that truth is relative to the position in social space, or interests of the person or group concerned.

Heidegger, Martin (1994) *Basic Questions of Philosophy. Selected 'Problems' of 'Logic'*, trans. Richard Rojcewicz and André Schuwer, Bloomington and Indianapolis: Indiana University Press.
Nietzsche, Friedrich (1968 [1901]) *Will to Power*, trans. Walter Kaufmann and R.J. Hollingsworth, New York: Vintage.

See EPISTEMOLOGY

U

UNCONSCIOUS

'Unconscious' in the psycho-analytic sense first occurs in 1893 in Sigmund Freud (1856–1939) and Joseph Breuer's (1842–1925) work on hysteria (1974: 100), where it was a way of explaining the symptom in neurosis. Although often used collo-quially to refer to actions that are carried out spontaneously and unre-flectively, Freud gave it a much more technical meaning.

Initially, the unconscious (Ucs) was equivalent to the 'id' as the reserve of unbound sexual energy and impulses of maximum pleasure-seeking. In the id–ego–superego schema, looked at economically, the energy of the id and of the superego – as a force for repres-sion – has to be mediated by the ego. The more energy goes to one agency, the less is available to another.

From a topological, or descriptive point of view, Freud speaks of the pre-conscious (Pcs) as the place of material that can be accessed by consciousness (Cs) (Freud 1964), if need be. The id (the place of repressed energy), gives rise to the formation of the uncon-scious (dreams, phantasies, symptoms, repetitions), while the ego is the point of consciousness *par excellence*, and the superego the source of moral impera-tives and so-called normal social behaviour, and the bridge between the individual, inner world, and the external, outer world. Topographically, the ego acquires its moral sense from the superego, while, at the other extreme, the id strives to achieve pleasure.

The topographical view thus gives way to a dynamic view, where the ego becomes the mediating point between the id and the superego. Although con-sciousness seems to claim the contrary, the ego is, on this view, nothing in itself, and is simply the third element enabling a synthesis to be articulated between pleasure and morality. Or, to put it another way, the ego is a realist: too much pleasure is imprudent, because it might lead to death, while, by contrast, the pursuit of an ethic of absolute ends, as Weber would call it – the ethic of fundamentalism – is also a danger to the organism. The ego thus works for balance.

It is also true to say that Freud, in *The Interpretation of Dreams* (1976), and elsewhere, theorises and analyses the unconscious as a domain in its own right. Thus, displacement and conden-sation in dream work – the mecha-nisms which turn the more laconic, manifest dream content into a disguise – are also mechanisms through which the unconscious dream thoughts can be deciphered. Generally, Freud said that dream interpretation was '*the royal road to a knowledge of the unconscious*'

(Freud 1976: 769. Freud's emphasis). In other respects, Freud's conception of the unconscious prior to *The Interpretation of Dreams* tends to be biologically based: Freud was aiming at the time to find a biological explanation for the psyche.

After 1900, the unconscious becomes related to symbolic formations (or 'parapraxes': slips of the tongue; repetitions of words; memory lapses; dream images) and to natural language as the main vehicle for these. But of course the prime vehicle for the unconscious becomes what is, and is not, said in the psychoanalytic session. What is revealed, or remains concealed, there is unconscious desire, which inevitably has a sexual aspect.

The French psychoanalyst, Jacques Lacan (1977) has taken up this recognition of the primacy of language in revealing the unconscious. Lacan (1901–1981), strongly influenced by structuralism, famously described the unconscious as being 'structured like a language', with the two technical terms invented by Freud to describe dream work – condensation and displacement – being equated by Lacan, in light of the linguist Roman Jakobson's (1896–1982) work, with 'metaphor' and 'metonymy' (Jakobson 1990: 115–133).

The exact meaning of Lacan's aphorism relating the unconscious and language has never been fully interpreted. However, if the unconscious is revealed in language, the speech of the analytic session becomes crucial. Moreover, if language is understood as a structure (syntax, grammar, person, etc.) rather than content (the equivalent of the French word, *langue*), the unconscious approximates this structure. In other words, the unconscious

is the key to the kind of logic that emerges once one listens in a different kind of way to the apparent 'incoherencies' of unconscious phenomena. The unconscious, then, borrows the content of existing speech in order to give it different syntax and grammar. Particular weight here is attached to the relations between elements rather than to the nature of the elements themselves.

Such a view of the unconscious is close to Freud's view when he said that his approach to dreams was different to what had gone before because he did not interpret dreams according to a pre-existing code*. For the dream itself, Freud proposed, constitutes its own code. The dream – the royal road to the unconscious – is thus 'structured like a language'.

Breuer, Joseph and Freud, Sigmund (1974 [1893]) *Studies in Hysteria*, in *The Pelican Freud Library, Volume 3*, trans. James and Alix Strachey, Harmondsworth: Penguin.

Freud, Sigmund (1964 [1915]) 'The Unconscious', trans. James Strachey in *The Freud Pelican Library, Volume 11: On Metapsychology: The Theory of Psychoanalysis*, Harmondsworth: Penguin.

Freud, Sigmund (1976 [1900]) *The Interpretation of Dreams*, in *The Freud Pelican Library, Volume 4*, trans. James Strachey, London: Penguin.

Jakobson, Roman (1990) *On Language*, ed. Linda R. Waugh and Monique Monville-Burston, Cambridge, Mass., and London: Harvard University Press.

Lacan, Jacques (1977 [1966]) 'The Agency of the Letter in the Unconscious, or Reason since Freud', in *Écrits: A Selection*, trans. Alan Sheridan, London: Tavistock.

See FANTASY/PHANTASY, FANTASM

UNIVERSAL

'Universal' is a term with a long history in philosophy and political thought. In Plato's and Aristotle's philosophy, the realm of the universal is the realm of the pure form of the entity, whether this be human, animal or thing. In the realm of forms, things are free of any difference: so, the form of the horse is the ideal to which all manifestations of horse aspire. Although this pure form is independent of empirical reality, Plato and Aristotle are realists because the realm of forms is deemed to be a truly existing realm.

A realist approach to universals can be contrasted with a nominalist view, first put forward in the Middle Ages. With nominalism, the universal does not exist as such but is the name, word or symbolic form organising a range of things. What the name names is real, but a name is not real – such is the nominalist credo.

Another dimension of the universal concerns the universality, or otherwise, of moral and political principles. Here, the universal corresponds to what is essential by comparison with what is contingent and particular. Or, more bluntly, it is sometimes contrasted with relativism. If torture is wrong, and judged to be a violation of universal human rights in societies with an Enlightenment heritage, is this principle truly applicable to all societies? The same applies to notions of democracy. Regarding the latter, certain countries on the 'way to development' (like Malaysia and Indonesia) have claimed that once the economic problems are solved, concern for human rights and democracy can then follow. In the view of these countries, to put pressure on such nations to respect human rights is to violate national sovereignty and to impose European cultural values.

China has used a similar argument. Issues arise in relation to the human rights of women in cultures and nations with a very marked sexual division of labour established by tradition. Should tradition be supported if it leads to injustice? Who is to decide here what is just and what is unjust and oppressive? Such are the key questions a universalist approach opens up.

Opponents of the defence of human rights have sometimes argued that the claimed universality of the rights being defended are in fact specific to the West – and even to the West's self-interest, as led by the United States. Possibly the most important defence of universalism in relation to such an argument has come from Edmund Husserl (1859–1938). Husserl's philosophical mission was to establish the essential foundations of thought, in contrast to contingent knowledge. The stakes here are cultural and political, as well as philosophical, as the following question serves to highlight: Is the European tradition of philosophy which is essentially transcendent and universalist since Plato, and certainly since Descartes, in fact ethnocentric in its claim concerning the essential nature of the transcendental realm? An affirmative response might well see itself as validated by the objection cited by Husserl towards the end of his *Origin of Geometry*:

> One will object: what naïveté, to seek to display, and to claim to have displayed, a historical a priori, an absolute, super-temporal validity, after we have obtained abundant testimony for the relativity of everything historical, of all historically developed world-apperceptions, right back to those of 'primitive' tribes. Every people, large or small, has its world in which, for that people, everything fits well together, whether in mythical-magical or in European-rational terms, and in which everything can be explained

perfectly. Every people has its 'logic' and, accordingly, if this logic is explicated in propositions, 'its' a priori. (Husserl 1989: 175)

It is therefore inadmissible to 'privilege' a single, European way of understanding cultural forms.

Husserl's response to this objection is clear and to the point, whether one agrees with it or not. It is that knowledge which is specific to a given time and place (knowledge deriving from myth or magical powers, for example) – 'all merely factual' knowledge, in effect – is unable to account for its foundation. More than this, however, the failure to account for the foundation means that the presuppositions underpinning a given form of scientific endeavour also remain unthematised and invisible, even when the necessity of these presuppositions is no less incontestable. How, Husserl thus puzzles, does one establish that there are different knowledges, different histories, different cultural presuppositions if not through some sort of transcendence? The above objection, therefore, has at least two levels. One of these concerns the 'facts of the case' (the fact of different logics and thus of historical relativity), while the other level concerns the preconditions of this knowing itself. For Husserl, the 'facts' presuppose the preconditions of these facts. Consequently, there are no autonomous facts for the good reason that the establishment of the relativity of factual knowledge entails a comparative approach that raises the question of how insight into, or knowledge of, the relativity of knowledges is possible. Put another way: it is necessary to know how differences in knowledges could be established from a particular position.

On this basis, the claim that, *de facto*, Eurocentrism colours all attempts to found universal premises, does not, *de jure*, invalidate the necessity for such universal premises. Thus even if the attempts at universalism are found wanting, the well-foundedness of a universalist insight is not thereby refuted. This would apply to moral and political rights as much as to knowledge.

It is very likely, then, that universalism cannot be avoided simply by arguing against it. For an anti-universalist philosophy is inconceivable. To question it is, in relation to it, to maintain a transcendent or metalinguistic, universal position.

To follow Husserl in his encounter with sceptical empiricism is also to work towards recognising the line dividing the essential Idea from the inessential, contingent moment. The contingent moment is also the existential moment: the moment of worldly existence that so fascinated the existentialists. Such a dividing line – such a border – current thinking has argued, is susceptible to breaches of all kinds. The integrity of the essential realm is thus at risk. Contingency intrudes into the essential and threatens its purity. Chance*, too, plays a part in the rupture of boundaries, and so the repressed (the negative) returns. All this is appreciated. And yet…this division cannot but be maintained; this is precisely why it can be threatened. Thus, the challenge to universalism could be the surest sign of its viability.

Husserl, Edmund (1989) *The Origin of Geometry*, trans. David Carr with an Introduction by Jacques Derrida, Lincoln and London: University of Nebraska Press.

See CULTURE; HISTORY

V, W

VALUE 'Value' has a number of meanings in philosophy and economics. In Nietzsche's philosophy, value assumes prime importance; for truth* itself becomes a value. In other respects, Nietzsche (1844–1900) set out to 'revalue all values' in terms of the 'will to power', where pure, form-giving, Apollonian ideals are devalued, and there is a revaluation of intoxication – or Dionysian realities – in relation to health, the body, beauty*, art, and in particular in relation to life*, or the world as it is – even its most terrible aspects. Because the old moral, largely Christian values (kindness, unselfishness, obedience, sobriety) devalued life (and truth in this sense), they are, in Nietzsche's philosophy, devalued in their turn (Nietzsche 1968).

Value has also been the subject of the famous fact–value distinction, which is reflected in the idea of a difference between what is, and what ought to be. While a positivist approach tends to adhere strongly to this distinction, the critics of positivism (e.g. the Frankfurt School) argue that the determination of what is (the facts) is implicated in the ideological position (value) of the one making the statement, or observation. In other words, so-called objectivity inevitably includes a value judgement at its heart, even if this is only that something is worth knowing.

However, the critics have, in their turn, been superseded by approaches informed by psychoanalysis and structuralist linguistics, where the humanism implicit in the notion of ideology* has been shown to be a limitation. This is because the humanist approach tends to privilege consciousness and the idea of the intrinsic nature of things, and neglects the unconscious* and the relationship between elements. In other words, access to the agent of the judging consciousness does not go without saying.

But maybe we should now listen to the critic of value as relational or subject to interests and desires of those involved. Here, it is not so much a matter of objective value, as of value as intrinsic, as an end in itself, not just as a means. At this point the market view of value is at issue. For value in market exchanges as represented by price is entirely relational. In addition, market price is very much linked to the exchange-value of the thing in question. The affective dimension – the love for the object – becomes irrelevant, and the issue becomes one between love* *or* money*.

Nietzsche, Friedrich (1968 [1901]) *Will to Power*, trans. Walter Kaufmann and R.J. Hollingsworth, New York: Vintage.

See EXCHANGE; MONEY

VIRTUAL (see CYBERSPACE)

VIRUS

The word 'virus' is a Latin word that meant slimy, liquid, poison or venom with offensive odour or taste. In disease terms, a virus is a tiny packet of genic information wrapped in protein, hundreds of times smaller than a bacterium, which shows no signs of life until it gets inside a living cell. Because of its exterior protein material, the virus is often accepted into the cell. It then confuses the cell's own genetic instructions and gets itself reproduced. It becomes aberrant, with new genes building their own protein shells. Consequently, a virus can deceive the body's immune system. Because a virus becomes part of the cell itself and thus part of part of the body's own system, a viral infection cannot, as is becoming increasingly well known, be treated successfully with antibiotics, which are designed to kill foreign bacteria. The characteristics of a virus then include a capacity to disguise itself because it has no identity of its own, and to be a parasite and to use another environment as its own, and to mutate rapidly, thereby putting pressure on the host environment.

The idea of a virus as inseparable from the system which it infects also applies to computing. Here, a virus is an aberrant set of instructions that become indistinguishable from the authentic instructions of the target software. Very often, a virus will destroy files or cause files to proliferate. It can only be destroyed at the risk of what one wants to save.

In light of this, Jean Baudrillard has argued that the old forms of political and social protest, where there were clear lines of demarcation between opposing forces, are no longer relevant. Irony – using the enemy's weapons – becomes a viral strategy (Baudrillard 1993: 158, 175; 1990: 71–110). The enemy is within, more than it is without. Terror is viral in this sense, since it strikes at targets which may have no attraction for the terrorist other than their vulnerability. In bombings in Northern Ireland the perpetrators have also, on occasion, killed their own supporters. The same occurred with the destruction of the World Trade Center on 11 September, 2001. Some victims were people of Muslim origin.

Establishing who is responsible for terror is also a 'viral' problem, because the causes are never entirely external. Does responsibility lie with the one who explodes the bomb? Does it lie with the organisation or government that gives the bomber support? Is terror due to the repressed sadism of the individuals involved, or to the sadism in all humans? Are the political and social conditions themselves to blame, as is often said of the Israeli–Palestinian conflict? Are the suppliers of the weapons used really the ones responsible? An answer to any of these questions is bound to be both intricate and complex, since fighting terror has often required the use of certain forms of terror. It is not that such complexity* was absent in the past, but that the symbolic order was much more robust in enabling the world to be described and perceived in a specific way. A clear and credible language and terminology was available for expressing complexity; with viral politics, this is no longer the case. The failure to invent a new language for understanding viral phenomena means that we risk being left to languish in our perplexity and melancholia.

Baudrillard, Jean (1990 [1983]) *Fatal Strategies*, trans. Philip Beitchman and W.G.J. Niesluchowski, New York: Semiotext(e); London: Pluto.

Baudrillard, Jean (1993) *Baudrillard Live: Selected Interviews*, ed. Mike Gane, London and New York: Routledge.

WORK

WORK Work derives from the Old English, *weorc*, German *werkham*, and the Greek, *ergon*. The latter connotes work as energy, evoking work as understood in physics.

From a social and historical perspective, work is often used to describe the labour of people during the Industrial Revolution who worked under conditions of an increasingly differentiated division of labour; however, a better term here is labour-power*. Work, Hannah Arendt points out, is better reserved for *homo faber*: man the tool-maker and craftsman (Arendt 1958: 136). Here, work would be midway between the bare labour-power needed to sustain physical life (this is labour-power as a means), and something more creative: work as, in part, an end in itself. This is also work as technology.

In a more colloquial sense, work is talked about in relation to employment. In this regard the nature of work, in terms of the forms of employment available, becomes an issue. Within the same context, the history* of work shows that its nature as a form of activity and employment is extremely varied. At the present moment, two aspects of historical evolution have affected the nature of work: the first is the radical change from industrial technology, based on the steam engine and manual labour, to computer-based information. Computers lead to the displacement of manual labour, including some relatively skilled labour.

One commentator has even said that computer technology reverses the efficiency equation of increased output requiring increased input. Now a greater output can be achieved with a lesser input.

The second important aspect of the history of work is that a generation is emerging for whom work is no longer an end in itself. The instrumental rationality, which dominates the work ethic, is itself being instrumentalised. While in former times life centred around work (think of the coal miners), now work is centred around a lifestyle. The latter can include artistic and intellectual activity. Work, as employment, thus becomes a means to enable work as creative endeavour. A side effect of this is that the solidarity that work as the centre of life encouraged is giving way to a more individual – not to say individualist – attitude, an attitude that is often in tension with the solidarity represented by trade unions and socialist politics.

Arendt, Hannah (1958) *The Human Condition*, Chicago: University of Chicago Press.

WRITING

WRITING To write, in English, formerly meant to 'delineate with an instrument', thus to make a mark by scoring. 'Writing' comes from 'writ', meaning stroke, and the Old English, 'written' to scratch. More generally, writing is any form of inscription where two elements – a mark and a surface, or a script and its support – come together.

Historically, the most widely discussed forms of writing scripts are pictographic: the best known forms are Egyptian hieroglyphics (3000 BC), ideographic writing, of which Chinese (1500 BC) is an example, and the familiar phonetic script, first invented by the Phoenicians around 1300 to 1100 BC, and refined by the Greeks in 500–400 BC.

The earliest writing (Sumerian cuneiform, 3500 BC) was probably invented to create tables, charts and lists (Goody 1977), of which the calendar is an example. This is in keeping with the notion of writing as an *aide-mémoire* and a technology. Modern databases are no doubt an extension of the list.

One of the great philosophical limitations in the study of the history* of writing is the idea that writing evolved from primitive, mimetic forms, represented by forms of pictographic script, to a sophisticated code*, where the relationship between a script and what it signifies is entirely conventional. This idea has been crucial in allowing societies to be classified as those with, and those without, phonetic writing, the latter being used as a marker of civilisation proper. Following this approach, primitive 'forerunners' to writing emerged before writing proper was born. But not only can pictographic scripts be highly complex, what counts as strictly pictographic script is also often open to debate (Gelb 1954: 35).

Limited writing systems are represented by Aztec and Mayan scripts. Despite appearances, these, according to Gelb, 'are not on a much higher level of development than are the primitive systems of North America and Africa. What can be clearly understood in the Central American inscriptions are first and above all the mathematical and astronomical systems of notation' (Gelb 1954: 51).

Phonetic writing was often limited to the writing of proper names. In Australian Aboriginal society names were forgotten, or kept secret, to avoid making people vulnerable to their enemies. The name becomes part of a system of prohibitions and taboos. The sobriquet used by individuals thus conceals another name, and could even be understood as the trace of another name, thereby giving rise to a key principle of writing from a grammatological point of view. As such, the well-worn distinction between societies with, and those without, writing begins to break down.

Furthermore, the problem with pictographic and other mimetic forms being equated with writing's origin is that there is a fundamental qualitative difference between pictographic and phonetic forms based on an alphabet of conventional letters. Pictographic forms are analogical and thus tied to the context in which they appear; they are untranslatable into different linguistic media, even if their realist nature obviates the need for translation. The phonetic alphabet, by contrast, is digital* and so open to translation. As a code, its form is in no way tied to the meaning it conveys. If 'pictographic' is the opposite of 'code', which is the basis of writing, it becomes impossible to see how writing developed out of pictographic script proper.

Another idea that has dominated the history and linguistics of writing is that phonetic writing, as a representation of the sounds of speech, is secondary to speech, speech being deemed the original form of language. The father of modern linguistics Ferdinard de Saussure (1857–1913), puts it this way:

A language and its written form constitue two separate system of signs. The sole reason for the existence of the latter is to represent the former. The object of study in linguistics is not a combination of the written word and the spoken word. *The spoken word alone constitutes that object.* (Saussure 1983: 24–25. Emphasis added)

Again, this is a principle that has been challenged by grammatology, which argues that if language is a system, as Saussure said, writing rather than speech is a better model of language in general.

Of great interest to sociologists and cultural historians is the idea that forms of writing condition culture* and consciousness. For instance, when faced with the task of learning over 40,000, often complex, ideographic characters, Chinese language users quickly divide into those who have been able to learn a large enough proportion of these to be called literate, and those who have not. For this reason Chinese is less democratic than languages based on the Greek phonetic alphabet. The latter is relatively easy to learn and enables languages based on it to be translated into one another. The possibility of broadly based literacy derives from such an alphabet.

Even more to the point is the fact that the development of writing 'restructures consciousness' (Ong 1997: 78–116). Thinking in an oral culture is a very different matter from thinking in a literate culture. Or more precisely, the structure of thinking is influenced by the kind of writing that is put in place, as we saw with the case of Chinese. In the West, writing in general has given rise to the dominance of analytical thought. This can be illustrated in two ways. In the first place, writing enables what Goody (1977) has called 'backward scanning'. A text – unlike speech – can be scrutinised and corrected after the initial draft is written. Corrections can thus be made (even more so with the computer), and these can be productive. As a result, writing leads to anticipation and identification: the writer has to anticipate all possible meanings. Clearly, all that has been attributed to writing involves, above all else, analytical procedures. This is reinforced by the fact that written words can be read either forwards or backwards. As Ong shows, ' "p-a-r-t" can be pronounced "trap"' (Ong 1997: 91). This is also an analytical truth, which opens up the vista of anagrams, where letters can be seen (and analysed) in a variety of arrangements.

Recorded speech, by contrast, is an event tied to a context (though digital recording is changing this). When speech is played backwards the result is noise. Speech, then, is an event, while writing turns words into things that can be examined from a variety of analytical perspectives.

Even a culture where writing has not proceeded much beyond the creation of lists and charts entails very different intellectual modes from that of an entirely oral culture. Print intensifies this distinction. Ong points out that 'the extensive use of lists and particularly of charts so commonplace in our high-technology cultures is the result not simply of writing, but of the deep interiorisation of print' (Ong 1997: 101).

Also noted by Ong is the fact that a written text can outlive its author. Whether the author is alive or dead is irrelevant to the possibility of meaning (even if this meaning differs from what the author intended). Whereas the orator's audience was mostly real, the writer's audience is always fictive. Even with a personal diary, the audience of one (the self) must be objectified, and therefore fictionalised. Indeed, keeping a diary is part of the development of the individual narcissistic self; this is a self derived from writing. Print leads to small books that can be read in private. Print, not writing, has led to the reified the word. Print leads to greater legibility.

With James Joyce (1882–1941), and other great novelists (cf. Marcel Proust 1871–1922) the novel itself creates the world for reading, not the external world.

With writing, too, there is the emergence of a 'new noetic world', which leads to the quantification of knowledge.

FORMS AND THE FORM OF WRITING

Absolutely formal, mathematical systems of notation can also be called writing, even though such systems only represent themselves. Being purely formal and abstract, mathematical writing is independent of any context whatsoever; it is therefore indeterminate. Mathematical writing, as the philosopher Husserl (1859–1938) recognised, enabled ideal objects – so crucial to the development of science – to be constructed.

Computer programs are also a form of writing. They are sets of instructions (or algorithms) constructed through zero–one switching that enables tasks (retention of data; creation of texts; imaging, etc.) to be realised. Such programs can be determinate and analytical, as in artificial intelligence (AI), where outcomes are programmed on an a priori basis, or indeterminant and synthetic, as in artificial life* (AL), where the outcomes cannot be predicted. Writing is the virtual itself as

delay, and thus as time, as opposed to a representation of presence. This version of writing in the grammatological sense connects it to computing in an essential, and not just an accidental way.

Finally, the material incarnation of writing – its signification, as opposed to its meaning – is also of great importance when coming to understand the nature of writing. Indeed, since writing originated as a mark or incision, materiality would seem to be even more significant. This opens up the importance of an analogical and contextual element in writing. Thus, the fact that Σστιατσριο (Restaurant) is in Greek script on a restaurant outside Greece can be a sign, to a non-Greek-speaker, of a Greek restaurant. Similarly, a text written in blood will have a different signification to one that is typewritten, even if the same meaning can be attributed to both texts.

Gelb, I.J. (1954) *A Study of Writing: The Foundations of Grammatology*, Chicago: University of Chicago Press.
Goody, Jack (1977) *The Domestication of the Savage Mind*, Cambridge: Cambridge University Press.
Ong, Walter J. (1997 [1982]) *Orality and Literacy: The Technologising of the Word*, London and New York: Routledge.
Saussure, Ferdinand de (1983) *Course in General Linguistics*, trans. Roy Harris, London: Duckworth.

See ANALYTIC–SYNTHETIC; GRAMMATOLOGY; MIMESIS

X, Z

XENOPHOBIA The concept of xenophobia – a morbid dislike or dread of foreigners – derives from the Greek, *xénos*, meaning stranger, or foreigner, and *phobos* meaning, 'fear'. For the Greeks, the *xénoi*, were not members of the community*. They were other*. As the other, refugees in the late twentieth and early twenty-first centuries have often been the target of xenophobic outbursts. Thus, the Turks in Germany, the Kurds in Turkey and Iraq, the Ethiopians in Italy, along with asylum seekers trying to get into first world countries, have been the focus of xenophobic attacks, although in the Australian case, political and bureaucratic intransigence rather than violence has been the vehicle of this xenophobia.

Xenophobia, as the name implies, is related to a danger that is more imaginary than real. It seems that there has to be an underlying, residual anxiety and paranoia manifesting itself in society in a variety of ways before fully-fledged violence is likely to occur. Hostility towards political opponents (cf. the Cold War and the McCarthy trials, and hostility towards the counter-culture), women, homosexuals, intellectuals and the avant-garde, the unemployed, the disabled, and indigenous minorities, is often an index* of an underlying xenophobia. In fact, this list includes all the pet hates of the Nazis, hates adding up to a general hatred so all-consuming that it culminated in the Holocaust – which is xenophobia gone completely out of control.

Groups with xenophobic tendencies have experienced increased pressure in modernity because there is no longer – if there ever was – a substantive community legitimised by tradition ready to support their hatred. Individuals cannot, today, so easily invoke collective solidarity as a way of bringing about xenophobic behaviour: if only a few extremists manifest xenophobia, the result is pathetic. And if, as Julia Kristeva (b. 1941) has written, the other, hated by the xenophobe, is 'in us' (Kristeva 1991), the xenophobic project is doubly guaranteed to fail: first, because marshalling what community opposition exists against foreigners is a full-time task, and destined to fail if past history is any guide; but, secondly, because the hatred in xenophobia derives from an unconscious hatred of oneself. This is reinforced by the insights of Levinas's philosophy (1989). And so if, ultimately, self-hatred is at the core of xenophobia, the way to combat it is to increase individuals' level of self-knowledge, a fearsomely difficult thing, but at least it clarifies where the task in this area lies.

Kristeva, Julia (1991 [1988]) *Strangers to Ourselves*, trans. Léon Roudiez, New York: Columbia University Press.
Levinas, Emmanuel (1989) 'Ethics as First Philosophy', in *The Levinas Reader*, ed. Seán Hand, Oxford: Basil Blackwell, 76–87.

ZENO'S PARADOX

The importance of Zeno's paradox regarding movement has grown since the resurgence of interest in the relationship between cinema and time*. For Zeno of Elea (fl. c. 450 BC), all movement was an illusion because the ultimate unit of movement was the stationary instant, or immobile section, as Bergson (1859–1941) called it (Bergson 1991). Thus, the arrow in flight is really passing a specific number of immobile sections which, in themselves, are static. Consequently, the paradox of movement is that its essence is non-movement. The case is similar with the apologue of Achilles and the tortoise. Achilles, the fastest runner, gives the tortoise, the slowest of creatures, a head start, but can never overtake the tortoise because the Zeno theory of movement says that movement, being divisible into its smallest parts, enables one fraction of a step by the tortoise to compare with Achilles' fraction of a step. The paradox emerges because movement is treated as a series of static steps and not as a fluid progression.

The importance of Zeno now is that his paradoxical views of movement and time are a similar kind to those invoked in relation to the photographic image*. The photographic image, it is said, 'freezes' a moment of time; it 'captures' time. This, again, is to treat time as a series of discrete, discontinuous steps, rather than as a continuous flow. The main reason that the idea of time as discontinuous has gained such prominence is that it is the analytical version of time, time divided into a finite number of minuscule, durationless moments, or time supposedly reduced to its basic elements. In fact, this spatialises time. The next step is to move beyond this spatialisation. Perhaps cinema can do it.

Bergson, Henri (1991[1939]) *Matter and Memory*, trans. Nancy Margaret Paul and W. Scott Palmer, New York: Zone Books.

See ANALYTIC-SYNTHETIC